The Internet Marketing Plan

Kim M. Bayn

WILEY COMPUTER PUBLISHING

John Wiley & Sons, Inc.

New York • Chichester • Weinheim • Brisbane • Singapore • Toronto

This book is dedicated to my mother, Rita,
for teaching me to trust my heart,
and to my father, Haaren,
for teaching me to trust my head

Copyright © 1997 by Kim M. Bayne.

Published by John Wiley & Sons, Inc.

Library of Congress Cataloging-in-Publication Data:

ISBN: 0-471-17295-2

Printed in the United States of America

10 9 8 7 6 5 4 3 2 1

contents

ABOUT THE AUTHOR   xiii
ACKNOWLEDGMENTS   xiv
INTRODUCTION   xvi

Chapter 1   Writing the Internet Marketing Plan: An Introduction   1

WHAT IS AN INTERNET MARKETING PLAN?   2
ABOUT WRITING THE PLAN   3
    How to Use This Book   3
HOW THE INTERNET MARKETING PLAN
AND THIS BOOK ARE ORGANIZED   4
    Part 1   Creation: Building Your Internet Marketing Plan   4
    Part 2   Implementation: Fitting the Internet into Your Marketing Communications Mix   6
    Part 3   Evaluation: Reviewing Achievements and Improving Future Performance   7
    How Much Should You Write?   8
GENERAL INTERNET MARKETING IMPLEMENTATION STRATEGIES   8
    1. View the Internet as an Adjunct   9
    2. Use E-mail Strategically   14
    3. Cross-Pollinate   16
    4. Provide Extra Value   17
    5. Analyze Content and Use   18
    6. Repurpose Materials   19
    7. Design with Online in Mind   20
    8. Plan Frequent Revisions   22
    9. Manage for the Long Term   23
    10. Set Reasonable Goals   23

PART 1
CREATION: BUILDING YOUR
INTERNET MARKETING PLAN

Chapter 2   Preparing the Business Overview and Executive Summary   27

SECTION ONE: BUSINESS OVERVIEW AND EXECUTIVE SUMMARY   27
Getting the Most out of This Chapter   28
Reusing This Section of Your Internet Marketing Plan   28
COMPANY OVERVIEW   28
Some Activities You Can Do Now   29
What Is the Name of Your Company?   30
How Long Has Your Company Been in Existence?   33
What Type of Business Is Your Company Engaged In?   36
PRODUCT AND MARKET DEFINITION: IS IT TIME TO GET ONLINE?   39
Some Activities You Can Do Now   40
Where You'll Find This Information Helpful   40
Why Are Some Companies Online?   40

Chapter 3   Analyzing Internet Market Statistics   49

SECTION TWO: ANALYZING INTERNET MARKET STATISTICS   50
Getting the Most out of This Chapter   50
ACTIVE VERSUS PASSIVE INTERNET MARKETING   51
GATHERING AND APPLYING DATA   52
FUN WITH INTERNET STATISTICS   53
Misusing Numbers and Other Mistakes   54
Who Cares How Many Web Sites There Are?   55
Estimates of Worldwide Users or Hosts   56
Growth of the Internet   59
International Reach   61
Internet Users by Gender   62
HOW DO THESE NUMBERS APPLY?   62
ADDITIONAL RESOURCES   62
Organizations and Associations   68
Trade Magazine Publishing Companies   69

Chapter 4   Formulating Marketing Communications Strategies   81

SECTION THREE: FORMULATING MARKETING
   COMMUNICATIONS STRATEGIES   82
     Getting the Most out of This Chapter   82
OBJECTIVES, STRATEGIES, AND TACTICS: WHAT'S THE DIFFERENCE?   82
TRADITIONAL MARKETING PRINCIPLES REVISED   84
     Revisiting Old Marketers' Tales   85
     Establishing an Internet Marketing Vision   103
ADDITIONAL RESOURCES   107
     Studies   107
     Publications   108

Chapter 5   Planning Your Internet Marketing Budget   109

SECTION FOUR: PLANNING YOUR INTERNET MARKETING BUDGET   110
WHY YOU NEED AN INTERNET MARKETING BUDGET   111
WAYS TO DETERMINE A BUDGET: A LOOK AT METHODS   111
     The Internet Marketing Budget Is Based on
       Last Year's Internet Marketing Budget   112
     The Internet Marketing Budget Is Based on
       a Percentage of Company Sales   112
     The Internet Marketing Budget Is Based on
       a Percentage of the Total Marketing Budget   113
     The Internet Marketing Budget Is Based on
       a Reallocation of Marketing Dollars   113
     The Internet Marketing Budget Is Based on
       What Other Companies in Your Industry Are Spending   114
     The Internet Marketing Budget Is Based on
       Creating an Effective Online Presence   115
     The Internet Marketing Budget Is Based on
       a Graduated Plan Tied into Measurable Results   115
     The Internet Marketing Budget Is Based on
       a Combination of Several Factors   116
DIALING FOR DOLLARS: HOW MUCH DOES EVERYTHING COST?   116
     Internet Service Options (ISPs)   116
     Internet Service Options: In-House Web Servers   117
     Web Design Services   120

ADDITIONAL RESOURCES   120
> Internet Service Providers   122
> Computer Systems   123
> Web Hosting Services   126

Chapter 6   Forming the Internet Marketing Task Force   127

SECTION FIVE: FORMING THE INTERNET MARKETING TASK FORCE   127
> Getting the Most out of This Chapter   128
DO WE WANT TO FARM THIS OUT OR NOT?   128
HIRING STAFF MEMBERS   131
EVALUATING OUTSIDE VENDORS AND SERVICES   134
> Internet Marketing Services   135
WORKING WITH COMPUTING SERVICES   136
EVALUATING INTERNET SERVICE PROVIDERS   137
THE BUSINESS CARD LITMUS TEST   137
SELECTING AN INTERNET MARKETING AGENCY   141
HIRING A WEB BOUTIQUE   141
HIRING A GRAPHIC ARTIST   147

PART 2
IMPLEMENTATION: FITTING THE INTERNET INTO YOUR MARKETING COMMUNICATIONS MIX

Chapter 7   Designing Advertising and Direct Mail Campaigns   153

INTRODUCTION TO PART 2: IMPLEMENTATION   154
> Internet and Traditional Marketing: The Perfect Marriage   154
SECTION SIX: INTERNET MARKETING PROGRAM IMPLEMENTATION (CHAPTERS 7 THROUGH 14)   156
WHAT THIS SECTION OF YOUR PLAN MIGHT INCLUDE   156
MEDIA PLANNING WITH INTERNET RESOURCES   157
TRADITIONAL ADVERTISING AND THE INTERNET   158

NOW FOR A FEW DEFINITIONS **163**
    Ad Banners *164*
    Hyperlinked Banner *165*
    Clickthrough Ratios *165*
    Clickstreams *166*
    Headers *166*
BUDGET CONSIDERATIONS **169**
THE REALITY OF INTERNET ADVERTISING **170**
    Littering the Information Superhighway *171*
    Acceptable Online Advertising *171*
    Advertisers Prevail *173*
    Internet Advertising Is Not Alone *173*
    Advertising Management Firms Abound *173*
CREATING YOUR OWN ADS **174**
    Banner Design Services *177*
PLACING ADVERTISING ON THE WEB **178**
SELLING ADVERTISING ON THE WEB **179**
    Attracting and Retaining Advertisers *180*
    Why Should You Place Advertising on the Internet? *187*
ADVERTISING SPECIALTIES **194**
DIRECT MAIL AND HOW TO MAKE ONLINE ENEMIES **196**
    Three Cheers for AOL *197*
    The Impact of Unsolicited E-mail *198*
    Deciding to Use Bulk E-mail Lists *199*
    Some Closing Advice *200*
RESOURCES **201**
    Advertising Placement and Sales *201*
    Direct Mail *202*

Chapter 8   Utilizing Collateral Materials/Sales Literature   203

EFFECTIVE SUPPORTING MATERIALS FOR THE PLAN **204**
INTEGRATE THE INTERNET INTO YOUR COLLATERAL MATERIALS **204**
INTEGRATE YOUR COLLATERAL MATERIALS INTO THE INTERNET **205**
WHY PUT YOUR LITERATURE ON THE WEB? **205**
WHAT SHOULD YOU PUBLISH ON THE WEB? **210**
    Document Formats *212*
    Annual Reports and Other Financial Data *213*
EQUIPMENT NEEDS **213**

How Much Are You Going to Put Online?   216
Password-Restricted Access   218
The Web Demands More   220

Chapter 9   Developing a Corporate Identity   221

Effective Supporting Materials for the Plan   222
   Getting the Most out of This Chapter   222
Applying the Internet to Your Corporate Identity   222
How Corporate Identity Guidelines Change Online   223
Take Advantage of Your Identity   224
Domain Name Ownership and Trademark Issues   226
   Why Can't the Federal Government Do Something?   227
   How Did Everything Get So Messed Up?   228
   Whose Responsibility Is Your Identity, Anyway?   229
   Action Item 1   230
Creating an Internet Style Manual   234
   Contact Information   241
   Signature Blocks   242
   Logo   243
   Typeface   244
   Horizontal Rule   244
   Navigational Links   244
   Colors   244
   Signage   245
   Designing for a Specific Browser   246
Answers to the Riddle   246

Chapter 10   Conducting Market Research   249

Effective Supporting Materials for the Plan   249
   Getting the Most out of This Chapter   250
Market Research, the Internet, and Business Ethics   250
Searching Tips   252
   What Search Strategy? Oh, I'll Just Surf until I Find It!   252
   Resources   253
Conducting Market Research via E-mail   259

Chapter 11   Executing Public Relations and Promotional Programs   263

EFFECTIVE SUPPORTING MATERIALS FOR THE PLAN   263
> Getting the Most out of This Chapter   264

INTERNET COMMUNICATIONS AND THE CHANGING FACE OF PR   264
> Risk and Opportunities   265
> Working Tips for Internet PR   266
> Use the Internet to Enhance External Communications   266

HOW MUCH ARE YOU GOING TO PUT ONLINE?   267

RESOURCES   274
> Media Directories, Mailing and Clipping Services   274
> News Distribution and Wire Services   276
> Miscellaneous PR Resources   277

Chapter 12   Incorporating Sales Support Functions   279

EFFECTIVE SUPPORTING MATERIALS FOR THE PLAN   279

APPLYING THE INTERNET TO SALES SUPPORT   280

AUTORESPONDERS, MAILBOTS, AND OTHER DEVICES   280
> A Quick List of Autoresponder Applications   283

TAKING ORDERS ON THE INTERNET   285

SALES LEADS MANAGEMENT   285

FUN WITH JAVA AND FRAMES   286

RESOURCES   290
> Secure Payments   290

Chapter 13   Planning Trade Shows   293

EFFECTIVE SUPPORTING MATERIALS FOR THE PLAN   294
> Getting the Most out of This Chapter   294

APPLYING THE INTERNET TO THE TRADE SHOW FUNCTION   295
> Dressing for Success   295

THAT'S IT? I JUST REPRODUCE MY WEB URL ON EVERYTHING?   298

SHOW SELECTION   299

EXHIBITOR SERVICES FIRMS   301

DISPLAYS FOR RENT   302

ACCOMMODATIONS AND TRAVEL   303

INTERNATIONAL EXHIBITS   306
CONVENTION FACILITIES AND AMENITIES   307
GRAPHICS CREATION   308
BOOKING ENTERTAINMENT   308
KEEP CURRENT ON TRADE SHOW DEVELOPMENTS   309
GETTING THE WORD OUT ABOUT YOUR EVENT   309
VIRTUAL TRADE SHOWS AND OTHER IDEAS   310
    Some Activities You Can Do Now   312
    Cross-Pollinate   314

Chapter 14   Launching Your Internet
             Marketing Program   321

EFFECTIVE SUPPORTING MATERIALS FOR THE PLAN   322
    Getting the Most out of This Chapter   322
PLAN OF ACTION: THE SCHEDULE   322
ONLINE PROMOTIONAL PLAN   327
    Read Relevant Newsgroups   327
    Join Relevant Mailing Lists   328
    Submit Your URL to Search Engines and Indexes   329
    Include Commercial Online Services   330
    Trade Reciprocal Links   331
    Distribute the News   333
    In the Future Everyone Will Be Famous for 15 Minutes   336

PART 3
EVALUATION: REVIEWING ACHIEVEMENTS AND IMPROVING FUTURE PERFORMANCE

Chapter 15   Measuring Internet
             Marketing Results   341

REVIEW OF PART 2: IMPLEMENTATION   341
CHAPTER 15.   MEASURING INTERNET MARKETING RESULTS   342
    Getting the Most out of This Chapter   342

WHAT IS MARKETING MEASUREMENT?   342
    Advertising Equivalence   343
    Editorial Slant   344
    Key Message   344
WHAT TO MEASURE IN YOUR INTERNET MARKETING PROGRAM   344
    Where Did They Go and How Did They Get There?   345
    Knock, Knock. Who's There?   346
    How Many Browsers Does It Take To . . .   346
    Yes, I Did See Your Web Address in That Ad!   346
    Is It Sales Yet?   346
    Counting Beans and Other Pastimes   347
    Measurement Tracking Firms   347
    Off-Line Tracking Methods   349
SUMMARY   350
YOUR INTERNET MARKETING PLAN SUMMARY   351

Appendix A   Internet Marketing Plan   355

SECTION ONE: BUSINESS OVERVIEW AND EXECUTIVE SUMMARY   355
SECTION TWO: APPLICABLE INTERNET MARKET STATISTICS   357
SECTION THREE: MARKETING COMMUNICATIONS STRATEGIES   358
SECTION FOUR: INTERNET MARKETING BUDGET   358
SECTION FIVE: THE INTERNET MARKETING TASK FORCE   361
SECTION SIX: INTERNET MARKETING PROGRAM IMPLEMENTATION   362
SECTION SEVEN: INTERNET MARKETING PLAN SUMMARY   364
SECTION EIGHT: SUPPORTING DOCUMENTS   364

Appendix B   Marketing Plan Software   365

Appendix C   Periodicals Covering the Internet and Marketing   367

INTERNET   367
MARKETING COMMUNICATIONS   370

Index   373

about the author

Since 1981, Kim M. Bayne has been professionally active in business-to-business marketing communications. Her experience includes a diverse blend of both advertising agency and company experience, as a freelance copywriter, an agency and company employee, and an independent consultant. Currently she is president of wolfBayne Communications, a high-technology business-to-business consultancy specializing in computer and electronics media relations, marketing communications, and Internet marketing. Prior to her current position as a consultant, author, and speaker, Kim was marketing communications manager for Array Microsystems, a manufacturer of digital signal-processing boards and software development tools.

Kim Bayne's agency experience includes planning and implementing public relations and advertising programs for international manufacturers of mass-storage peripherals, software, board-level products, semiconductors, instrumentation, telecommunications, and biomedical equipment. In addition, she held positions of increasing responsibility in marketing communications with Philips/Laser Magnetic Storage and Information Storage, mass-storage-device manufacturers.

Before entering the world of high-technology marketing, Kim Bayne served as reference services coordinator and interlibrary loan paralibrarian for the academic library of a small, midwestern, private college. During this time, she received on-the-job training in the use of traditional reference tools for academic and business research purposes, and also attended classroom instruction in techniques for computer-assisted retrieval. As an extension of her interlibrary loan responsibilities, she conducted online research for undergraduate and faculty library patrons, through such services as Dialog and OCLC. The addition of the Internet has greatly enhanced her skills in market research.

Ms. Bayne is the recipient of multiple awards in copywriting, product marketing, and public speaking, and she holds a Masters degree in computer resources management. She is the owner of the Internet's HTMARCOM list, the premier e-mail discussion group for high-tech marketing communicators, which has been featured in *Advertising Age, Marketing Computers,* and *Business Marketing* magazines. Bayne publishes Marketing Lists on the Internet, a comprehensive directory of marketing-related lists, newsgroups, and online forums.

She also writes regularly on Internet marketing and marketing communications for such publications as *Marketing Tools* and *Internet Marketing and Technology Report,* and speaks frequently at worldwide conferences, seminars, and classes, including UCLA Extension, Internet World, Email World and Internet Expo Conference, Mobile World Exposition, Mecklermedia's Web Seminars, the Business Marketing Association, and the International Association of Business Communicators.

Acknowledgments

My decision to write *The Internet Marketing Plan* was inspired by enough individuals to fill an entire encyclopedia. Unfortunately, I can only scratch the service in these pages. My thanks and appreciation to the following:

> My husband, Bruce Davis Bayne, for patiently listening to my endless ramblings about minute aspects of the Internet, for putting up with my incredibly late hours during the writing of this book, and for never letting me forget how important it is to laugh
>
> My daughter, Kaitlyn Ruth Bayne, for reminding me to take a break when I needed it most, for showing me how gratifying it is to learn new things, and for telling me to "put it on my Web page."
>
> Tony Donohoe, for the inspiration to write by his example
>
> The librarians and staff members of Charles Leaming Tutt Library at The Colorado College, for teaching me the values

of and techniques for effective research, both online and otherwise

The late Professor Albert Seay, for recognizing that I had to find my own path, ruling passion and all

Richard Zech, for hiring me for my first in-house marketing communications position

The Colorado Marcom Network and Silicon Mountain Symposium, its founders and members, for influencing my creation of the HTMARCOM List

Doug Mitchell, for his support in my career and for his never-ending entrepreneurial spirit

Kristin Zhivago and Mac McIntosh, for encouraging me to venture out on my own

Jim Sterne, for inviting me to join the faculty of his very popular Marketing on the Internet seminar series

Glenn Fleishman, for spinning off the Internet Marketing list from HTMARCOM and maintaining it with dedication

The rest of my immediate family and very close friends for helping me put things in perspective

introduction

A feeding frenzy has surrounded marketing on the Internet. There's little doubt that the Internet appears powerful, captivating, and dangerous to the novice online marketer. Frequently, companies jump online without much forethought or are forced into the situation by outside forces. Customers ask for Web page addresses, colleagues brag about their latest online achievement, and competitors aggressively launch an in-your-face Internet campaign. A company's ad agency starts pitching its Internet development services. A local Internet service provider mails out brochures telling everyone how inexpensive it is to set up an account. All these factors can and do force a marketer to make hasty decisions regarding a company's Internet presence.

Sometimes a marketer, such as yourself, chooses to upload a quick-and-dirty Web page in response to repeated in-house requests. You tell yourself that it's merely a placeholder, just until you "get around to it." As time passes and the pressure builds, so does the ad hoc web site. Like a patchwork quilt, with leftover bits of fabric, you piece together your Web site. The final result: We've covered ourselves. That's about it. You virtually ignore the big marketing picture. And that is where most companies fail. The development of your Internet marketing presence shouldn't be an on-the-fly proposition just because technology makes it possible.

With *The Internet Marketing Plan* you will be able to create a coherent and integrated Internet marketing presence to enhance your overall general marketing communications program. *The Internet Marketing Plan* is a hands-on workbook, which includes discussions, tips, and techniques for combining traditional marketing concepts with new Web marketing methods. This book is chock-full of little anecdotes, worksheets, checklists, and brainstorming ideas. *The Internet Marketing Plan* book and disk set will help you create a blueprint that you can use to effectively design, implement, and evaluate your Internet marketing programs.

Who Should Read This Book?

Your job title might be vice president of marketing and sales or even trade show administrator. You might be responsible for your company's advertising, sales literature, public relations, or even every aspect of marketing communications. You now are responsible for your Internet marketing presence as well. This book answers questions for those of you who have amassed a lot of experience in traditional media but have little expertise in applying the Internet to your traditional marketing program. It also answers questions for those of you who have a lot of hands-on Internet experience, but little expertise in applying traditional marketing communications strategies and tactics to Internet tools.

Getting the Most Out of This Book

The activities in this book include reviewing and comparing examples of how companies have created their Internet marketing presence. These exercises also include steps for deciding upon and inventing your own approach. During this process, you will take notes on information that is useful for your company to include—as well as to ignore—in your Internet marketing plan. Which brings me to the subject of how you might choose to read this book.

I'm not one to dictate how someone should read a book. It would be silly of me to expect everyone to read this one in the exact order in which it was conceived. After all, *I* read consumer magazines from back to front cover, for some unknown reason. Sometimes I just skip around and look at anything that happens to catch my fancy, which is pretty much how many people watch television, too.

If you're one of those people who likes to "surf," whether it be online, in front of the TV, or with this book, you'll still get a lot out of this. You may even decide to read it from beginning to end someday. Since I can't be sure how you'll approach *The Internet Marketing Plan,* I have included quite a bit of repetition throughout. By doing so, this book becomes a combination reference tool and workbook, one that you will be able to refer to repeatedly, long after your plan has been finalized.

How to Use This Book

Now that I've said all that, here is my *recommendation:*

- ◆ Gather all the material you have that addresses how your company does business and markets its products.
- ◆ Read the articles throughout the book.
- ◆ Read lots of other articles in Internet and marketing publications.
- ◆ Visit the Web sites included on the inetplan.htm bookmarks file.
- ◆ Explore how successful companies present both image and information at their Web sites.
- ◆ Learn by example.
- ◆ Decide what works for your company and what doesn't.
- ◆ Take copious notes.
- ◆ Complete the worksheets in each chapter.
- ◆ Draft each section of your Internet marketing plan.
- ◆ Open a duplicate copy the Internet Marketing Plan template found in Appendix A, which is a basic outline for your plan. Insert each section of the plan as you complete it.

How to Use the Worksheets, Forms, Checklists, and Questionnaires

Each of the forms in this book require you to perform one or more of the following actions:

- ◆ Perform research.
- ◆ Ask questions.

- ◆ Answer questions.
- ◆ Make choices.
- ◆ Write text.

Your choice to complete every worksheet is up to you. Decide for yourself how detailed you want your plan to be or how much time you have to devote to this process. You might even want to do an in-house survey of everyone's tolerance level before you embark on a 100-page tome.

It's simply not possible to cover all the variations in marketing plans that can exist in the world. There are variations for every type of marketer, company, product, or industry imaginable. In appreciation of this fact, I have included all of the forms that appear in this book on disk. You can modify them to your heart's content. If you have spent quite a bit of time modifying or enhancing a form, you may wish to submit your version for inclusion in the next edition of this book. If I include your form, I will be sure to include a credit line for you.

How to Use the Disk Included with This Book

Included with this book is a disk in PC format. The disk is provided for your convenience in drafting your Internet marketing plan. The disk contains the following files.

Document

Included on this disk is a template labeled inetplan.txt, which is a document containing the basic outline for your Internet marketing plan. Open this document and insert each section of the plan as you complete it. Format your plan according to your company's style for proposals, or invent your own format. After you have completed writing your entire Internet marketing plan, you may wish to create a table of contents and/or index to make it easier for others to read.

Spreadsheet

Included on this disk is a template labeled budget.xls, which is a spreadsheet containing a basic outline for your Internet marketing budget. This outline is only a skeleton, which you will complete with your own numbers. Open this file and insert costs as you go along. Format your worksheet according to your company's style, or invent your own. After you have completed drafting your budget, include it somehow in your Internet marketing plan.

Forms

Included on this disk are all of the forms you need to complete in order to write your Internet marketing plan. Illustrative tables and graphics appearing in the book are not included on the disk. For your convenience in locating, modifying, and/or printing out the forms, the disk files are labeled exactly like the figures in the book. For example, Figure 2.5 is in the file labeled fig2-5.

Bookmarks

Included on this disk is a bookmark file labeled inetplan.htm that you can either import into your Web browser software or access from your disk or hard drive by opening it as a file. If you decide to use it as a file, open your browser and select it by name, rather than open any other type of program. Using it as a file will also allow you to click on each of the links, as long as you are connected to the Internet.

The bookmark file is arranged by chapter and contains all of the URLs referenced throughout the book. It will save you time in locating various addresses on the World Wide Web.

All of the URLs referenced in this book and in the bookmarks file were working at the time I submitted my manuscript for publication. Keep in mind that URLs change frequently on the Internet. By the time this book is published, some of the URLs will already be out of date. If a URL has changed and you find that you are no longer able to locate the corresponding Internet resource, I would welcome a note from you. Please send e-mail to me at kimmik@wolfBayne.com. I will catalog the new URL for any future editions of this book.

chapter one

Writing the Internet Marketing Plan: An Introduction

Practically every traditional marketing project you undertake will have a beginning, a middle, and an end. You write copy for a piece of sales literature. You have it designed, typeset, and printed. Finally, you arrange for literature distribution. You'll probably experience this same exact project over and over again for the life of each particular product. Most important, the final result, the printed data sheet, brochure, or direct-mail circular, is a tangible piece of marketing evidence that you have indeed completed an activity. Not so with the Internet.

   The nature of the Internet is volatile. It not only lends itself to frequent, sometimes hourly, updates and revisions, but it demands it. It's a work-in-progress that is constantly evolving. It is very rare that a Webmaster says with confidence that he or she has completely finished. If a Webmaster does say that, it may mean that he or she has gotten a better offer and starts the new job on Monday. There will always be one more change that is worth making, regardless of how happy everyone is with the so-called final result. That is why creating a written Internet marketing plan is even more important. An Internet marketing plan will improve your ability to manage your Internet marketing presence more effectively, not only for your own sanity but for that of your company's as well.

What Is an Internet Marketing Plan?

In the world of traditional marketing, you propose or justify a new program or its continuation through its relationship to several different elements, including the company, its products, the market, a budget, and staff considerations. In order to successfully execute any type program at all, you need a plan. You need a detailed road map of sorts. An Internet marketing plan *is* that road map. That's where this book enters and your work begins.

The elements of an Internet marketing plan are not much different than the elements of a traditional marketing plan. OK, they're practically identical. Why shouldn't they be? It's very simple. Without an Internet marketing plan that at least resembles something you've seen or worked with before, you've got a smaller chance that your marketing staff and management will understand what you're trying to accomplish. The Internet marketing plan (Appendix A) upon which this book is based includes these sections:

- Section One: Business Overview and Executive Summary
- Section Two: Applicable Internet Market Statistics
- Section Three: Marketing Communications Strategies
- Section Four: Internet Marketing Budget
- Section Five: The Internet Marketing Task Force
- Section Six: Internet Marketing Program Implementation
- Section Seven: Internet Marketing Plan Summary

This book represents but one way to prepare your marketing plan. If you've written a plan before, then you may have your own way of organizing your final document. For example, you could decide to move the section on budget to the end. The choice is yours. Bottom line: Don't strain trying to find a new marketing plan format for the Internet when, after all, it's just another type of media. Once you and everyone in your organization feel comfortable with using the Internet for marketing purposes, you can experiment with different ways to present your program.

If you absolutely have to have a sexy new way to present your Internet marketing plan, here's a good technique for impressing your colleagues:

- ◆ Step 1.   Edit each section of your plan down to bullets similar to a slide show outline.
- ◆ Step 2.   Convert each section into HTML with a 20-second refresh per page.
- ◆ Step 3.   Stick the plan on your company's intranet for everyone to see.
- ◆ Step 4.   Add an e-mail comment form for immediate feedback.
- ◆ Step 5.   Get back to work. You have a plan to execute!

One more thing. Keep the text of your plan as readable as possible. As you use new terms that may or may not be familiar to the readers of your plan, define them in the simplest terms possible. You really have nothing to gain by emulating someone intent on overwhelming staff members with a newly attained command of online vocabulary.

About Writing the Plan

Writing a marketing plan, whether it is for traditional or new media, requires time, research, and patience. An Internet marketing plan, like the World Wide Web it discusses, is a constantly developing document. The execution of that plan involves continually updating the plan's content and adapting to the changing marketplace and technology that drives the online world. Don't be surprised if you find yourself revising sections of the plan to improve it. After all, the Internet marketing plan is your working document for success.

How to Use This Book

- ◆ Read the articles.
- ◆ Look at the illustrations and figures.

- Visit the Web sites included on the inetplan.htm bookmarks file.
- Explore how each company used this information.
- Explore how your company can use this information.
- Take copious notes.
- Complete the worksheets in each chapter.
- Open a duplicate copy of the Internet Marketing Budget found on the disk file budget.xls. Insert cost data as you discover it.
- Open a duplicate copy of the Internet Marketing Plan template found in Appendix A, which is a basic outline for your plan. Insert each section of the plan as you complete it.

How the Internet Marketing Plan and This Book Are Organized

Let's take a look at the different sections, which coincidentally are the outline for your own Internet marketing plan. This book is divided into three major parts.

Part 1 Creation: Building Your Internet Marketing Plan

In Part 1, you'll spend time gathering data that, in most cases, already exists in other forms. For this section, you'll need your company profile, your annual report, your marketing budget, your sales literature, and perhaps some reports by industry analysts that dissect your market. While you're at it, dig out the competitive literature you picked up at that last trade show. You'll need this when we get to the chapter on market statistics.

When you decide to address budget issues, enlist the help of your MIS department, local computer store, and/or local Internet service provider. Pull out your address book with your ad agency's number or that of your local Web design boutique. While you're grabbing phone numbers, don't forget your company's internal extension list as well. Guess who you'll be calling to recruit for your Internet marketing team? Yep, your coworkers. At the very least, if they don't end up on your team, you can pick their brains. Believe it or not, their seemingly uninitiated ideas can help you sell your plan to as many people as possible. The chapters in this section include the following.

Chapter 2.   Preparing the Business Overview and Executive Summary

You may have to ask management for the money to launch your Internet marketing program. In order to address this particular readership of your plan, this book includes how to tell the bigwigs who you are, where you've been, what you're doing, why you're doing it, and how to proceed from here. It's basically a history lesson drafted in business review terms.

Chapter 3.   Analyzing Internet Market Statistics

In order to properly justify your Internet marketing program, you'll need to gather information that supports the use of the Internet. You can do this in the following ways:

◆ Demonstrate the successful use of the Internet.

◆ Demonstrate the successful use of the Internet in your market.

◆ Demonstrate the successful use of the Internet in your market for your product or service.

In this section, we'll point you to resources that will help you in this endeavor. And if you didn't get enough of browsing the Net for your initial answers, we'll spend even more time with you in the chapter on market research, just to keep you on your toes.

Chapter 4.   Formulating Marketing Communications Strategies

An approach to your Internet marketing would be nice. In this chapter, we'll get you in the mood to start thinking of strategies and tactics you can use.

Chapter 5.   Planning Your Internet Marketing Budget

Budget issues are always of interest to upper management, regardless of the media, so our plan will include that information as well. You'll know which questions to ask staff members and outside suppliers so you can get the numbers right, or at least as close as humanly possible. A word of warning: This chapter does not stand alone. You will need to review other chapters for your actual Internet marketing activities *first* before you can even come close to completing your Internet marketing budget.

Chapter 6.   Forming the Internet Marketing Task Force

Before you start getting overconfident about your Internet marketing venture, remember this: Anything that can go wrong will. It's even more likely because of the continuously changing technical aspects of the Internet. That's why you're going to want to form an Internet marketing task force or team. You will have to decide whether or not you want to form your team before or after you put your plan together. Maybe management will even decide that for you. Regardless, the formation of your team will be one of the plan elements that will drive your budget as well.

Part 2   Implementation: Fitting the Internet into Your Marketing Communications Mix

In Part 2, you'll continue drafting portions of your plan, but you'll also take into account the actual activities associated with executing it. You'll also receive practical help in the actual implementation phase.

Eventually, you'll need to address how the Internet fits into your overall marketing communications program. Be ready to review everything you've done with traditional media up to now. Defining activities that relate to the rest of your marketing program will keep you from duplicating efforts or overlooking the obvious. You will soon realize how easy it becomes to leverage your other marketing programs when the Internet becomes part of the picture. The Internet marketing plan is no different. We'll apply the Internet to these selected marketing communications activities:

◆ Chapter 7.   Designing Advertising and Direct-Mail Campaigns

- ◆ Chapter 8. Utilizing Collateral Materials/Sales Literature
- ◆ Chapter 9. Developing a Corporate Identity
- ◆ Chapter 10. Conducting Market Research
- ◆ Chapter 11. Executing Public Relations and Promotional Programs
- ◆ Chapter 12. Incorporating Sales Support Functions
- ◆ Chapter 13. Planning Trade Shows

The marcom programs in this list are only the tip of the iceberg. I know that many of you have responsibilities in other areas that I have failed to mention. Marketing communications responsibilities differ by company, and I hope the areas outlined in this book will, at the very least, cover the average marketing communications agendas.

Also included in Part 2 is Chapter 14, *Launching Your Internet Marketing Program.* A schedule is a schedule is a schedule. Please, let's not get into a philosophical discussion about how deadlines are negotiable. I wouldn't recommend taking on an Internet marketing program unless you are serious about completing certain elements within a reasonable period. There's just too much competition out there to let the time get away from you.

If you don't know definitely, come up with your best guesstimate of when you'll get everything done. Putting together your timeline for launching your Internet marketing program is essential. Of course, if you can afford to spend your days just surfing the Net and fit in your marketing whenever it occurs to you . . . more power to you. (Don't laugh. I know plenty of people who still operate in this mode . . . even today.)

Part 3   Evaluation: Reviewing Achievements and Improving Future Performance

In Part 3, you'll determine how to measure your Internet marketing program against the goals you previously established. Measurement will help you justify a continuation of your program in the next fiscal year. The final chapter in the book is included in this section.

Chapter 15.   Measuring Internet Marketing Results

Measurement always seems to be the poor forgotten relative when it comes time for action. A word of warning: *Don't, don't, don't* ignore this part of your program. In many cases, putting a measurement function into place after the fact is more difficult than you think.

If you forget measurement on traditional programs, you can always reconstruct the data somehow. Perhaps your public relations program will benefit by a retroactive analysis of press clippings done by an outside firm. You just don't have that option when it comes to the Internet. To put it bluntly, if you ignore measurement and its associated software programs, adding it in later, you may have no way to recover any of the lost data. Not unless you somehow invent a time machine and manage to travel back to correct your mistake. (If you do, let me know, there are some lottery numbers I'd like to buy tickets for.)

How Much Should You Write?

Most company executives do not have a lot of time to read lengthy documents. Sometimes your wonderfully crafted Internet marketing plan will become part of a larger, more extensive marketing plan for the company, a division, or an entire network of interconnected companies. Another marketing professional like yourself may have the task of editing plans down to the bare essentials, leaving out all your hard work and finely tuned prose. That's why it's important for you to keep your plan as concise as possible.

Keep each section of your plan to one page or less. Supplement your written word with easy-to-read diagrams, charts, and schedules. Most of the information you wish to include in your Internet marketing plan may already appear in other company documents. Save time, money, and space. Refer to these other documents and get to the point about the Internet while you have the reader's attention.

General Internet Marketing Implementation Strategies

Now you know what you've gotten yourself into. Before you start putting your thoughts down on paper, it's time to create a unique state of mind with which to approach our Internet marketing plan.

As marketers devise ways to fit the Internet into their traditional marketing communications mix, they must include both strategic and tactical approaches in their use of this exciting new medium. Along those lines, here are my favorite 10 strategies for Internet marketing. These apply whether you decide to use e-mail, the Web, FTP, newsgroups, or all of these.

1. View the Internet as an Adjunct

When marketers embraced the Internet and started making advertising and promotion a reality, no one intended it to become the only element in your marketing mix. How many times have you heard company representatives say, "We don't have much budget. The Internet is cheap enough and print advertising is so expensive. Let's just put up a Web page and cut back on our other activities." Think about this. Did the rules of marketing change overnight when businesses discovered the Internet? For the sake of this argument, the answer is no.

Off-Line and Online Media Are the Perfect Couple

There exists a synergistic relationship between traditional media and online media. You need to marry them in a complementary way. The Internet is not designed to be the only element in your marketing mix. Successful businesses still continue to plan well-rounded marketing communications campaigns. Successful businesses investigate every opportunity and shine like industry stars when they do. Marketers at these companies leave no stone unturned. They have used and will continue to use every available marketing vehicle that suits their particular needs.

This advice becomes all too clear when you realize that the Internet is one of those marketing elements that requires the presence of other marketing media in order to work most effectively. Think of it as throwing a holiday party. Sure, we all know it's New Year's Eve, but if you don't send me an invitation, how will I know *you* are having a celebration?

Old marketers' tales. Marketers sometimes claim that the Internet didn't work for them because no one visited their site. One Internet marketing myth says that putting up a Web page constitutes creating an Internet marketing presence. Yes, there are robots out there that search and catalog pages on the Web, but why leave your promotion to chance? Another Internet marketing myth claims that registering in online search engines will cover just about any promotion you'll ever need. Well, I already know that *you* don't believe any of that, because you're reading this book.

Most people won't know about or even notice your online presence unless they are already online looking for you or your type of product. How do you get them to notice your online activities? One way is by flaunting your presence in off-line media. I *love* to hear this statement after someone looks at a company brochure with the URL prominently displayed, "I didn't know they had a Web page. Great! I'll have to look at it the next time I'm online."

How Do You Spell Information?

Now let's take this one step further. You've become excited about the potential for creating a very powerful online presence. You've become less enthusiastic about the potential of your print advertising in trade publications. You're not too interested in spending time on your ad placement anymore, since you know that the Internet is the wave of the future. Mr. Bob Big Bucks, CEO, *doesn't* have time to get online, but he *does* influence buying decisions. How are you going to continue to reach him?

Companies who decide to eliminate a portion of their marketing program in favor of an Internet marketing presence may be selling their customers and clients short. The keyword here is *eliminate.* Ask your customers how many different ways they get their information before they purchase. They each tell a different story about how they gather their product and service features and benefits on a daily, weekly, or monthly basis. For example, I receive my consumer product news through print magazine ads, TV commercials, and coupons and offers in the Sunday paper. I receive my technical product information, such as that needed for my computer and its peripherals, through print manuals, and occasionally I'll look for it on the Internet. I may even pick up the phone and dial some company's toll-free number if I'm really desperate.

News on current world events comes to me through a variety of sources. My cable TV subscription includes *CNN Headline News.* *The Denver Post* newspaper is delivered to my door each morning. When I haven't had time to read the paper or turn on the tube, I go to InternetMCI or Reuters newswire while I am online just to verify that aliens from another galaxy haven't landed, or that Pikes Peak isn't going to erupt any minute. When I'm on vacation, I turn on the TV in my hotel room. If I'm camping, I turn on the car radio. Believe it or not, sometimes I actually ask another human being what's new. That's exactly how I found out President Reagan had been shot way back when. At breakfast one morning, I asked someone staying in my London bed-and-breakfast if they'd seen the paper. I gathered my news that morning by word of mouth. I would bet that I am not unique in using a variety of resources, both traditional and new media, to collect news and information. I weigh these separately gathered facts whenever I have to make a decision or form an opinion.

Humans Are Driven by Routine

In this century, particularly in the past few decades, we have advanced tremendously in the technological arena. In spite of it all, we're still just creatures driven by habit. Most people use what's convenient and/or what they're accustomed to, and I wouldn't be surprised, if they continue to do so for quite some time. You could be making a big customer-service mistake if you choose to eliminate a certain type of media from your marketing program in favor of a hot new one.

Unfortunately, the attitude of some companies, and the ad agencies that represent them, smacks of elitism when it comes to discussing how they'll approach Internet marketing. While consulting for a well-known Denver-based advertising agency, I was amazed by remarks regarding which customers were worthy of the company's time. Here were people discussing strategies for pitching several of their big accounts, as well as several well-coveted prospects, on the advantages of creating an Internet marketing presence. First we discussed how the agency would approach its own Internet presence. After all, how can you convince someone to join the club when you're not yet a member?

When the topic of the agency's site design was covered, I suggested that an option be included to allow customers, regardless of their connection speed or browser, to choose a low-tech version of the site. The agency's graphic artists had already decided their

Web site was going to be graphically intense, using the latest HTML extensions, long before this meeting. In defense of this view, someone commented, "Look, if these people haven't got a high-speed connection with Netscape, a multimedia setup, and experience surfing the Web, then we don't even want to talk to them." So there. In other words, they only wanted to bother with people who had the same taste in hardware and software. Or worse, they wanted only clients who were technologically savvy enough that they didn't even need to hire this agency. *Oops!* If you really needed this agency's help, you were out of luck.

Your Internet marketing presence is obviously going to reach a lot of online people. As in traditional media, you will not be able to control who eventually sees your message and who doesn't. This is not an undercover CIA operation, you know. So, as you decide how to approach your Internet content and presentation, keep the hidden market in mind. You wouldn't assume that all worthwhile customers are created equal. Don't assume that all worthwhile customers who just happen to be on the Internet are created equal, either.

If It's Not Broken, Don't Fix It . . . OK, Maybe Just a Little

Before you start making plans to reduce your marketing costs by thousands of dollars by eliminating a part of your program that is a proven sales generator, take an aspirin. If your direct-mail campaign is working, don't trade it for the Internet. If your TV campaign is working, don't trade it for the Internet. If your print advertising campaign is working . . . you get the idea.

When do you use the Internet? Use the Internet to help *enhance* those programs that are already working. If you notice a shift in how customers are gathering your literature and how they are contacting you, then it's time to regroup—but not before. If your marketing programs are *not* working, find out why not. Don't make the same mistakes online. Bad marketing is bad marketing, regardless of the media.

Be Responsible in Your Media Choices

Now, about that thought that you'll be able to cut down on print and literature distribution costs once you go online: Maybe you will, maybe you won't. I've talked to several companies who have claimed that the Internet saved them money in reprinting literature. I've also talked to several companies who have claimed that the demand for their literature is greater now that they have the international reach afforded by the Internet. I'm not going to guarantee what will happen to you one way or the other.

Here's the truth about literature and whether you should eliminate or reduce it. As a customer, if you make it difficult for me to get the help or information I need, I'm going to find an easier way and probably another company. You may end up being eliminated on major contracts you don't even know about. Your potential customer will complain to 10 buddies or business colleagues that you've stopped printing and distributing data sheets. If a customer walks into your trade show booth and asks for a piece of literature and you hand out your Web address, the person might get around to looking you up after the show and, then again, maybe not. He or she doesn't need to spend another hour of valuable time hunting down your online sales literature. All the customer wants is to pick up one crummy data sheet to read on the airplane.

Before you accuse me of being myopic, let me clarify my position. The reduction of printed literature may or may not happen anytime soon. You may be lucky enough to realize a cost savings on your printed literature immediately. You may not. The market has been talking about the paperless office since the days of the first optical disk drive, and we're still killing plenty of trees a decade later. However, if your goals must include lower literature distribution costs, be conservative in your estimate of how fast you will realize this savings.

I'm not saying that all budget dollars should stay the same and you should just invest more money to cover the Internet program. For many companies, that would mean instantaneous death to their dreams of an Internet marketing program. The money has to come from somewhere. Unless your company is very supportive or you are very lucky, the money will sometimes come from other marketing programs. Just be responsible about where you cut corners before you launch that prestigious Web page.

2. Use E-mail Strategically

Want to find customers on the Internet? E-mail is the first place to look. Before your customers use any other tool on the Internet, they'll use e-mail to send a message. And why not? E-mail is the easiest to use and the easiest to understand. The number of people who recognize that Mary-Mary@quite-contrary.com is an electronic mail address exceeds the number of people who recognize that http://www.quite-contrary.com is a Web page address. I still meet people who don't understand the difference between the two, and how that relates to the Internet as a whole . . . but that's another story altogether.

Very few communication vehicles allow you the flexibility and ease of response that e-mail does, especially when no one's there to take your call. Sure, you can always leave a voice mail or fax a note. Have you compared costs lately? I can send 25 or more targeted e-mail messages for the cost of one long-distance phone call to my mother in Florida. (Of course, Mom isn't on the Internet . . . yet.) Who isn't sick of telephone tag and voice mailboxes? E-mail helps you build customer relationships quickly. There is a definite sense of closure when you send an e-mail message that answers someone's questions quote by quote.

Another nice thing about electronic mail is the ease with which you can communicate with one, two, three, or multitudes of people at once. Besides being convenient, e-mail is even more powerful than the telephone, due to its potentially unlimited reach and low cost. E-mail can service customers, build one-on-one relationships, distribute newsletters, and automatically respond whenever a human is unavailable. Of course, the potential for abuse is just as great as its advantages.

If you have a customer's e-mail address you have his or her attention. Use it judiciously and respect its value. E-mail is the ultimate customer-relationship tool. Once you uncover your customers' e-mail addresses and where they hang out online, you're halfway to uncovering your competitor's customers. Newsgroups and lists are e-mail-driven. You can search these archives by a keyword that suits your area of interest and immediately find out where the good discussions are being held. Be careful. Strategic use of e-mail doesn't mean gathering up lists of addresses to add to your "shotgun" e-mail archives. It includes participating in these discussions in a useful and helpful manner. Yes, it takes time. Lots of people don't want to take the time. That's where they alienate potential customers.

Make a Million Dollars Overnight!

By now, you've probably come across advertisements that promise you the ability to reach millions of prospects on the Internet for little or no cost. These ads sell direct e-mail address lists. Online marketers who promote the use of these lists claim that they are *providing a service.* They claim that intelligent people *welcome* updates on information of interest to them. OK. I'm intelligent. You're intelligent. I'll buy that. But who decides what is interesting? I do. Marketers do, too. As a result, too many ads for solar-powered nose-hair clippers, professional dog-walking services, and swampland investment opportunities have ended up in my in-box, only to be met with a quick delete. My nose is fine, I don't own a dog, and I like living in the mountains, thank you.

How happy do you think your customers would be if you launched a telemarketing campaign that interrupted their work flow with annoying phone calls on a regular basis? How long do you think your customers would tolerate your continued waste of their office supplies (i.e., facsimile paper) while you tie up their incoming fax line with ads for your discounted products? While marketers who use the shotgun approach may reap *some* benefits from this type of advertising, the long-term effect is that they've created a reputation for reckless and inconsiderate marketing.

I've seen the result of many of these campaigns, and I have yet to believe that most people welcome unsolicited e-mail. With a 14.4 Kbps dial-up modem connection and a hundred worthless e-mail messages a day, I'm getting a lot of laundry done while my mail downloads. Before you decide to spend money purchasing someone else's bulk e-mail address list, think about whether or not there is a better, more professional way to approach your marketing.

If you choose to contact your customers via e-mail, do so with caution, incorporating business ethics and professional courtesy.

If someone has contacted you, you know they are already interested in your company. This is the time to ask them if they would
like to receive regular news through either e-mail or another
method. Think about offering customers the opportunity to
receive e-mail, just as credit card companies do when they
include a mail-removal form in your monthly statement. You
might even consider drafting a policy for e-mail communications
with customers. Spell out what types of e-mail messages are sent
and how often. Determine up front how you will respond to
requests for information. Make sure that there is a mechanism in
place for removing and/or flagging a customer's e-mail address
when asked to stop. If marketers don't take on this responsibility,
you can be sure that legislators eventually will.

3. Cross-Pollinate

Advertise that you're advertising. Few people will know you're on
the Internet unless you tell them. Recognize that the Internet can
be used in many different ways and not just online. You'll see
very quickly how your marketing use of the Internet can and
should be made visible. Your customers should be able to notice
that you are marketing on the Internet whether or not they're sitting in front of their computers looking at a Web page or in the
bathroom reading a favorite magazine. Think I'm joking? We talk
about television programs even when we're not viewing the tube,
don't we? The same goes for the Internet. The Internet can become
very visible when it is integrated properly into your preexisting
traditional marketing projects.

   A good way to get in this frame of mind is to sit down with a
list of all of your marketing communications activities. Take out a
blank sheet of paper (or open up a word-processing file if you prefer). Start listing every possible use for every possible marketing
element as it relates to the Internet. Do you print an 800 number
on your direct mailers? Include your Web address right next to it.
Do you tell your customers about upcoming trade shows? Mention
your e-mail address. By advertising your online presence in this
manner, you have increased your visibility many times, and you
will have stretched your marketing budget even more. You even

create added credibility by announcing your online presence in other media. If you're having trouble thinking in this manner, don't fret. We have lots of help for you later on in this book. Once you start making some efforts to incorporate your e-mail address and your URL into all your traditional marketing communications media, it will become second nature.

Product buyers don't have time to hunt around. Put your e-mail and Web page info on your brochures, in cover letters, and in your advertisements. Instruct sales and customer service to routinely promote your Internet addresses. Go out of your way to include traditional contact information online, as well. You can't assume you know every customer's comfort or technical level, or even their personal preferences. The Internet is a wonderful tool that has the potential of taking customers all the way through the sales process, from first inquiry to order processing. Guess what? It doesn't always happen that way. At some point during the sales process, customers will want to pick up the phone and talk to a human being. Maybe they'll even want to cue an RFP (request for proposal) already on their hard drive and fax it from their machine to yours. Perhaps they'll like to drop in for a demo, if you happen to be in the same city. The point is, not everyone will take advantage of that nifty order-entry system you've installed at your Web site . . . nor should they be forced to.

4. Provide Extra Value

Create a reason for customers to visit you online. With thousands of networks already connected and commercial use of the Internet growing at unparalleled rates every month, you must stand out to get noticed. If you can find something that doesn't exist anywhere else online, you've got it made. If you can find something that exists elsewhere, but can add your own unique and original spin to it, you've also got it made. There are lots of sites that fall short in this department in that they simply offer the basics. There's nothing wrong with that. Somebody has to supply the essentials. If you can go beyond that, you're providing extra value and attracting more visitors. If you can continue to offer something extra on a regular basis, you will continue to attract return visitors and new ones, long after the initial excitement about your Web site has diminished.

Try running a contest along with your other marketing programs. Offer an incentive, such as a customized service or give-away, for customers who register online. Consider offering something not available anywhere else, such as an online calculator for determining costs or making decisions. Consider a product drawing to give away to qualified, registered visitors. This is the same reasoning you apply when you prepare a trade show exhibit and it certainly applies here as well. How do you get people to your booth? Put on a show, do something creative, catchy, or wild, or offer a great demo or tutorial. How do you get them to your Web site and how do you get them back? Yes, you have the idea!

5. Analyze Content and Use

Think about how your customers react to your marketing literature or programs. Do they ask for additional materials, or do you supply them with everything at once? Decide whether or not you want to prequalify Web visitors or e-mail inquiries every step of the way. Companies sometimes take the tiered approach to distributing sales literature. They might choose to supply the essentials to initial contacts. Information gatherers or researchers would receive more detailed information. Finally, the most extensive collateral would be given to those who are truly in the buying mode. You can create tiers of online content as well. For example, you can create an area on your Web for free access by anyone, and provide even more data for those who register as legitimate buyers.

The Use of Your Literature Varies Greatly

Think about how your customers react to information that they gather. Think about how they use that information and the next step they take before they decide to buy your product or services. Use that thinking to create your flow of information on the Internet.

Think about how customers use your marketing literature and what the shelf life is for each piece that they take with them. Do you remember how you approached the development of your product literature? Did you decide to produce it in a three-hole-punched format because you knew that most buyers in your industry liked to file it in a binder? Did you decide to reproduce bulleted versions of individual product benefits on a wallet-size card for the new sales staff to carry? Did you leave plenty of white space or borders in the layout because you knew that your customers liked to have room to jot notes in the margins? If you did these or similar things, then you know what I'm talking about.

The Decision Process Varies as Well

When customers contact you online, what types of questions do they ask? Wouldn't those frequently asked questions be useful if put on your Web site? If you can identify a pattern, any pattern, of use, then you can decide how to approach your content, graphics, formatting, and layout for the Internet. Too many times, decisions to supply information on the Internet are made without this consideration. The Web site is designed in a vacuum, or worse, it detracts from other marketing material that has demonstrated success.

Determine how to supply content in a way that is logical, making sure that it complements or enhances your current efforts. Take into account your customer's work flow, decision-making process, and even purchasing time frame. With this strategic data in mind, you can determine the best way to present your material on the Internet.

6. Repurpose Materials

Do you want to speed up your Internet launch? Use shortcuts. *Repurposing* is an old multimedia term that means to take content from one media and reuse it on another. Repurpose or reuse the content from existing materials and revise it for the Internet. Your current library of literature is perfectly acceptable with some alterations.

Scenario 1: Do you keep getting the same routine requests and supplying the same answers? Excerpt text from your sales brochures in brief informational chunks that answer first-tier questions. These boilerplates can reside on your hard drive (if you use an off-line mail reader) or in your online files directory. Paste the documents into your response and *voilà!* You've just saved yourself hours of repetitive customer-service activities.

Scenario 2: Take a look at your data sheets and brochures. Open the accompanying file on your computer. Strip out the fluffy ad copy, expand on the facts, and reformat accordingly. Now you've just started creating materials that will work in your online document library or Web Page.

Let's not get too carried away with this idea of revising for the Internet, though. I'm not advising you to re-create your entire literature library on the Web and leave it at that. I'm not saying you should eliminate any key selling points or your personality from Internet copywriting, either. Enthusiasm for your product will win out over empty and unsupported claims any day.

Some customers will be more than glad to find your news release or company brochure in full-text version online. They'll grab it and forward it to someone else with their own comments, and you'll be glad you went to the trouble of uploading this information. On the other hand, you will have lots of people who expect to find something entirely different when they get to your coveted spot on the Web. And these people are not to be ignored.

7. Design with Online in Mind

Repurposing works fine for some portions of your online content, but you'll also need to create new materials specifically for online use. Remember, the Internet shouldn't be an online mirror of your off-line activities. It is acceptable to duplicate certain activities online, as I've mentioned previously, but creativity in capitalizing on the unique features of the Internet should be your ultimate goal.

Ads in cyberspace have a different touch and feel than traditional advertising. Ads on the Internet don't resemble print ads, and users access them differently. Print design elements, such as fancy die-cut shapes, varnishes, pop-ups, and holograms don't translate to online. Neither do double-page ads. Sure, you can scroll back and forth in certain browsers to view an extra-wide page, but you lose the impact you may have had with an identical print ad. That's why it's important to investigate the special features of the online world and take advantage of them. These features may include animated graphics or special scripts in Java.

To help you become familiar with how online layouts differ, I've included a preliminary comparison chart (Figure 1.1). This chart is not all-inclusive, but it will help you think in terms of the uniqueness of the Internet, along with its similarities. As you can see, on the Internet a marketer must deal with text-based multi-document links, computer-monitor width and height considerations, and graphics and file-size decisions. Not only must you become aware of online aesthetics, but you must incorporate them into your documents.

If creating a Web presence is another one of your many job responsibilities, don't be tempted to learn HyperText Markup Language (HTML) yourself unless you truly have the time to do it right. Hire a graphic artist and/or programmer with documented experience in designing for multimedia applications.

Print	Online
Fancy die cuts	Transparent GIF banners, tiled background textures
Double-page print ads	Web pages with frames, computer-monitor limits
Fractional consecutive page ads	Ad banners on unordered and multiple Web pages
Preferred advertising positions	Rotating ad banners at the top/bottom of pages
Catalog order forms	Online forms, HTML–to–e-mail functions
Beginning table of contents, appendixes	Hyperlinks, Java remote windows, search engines
Four-color printing process	Hardware, software, graphics, and HTML limits
Metallic colors and varnishes	Display variances that change or distort
Corporate typefaces	Browser font limitations, viewer display preferences

Figure 1.1 Print versus online design elements.

I'm not discounting all the wonderful tools that can help make HTML programming painless. There are some great programs on the market today that have helped make it easier for many people who don't have the time to decipher HTML code. Of course, assuming an HTML editor is going to create great Web pages is like assuming that a graphics program is going to create great art. Sometimes the amount of hours spent developing a layout and graphics for the Web is directly proportional to the appeal and effectiveness of the end result. In other words, if you don't have the time, don't waste your time. Hire a professional. Don't experiment on your image and budget with on-the-job training.

8. Plan Frequent Revisions

Computers can deceive you because online files are invisible. As you sit at your computer typing away, you may realize that there are tons of files on the network or on your hard drive that you haven't looked at in months. Gee, the filenames are pretty cryptic. Do you ever wonder if you need to do anything with them? You can fall into the trap of forgetting that your Internet files need updating as well.

Your online materials should be the first set of literature updated. Remember, it's a selling point to tell your customers that the "latest information is always online." Some sites, such as online newspapers, are updated daily. That's usually not a problem. It's the other Web sites and mailbot replies that worry me. If your site is one that grows and grows over a period of time, you may not get around to looking at those earlier pages.

In every single online file, include a comment on the date and person who last revised it. Do this with your boilerplate ASCII documents, the files in your FTP site, and your Web pages. If you keep a "golden copy" of each of your brochures for marking changes before the next print run, you already know what I'm going to tell you. Keep a master checklist of all your online documents. Make sure you note the filename, a brief description of contents, and the date each document was uploaded or revised. If at all possible, keep "golden copies" of these documents printed out and filed in a master notebook in a central location for noting changes or errors. Make sure you make those changes on a regular basis and remember to actually upload those changed files to your Internet server. This will help prevent your site from winning an Internet ghost award as an abandoned site.

9. Manage for the Long Term

Don't sign up for an Internet account with the intent that you'll try it out for a while. Unfortunately, some of you are wincing now. Your manager says, "Let's go on the Internet and see how it does for us. If we don't see a substantial difference in our sales over the next three months then we'll try something else." If you are working with someone who tells you this, here's some ammunition.

It could be that e-mail was the vehicle your hidden market needed to contact you. If you disconnect your e-mail, it's like telling the world you've gone out of business. You wouldn't disconnect your telephone and expect to keep your doors open, would you? If you aren't in it for the long haul, you won't make it for the short haul, either. Take your Internet opportunity seriously. Creating and maintaining an Internet presence takes dedication, time, ingenuity, time, resources, and time. Take and assign responsibility for your Internet program and proactively upgrade as your needs grow.

Also, if you can't put your Internet documents on a machine that's running around the clock, then consider using your access provider's machine. The Internet is a 24-hour mall. Your Web site becomes sorely conspicuous if it's closed when the customer is ready to shop.

10. Set Reasonable Goals

In spite of what some people would have you believe, this is not a get-rich-quick scheme. Your sales are not going to skyrocket overnight. Decide what you want your Internet presence to accomplish and plan how to achieve those goals. Measure results in reasonable terms, such as enhancing customer service, offering 24-hour access, or decreasing software distribution and packaging costs. Don't let external factors pressure you into believing that the Internet will help you attain something that wasn't possible for your service or product anyway. Be conservative, be fair, and be patient with your expectations.

The Internet has the potential to become equal to or greater than any other element in your marketing mix. By incorporating the preceding strategies into your thinking, you are prepared to begin tackling your online presence. By the time you finish this book, you will have improved your chances of creating the most effective Internet presence possible for your company.

PART ONE

Creation: Building Your Internet Marketing Plan

chapter two

Preparing the Business Overview and Executive Summary

Most typical marketing plans begin with a Business Overview and Executive Summary, a section that details what the company is all about and further defines the parameters for the company's existence. This chapter will help you better understand how your particular company's Internet marketing approach may be influenced by your company's philosophy, history, goals, and objectives.

In this chapter, you will draft the introductory section of your Internet marketing plan. Some of the steps in this chapter may seem unnecessary to you at first, until you see how other companies are reusing the content from this chapter in their Internet marketing activities. Once you analyze the real company examples and complete the exercises in this chapter, you'll be able to create this section of the plan on your own.

Section One: Business Overview and Executive Summary

Your Internet marketing plan is best supported by including data that reinforces your decision to market on the Internet. Section One of your Internet marketing plan may include any combination of the following:

- ◆ Internet marketing plan introduction
- ◆ Company overview

- ◆ Products and/or services overview
- ◆ Market or industry definition
- ◆ A summary of the risks associated with relying solely on traditional marketing activities

Getting the Most out of This Chapter

The activities in this chapter include reviewing and comparing examples of how companies have created executive overviews, whether they are used for corporate brochures, marketing plans, or Web pages. During this process, you will notice that some companies are very long-winded when introducing themselves, while others barely provide any insight at all. Some companies are conservative in their approach, presenting their company history in a very formal tone. Still others are relaxed, injecting humor at every opportunity.

Reusing This Section of Your Internet Marketing Plan

In Chapter 1, I mentioned repurposing materials, such as content, to get the most mileage out of your marketing activities. Here's what I mean. Portions of the content created for this section of the Internet marketing plan can be repurposed in one or more of the ways shown in Figure 2.1.

Company Overview

Don't know where you've been? Then how will you know where you're going? This variation on the old cliché applies neatly to the concept of reviewing your company's formation and activities. Nowhere else than in a written marketing plan is it more important to understand your company's history. In this section of your marketing plan, you will also provide a brief description of your company, tying it in with your purpose in creating an online visibility.

Most of the basic information can come from a company background document, such as a brochure. If you don't have a com-

Traditional	Internet
Opening statement of written marketing plan	Opening statement of written marketing plan
Company background brochure	Company background Web page, as in about.html
On-hold message for incoming telephone calls	E-mail autoresponder, as in info@wolfBayne.com
Boilerplate paragraph for product literature	Boilerplate signature block for e-mail messages
Company slogans or tag lines in print ads	Company slogans or tag lines in ad banners
Editor's notes for company news releases	Brief notes for online Web site announcement

Figure 2.1   Repurposing: how to reuse the business overview.

pany background, this will be your opportunity to create an outline for one that can always be used for traditional marketing purposes later.

Some Activities You Can Do Now

◆ Go to your favorite Internet search index or directory site. If you don't have a favorite search engine, start at Yahoo!, http://www.yahoo.com. If you don't get enough results from your search here, click on the other directory links found at the bottom of the page. Yahoo! will send your search with you to the next location.

◆ Search for pages that include the words "About this company," "Welcome," "Company profile," "Company overview," or "Company background."

◆ Read the corporate overviews at the various company sites. Excerpts from additional company overviews are found later in this chapter.

What Is the Name of Your Company?

Of course, you know your own company name. The question is . . . does everyone else? You may have been prudent in referring correctly to your company over the years, but everyone else has not been. Whether people are referring to your company correctly in print and especially online is part of your image management or public relations program. Whether you have the time, resources, energy, or inclination to correct everyone doesn't really matter here.

Why Is Your Name So Important?

My purpose in having you pay attention to your company's identity at this point in your Internet marketing plan formation is simple. Company and product confusion does occur on the Internet. In some cases, it occurs more frequently than in traditional marketing. Take the case of the domain name supplier who was offering vanity e-mail addresses closely resembling the domains of prestigious universities. The only difference in the legitimate university's domain name and the bogus one was the domain name extension, *.com instead of *.edu. For companies, this problem can significantly impact sales. Imagine a customer mistakenly sending e-mail to manufacturer.org when the intended recipient was manufacturer.com. Be aware of this phenomenon, and keep alert for potential problems and opportunities from the very beginning. You'd be amazed at the information you'll uncover online once you start experimenting with how your company and products are referenced.

Identifying your company's complete name and any variation thereof will help you when it's time to brainstorm about registering an Internet domain name (Chapter 9, *Developing a Corporate Identity*). Start thinking now about all the different possibilities, keeping in mind what customers and the press have called your organization. For example, Federal Express knew its customer base had already nicknamed it "FedEx." The company was able to capitalize on this market identification by changing its logo to match that image and publicizing its registered domain name of fedex.com.

You may wish to keep your company name list handy if you decide to put together a trademark page for your Web site. McDonald's has a very extensive trademark page, and if you ever have any doubts as to how much stock the company puts in its corporate identity, just drop by and check it out. For starters, McDonald's main home page is located at http://www.mcdonalds.com/. For a quick lesson in extensive variations on the name game, check out http://www.mcdonalds.com/legal.

A Rose by Any Other Name . . .

Here are some examples of organizations that have more than one name by which they are or have been known. These are variations that have been both spoken and written, in print and online. Notice that some companies are lucky enough to deal with only a few variations on their moniker, while others are not as fortunate. The most extreme case that follows is the result of multiple name changes and acquisitions of the company over the last decade or so. By the way, not all of the name variations listed are accepted and/or used by the companies involved. Sometimes a company continues to be referenced by an obsolete name for years after it has changed its identification. In many cases, it can be the customer or industry press that decides how the company is referenced, whether the company likes it or not. Of course, this problem is nothing that a good branding campaign can't repair . . . but not necessarily overnight. (In some of these examples the URL is not included in the bookmark file because the company did not have a Web site at the time of this book's publication.)

- ◆ *Business Marketing Association.*   Also referred to as BMA since 1993, formerly the Business/Professional Advertising Association or B/PAA (1973), formerly the Association of Industrial Advertisers (1959), formerly the National Industrial Advertising Association (1922), sometimes nicknamed the Business Marketing Club. Chose to register the domain name marketing.org because bma.org was taken by the British Medical Association.

- *Discovery Zone Fun Centers.* Also referred to as Discovery Zone, DZ, the Zone. They do *not* currently own the registered domain names of discoveryzone.com (registered to an adult site) or dz.com. Another domain name preference, zone.com, is registered by Microsoft Corporation.

- *Federal Express Corporation.* Also referred to as FedEx, Federal Express; may be used as a verb, as in "I'll FedEx this package to you." Registered domain name is fedex.com.

- *JCPenney Company, Inc.* Also referred to as J.C. Penney, Penney's. Besides the obvious registered domain name of jcpenney.com, the company has registered several domain names for its various divisions and brands, including Arizona Jean Company (arizonajeanco.com) and Hunt Club (huntclub.com).

- *McDonald's Corporation.* Also referred to as McDonald's, McDonald's Hamburgers, Mickey D's, the Golden Arches. Registered domain names are mcdonalds.com and mcd.com.

- *Philips LMS.* Also referred to as LMS International, LMS, LMSI, LMSIC, Laser Magnetic Storage International Company, Laser Magnetic Storage International, Laser Magnetic Storage, Laser Magnetics; formerly known as Optical Storage International. Registered domain name is lms.com.

- *United States Holocaust Memorial Museum.* Also referred to as USHMM, the Holocaust Museum, the Holocaust Memorial Museum, the U.S. Holocaust Museum. Registered domain name is ushmm.org. Oddly enough, the domain name of holocaust.org is registered to a Radio Shack in Louisville, Kentucky. Don't ask!

Where You'll Find This Information Helpful

Here's a summary of why you should pay attention to your company's name. By experimenting with variations on your company name, you can do the following:

- Find your company more quickly in online search engines.
- Find editorial coverage through a clipping service vendor.
- Find identity conflicts with existing companies worldwide.
- Find conflicting and misleading registered domain names.
- Find a better way to list your company in print and online in order to gain prominence.
- Brainstorm about possible company domain names.
- Brainstorm about corporate images you wish to create or enhance.
- Brainstorm about possible negative connotations in other languages.

How Long Has Your Company Been in Existence?

Why would anybody care how long your company has been in business? In traditional marketing terms, it speaks to your company's longevity. Older companies can claim that they are more likely to be around tomorrow if I need to return a product or buy more parts. Comparatively, in the Internet universe, three years is a long time. Internet service providers that have been in existence for only six months can boast a strong and growing customer base. The difference is that these types of companies emphasize their customer service and product features far more than they do their age. Take a look at Netscape. Do you think anybody cares right now how long they've been in business when they've got a major share of the browser market?

Somewhere along the line you will want to have this historical data on hand, but don't waste energy on compiling a detailed timeline for your Internet marketing plan. While it's nice to know that you're not just some fly-by-night company, most of the information related to company dates is of limited importance for Internet marketing purposes. Of course, including dates in your Internet marketing plan helps put things into perspective by reminding management and others of your progress . . . to a degree. You can always refer to the company birthdate as a starting point when you reference how many changes your company has or has not gone through over the years.

One tip: State your company's age by mentioning the year (e.g., established in 1922) you were established or founded rather than the *number* of years (e.g., 25-year-old company). The reason? For traditional marketing literature, you can avoid outdating your material before its shelf life expires. "Twenty-five years in business" is accurate this year, but what about the next? When you create a brochure, you'll be forced to wait until the inventory depletes or the content changes dramatically before you can fix the date on the next print run.

"So what? This is the Internet. I can update it immediately." Yeah, but do you want to? State it right the first time and it will be one less minuscule detail for you to overlook and for nitpickers to notice. If you have some hidden psychological agenda that indicates a preference to stating the number of years, then feel free to ignore what I just said.

If you're a brand-new company, you probably won't use very many reference dates when you repurpose materials for your Web site. "Established last month" doesn't sound so hot when you're trying to pitch your company's stability. This is a good opportunity to look at other company strengths, such as its leadership, technology, or product line. If you're still convinced that stating your company's age really makes a difference in your ability to sell your company in either traditional or online marketing, then be brief; include it and be done with it.

Where You'll Find This Information Helpful

Here's a summary of why dates are important to your company and your market: With dates, you can demonstrate longevity for your company, both for traditional and online marketing purposes; establish a track record in customer service over a long period of time; find companies with a prior claim to (and possibly registration for) your preferred domain name; exploit how your new company offers cutting-edge technology and products.

Real World Examples

Here are some examples of organizations that have publicized their organizational birthdate as part of their Internet marketing image. Some of these examples are helpful, while others leave you wondering why the company representatives thought it was important to publicize the information at all. The dates and descriptive sentences were gathered from a variety of sources, including Web site backgrounds and search engine descriptions. If you visit these sites and find yourself wondering why I chose them, let me clarify: The mention of a Web site here does not necessarily represent an endorsement of any type. I'm merely including them as differing examples of how some organizations use this aspect of their company's history as part of their Internet and traditional marketing presence.

- e-MATH home page of the *American Mathematical Society.* Founded in 1888 to further mathematical research and scholarship. Web site address: http://www.ams.org/.
- *Art Libraries Society of North America.* Founded in 1972, serves the interests of librarians, visual resources professionals, educators, and others interested in arts information. Web site address: http://www.uflib.ufl.edu/arlis/.
- *Contemporary Arts Museum, Houston.* Founded in 1948, CAM presents changing exhibitions of local, national, and international artists. Web site address: http://riceinfo.rice.edu/projects/cam/.
- *Cromwell Architects Engineers.* Cromwell is one of the oldest architectural-engineering firms in continuous practice in America today. Founded in 1885, Cromwell is a multidisciplinary firm with design principles that reflect the highest standards of quality and the latest of technology, while working within the constraints of time and budget. Web site address: http://www.cromwell.com/.
- *Flat Iron Cartoon Company.* The Flat Iron Cartoon Company was founded in 1908 in an abandoned grain

silo, 15 miles outside of Keokuk, Iowa. Trading their corn and beans for cotton, the Clacker brothers were able to process their spun raw cotton into thick, puffy short-sleeved shirts. Web site address: http://www.flatironcc.com/.

◆ *Harry Rubin Studio.*   Textile design since 1938, combining fine art, fashion trends, and the textile industry. HR Studio bridges the gap between designers and mills. Web site address: http://www.panix.com/~hrstudio/hrstudio.htm.

◆ *The Ross School in East Hampton, New York.*   An innovative laboratory school founded in 1991 by Courtney Sale Ross and her late husband, Steven J. Ross. Web site address: http://ross.pvt.k12.ny.us/.

What Type of Business Is Your Company Engaged In?

Use this section of your Internet marketing plan to identify areas of your company's products and services that would do well online for whatever reason. Take a good long look at your product and service line and its relationship to Internet marketing. You'll soon uncover some good opportunities on which to capitalize. This is where you get down to business and tell what you do for a living. This is the tip of the iceberg when it comes to deciding whether or not you should be online.

During a presentation at a local business conference, I was asked by someone in the audience whether or not he should market his services on the Internet. I asked the gentleman what he did for a living. He responded that he was a house painter.

Kim: Have you ever been asked for an e-mail address by any of your customers?
Painter: No.
Kim: The last time you went to your paint supplier, did anyone ask you for an e-mail address?
Painter: No.
Kim: What do you hope to accomplish with your business by marketing online?

Painter: I want to use it to increase my visibility in the community.

Kim: Do you know if any other housepainter in your area is marketing on the Internet?

Painter: I checked. I can't find any yet.

Kim: Bingo! Then start marketing on the Internet.

It doesn't hurt to be the first in your industry or the first in your market area to take advantage of the unique marketing power of the Internet. Even in a seemingly low-tech profession like housepainting, you can reap the benefits of the added credibility of being online. Potential customers may not browse the Internet looking for a housepainter, but painters can certainly take advantage of e-mail to provide bids in a fast and convenient manner. Of course, when you get to Chapter 4, *Formulating Marketing Communications Strategies,* you'll see that there really *is* more to marketing on the Internet than just being first. But it's a nice place to start.

While you're writing this section of your plan, avoid superlatives, such as "the greatest company on earth," "foremost in its field," and "an industry leader." If your company is all these things, everybody in your company knows it anyway. If they don't, and it's true, you should be able to demonstrate it rather quickly without puffery. Statistics are useful, as are sales figures and references to good product reviews.

Now you may be thinking, *"Hey, but this is an Internet marketing plan. I know I'm going to reuse some of this stuff and sweeten it during implementation, but management is going to read the real stuff first! They* like *superlatives."* OK, I'll grant you that. Management *is* going to read it first. Respect them enough to give it to them straight. Remember, you have to live with the final Internet marketing plan document. Save your personality and clever prose for online. If management chooses not to approve your plan because you took my advice, you've got bigger problems than a simple style issue.

Real-World Examples

Here are some examples of organizational descriptions and how they were translated into documents and keywords. Notice that keywords can consist of one, two, three, or more words and phrases. Keep in mind that these examples are from the final implementation result, as seen on the companies' Web sites, and not from their Internet marketing plans. Companies just don't give out proprietary information like they used to! See if you can tell the difference between the sweetened text (the advertising slant) and the facts (basic information that you'll start with for your Internet marketing plan).

- The American Academy of Ophthalmology (Web site address: http://www.eyenet.org/)

  Description.   The American Academy of Ophthalmology is an international member association of more than 22,000 ophthalmologists, physicians who provide comprehensive eye care, including medical, surgical, and optical care. This site provides authoritative information about eye care for the public, and serves the professional needs of the Academy's members.

  Keywords.   amblyopia, anterior segment, surgery, astigmatism, cataract, cataract surgery, contact lens, cornea, cornea external, disease, doctor, diabetic retinopathy, eye, eye care, eye disease, eye safety, eye surgery, eyeglasses, eyesight, glaucoma, glaucoma 2000, hyperopia, iris, laser, laser surgery, learning disabilities, lens, macular degeneration, M.D., medical, myopianeuroophthalmology, ophthalmic, ophthalmology, optical, optician, optometrypathology, pediatric ophthalmology, photorefractive keratectomy, plastic surgery, reconstructive surgery, plastic reconstructive surgery, presbiopia, PRK, refractive errors, refractive surgery, retina, retina vitreous, RK, sclera, strabismus, vision, vision care, care, vitreous, medical doctor, american academy of ophthalmology, academy, american

- Infoseek Guide home page (Web site address: http://www.infoseek.com/)

  Description.   From Infoseek's "About" page, located at http://info.infoseek.com/: "Search and browse the Internet for free! Infoseek Guide is your roadmap to the Internet! Search and browse Web pages, Usenet newsgroups, FTP and Gopher sites, and more!"

Keywords.   Infoseek Guide, search Web pages, Usenet newsgroups, articles, FTP sites, Gopher sites, search engine, World Wide Web search service, find information, locate information, get information, find Web pages, navigate Internet, browse subjects, navigation service.

◆ Microsoft Corporation (Web site address: http://www. microsoft.com/)

Description.   From its "Mission Statement" page, located at http://www.microsoft.com/jobs/guide/ mission.htm: "At Microsoft, our long-held vision of a computer on every desk and in every home continues to be at the core of everything we do. We are committed to the belief that software is the tool that empowers people both at work and at home. Since our company was founded in 1975, our charter has been to deliver on this vision of the power of personal computing."

Keywords.   From the description META HTML tag on its home page: Microsoft Corporate Information, Product Support, and More! (A META HTML tag allows search engines to catalog Web pages.)

Of course, Microsoft really doesn't have to say anything more than that to the rest of the world.

Product and Market Definition: Is It Time to Get Online?

Ask yourself if there exists an online market for your products and services. If you are unable to uncover any proof that Internet commerce currently exists for your company, this may point to some unique opportunities. The definition of your products and services, along with online factors related to them, will be included in brief in your Internet marketing plan. Let's begin by gathering some basic information now. If you already know that your products are being marketed online, then you're ahead of the game. If not, you'll need to do some preliminary research, such as searching online for the following:

- Examples of companies that are similar to yours
- Examples of products that are similar to yours
- Examples of services that are similar to yours

Some Activities You Can Do Now

- Select a search index or directory.
- Enter keywords for your company, products, services, and industry.
- Try searching the company names of your competitors, too.
- Your search will provide you with links to other sites. Go to these sites to find links to similar companies.
- Make notes for your Internet marketing plan.

Where You'll Find This Information Helpful

Here's a summary of how you'll be able to use keywords in your marketing program. With keywords, you can do the following:

- Select categories for product and company listings in industry publications and directories.
- Insert keyword META tags into your Web documents.
- Use keyword descriptions for registering with manually compiled Internet search indexes.
- Use keyword searches for finding your competitors in these same search indexes.
- Use keyword searches for sites that would be good prospects for swapping reciprocal links.

Why Are Some Companies Online?

Some quintessentially bad examples (or good, depending on your viewpoint) of why companies fail in their marketing efforts can be found on the Internet. By searching in any of a dozen directories, you can find companies that not only don't know why they are online, they don't even know why they are in business.

As I was watching television the other night, I noticed that the majority of commercials shown during prime time were of local car dealers. Most of these car dealers displayed a Web page address boldly on the screen while a talking head told the viewer how many cars they *had* to sell by "sundown tonight." I've always wondered why some auto dealers feel it is important to brag about how many cars they have to sell to meet their quotas. I'm much more impressed with low prices, quality products, personable customer service, and selection.

Some of these car dealer sites had no real reason to be online. I expected descriptions of the special services they offered to their online and off-line customers. What I found were ads. Pages and pages of ads. I wanted to know what I could hope to gain by shop-

Figure 2.2   Team Chevrolet Geo offers its e-mail customers a free lube, filter, and oil change.

ping at a particular car dealer. There was no reason for me to ever visit some of these sites again, even if I *were* in the market for a car. By contrast, Team Chevrolet Geo, http://www.teamchevy.com/, provided me with current financing options and a free offer just for setting up an appointment by e-mail (Figure 2.2). Until you can identify why you should promote your services and products online, and what customers will gain from your Internet presence, your site will be nothing more than a very pale imitation of your traditional advertising and public relations campaigns (Figures 2.3 and 2.4).

❑ Prior year marketing plan and schedules

❑ Annual report

❑ Clipping-service order

❑ Corporate brochure

❑ Corporate identity manuals

❑ Corporate news releases

❑ Customer newsletters

❑ Direct-mail pieces

❑ Executive profiles

❑ Stationery and business cards

❑ Editorial-clipping files

❑ Product literature: catalogs, data books, data sheets

❑ Miscellaneous literature on your company and products

❑ Literature title

Completed by: _____ Date: _____

Figure 2.3 Preparing to write your Internet marketing plan: a materials checklist.

Briefly explain why you are writing an Internet marketing plan. (Come back to this question if you are not yet sure.)

_____

_____

_____

_____

_____

_____

What are your company's goals, objectives, philosophies, and charter?

_____

_____

_____

_____

_____

_____

What is the name of your company? (Include parents, divisions, etc.)

_____

_____

_____

State significant dates and events related to your company and its marketing programs.

Date	Event
_____	Company founded _____
_____	_____
_____	_____
_____	_____
_____	_____

Figure 2.4 Drafting the business overview and executive summary (Plan Section One).

What type of business is your company engaged in?

_____

_____

_____

Briefly state your company's charter and/or philosophy.

_____

_____

_____

Comment on future business developments that may or may not affect your marketing plan (i.e., mergers, acquisitions, joint ventures, strategic alliances).

_____

_____

_____

_____

Write a brief company description.

_____

_____

_____

_____

_____

Write a brief description of your company's products and services.

_____

_____

_____

_____

_____

_____

Figure 2.4 (*Continued*)

List keywords for your company, products, services, market, and industry.

_____   _____
_____   _____
_____   _____
_____   _____
_____   _____
_____   _____
_____   _____
_____   _____

List significant key features of your products and services.

_____
_____
_____
_____
_____
_____

List the significant strengths and weaknesses of your products and services. (Some examples are included in italics to get you started.)

Product Name	Strengths	Weaknesses
ColorShift 3000 Laser Printer	*Three-hundred-year service agreement included in price*	*Programming glitch causes blue to print with greenish tint*
Lazy Daisy 2000	*Low price, free lifetime ribbons*	*Market peak reached years ago*

Figure 2.4 (*Continued*)

Summarize your current company sales figures.

_____

_____

_____

_____

State other companies in your industry that are serious competitors. Include the year each was founded.

Date Founded   **Industry Contenders**

_____   _____

_____   _____

_____   _____

_____   _____

_____   _____

Circle all of the companies listed above that are older than your company.

List advantages and disadvantages, opportunities and risks to establishing an Internet marketing presence for your company. (Some examples are included in italics to get you started.)

Advantages, Opportunities   **Disadvantages, Risks**

First company in industry to market online   *First company in industry to make mistakes online*

Reduced distribution costs for mail-order catalog   *Increased staff costs for order fulfillment*

Increased visibility in market niche   *Increased chance of bad online "press"*

Figure 2.4   (*Continued*)

What risks currently exist for your company by relying solely on traditional marketing activities?

_____

_____

_____

_____

_____

_____

_____

_____

_____

_____

Complotod byı _____ Datoı _____

Figure 2.4 (*Continued*)

chapter three

Analyzing Internet Market Statistics

Most typical marketing plans include a section on Analyzing Market Statistics, a section that details what the market is all about and further defines the parameters for a company's participation. This chapter will help you better understand how Internet market statistics vary considerably. Reviewing applicable and reliable statistics can help you determine if you are considering marketing on the Internet for the right or wrong reasons.

The single most important decision you'll make regarding your Internet marketing presence will be whether or not you *even have* an Internet marketing presence. For your company, your industry, or your products, Internet marketing may already be a foregone conclusion. For example, if you work for a computer or electronics manufacturer, most of the companies in your industry are on the Internet already. High-technology marketers were early Internet adopters; therefore market data on this industry's use of the Internet is fairly plentiful. If you're working in an industry that's familiar with Internet marketing, you can probably skip over parts of this chapter and just use the checklists. You have all the justification you need. Just start jotting down what you already know about the Internet and your market. After you've massaged the information into typical marketing plan prose, you can call it Section Two of your Internet marketing plan. However, if you're still trying to prove that the Internet is "the place to be," please keep reading.

In Chapter 2, *Preparing the Business Overview and Executive Summary,* you wrote Section One of your Internet marketing plan.

You reviewed your company history, your products, or your services. You also decided whether or not to continue developing an Internet marketing plan.

In Chapter 3, *Analyzing Internet Market Statistics,* you're going to write Section Two of your Internet marketing plan. This is where you tell everyone how your particular company, which you've previously defined, fits into the Internet marketing picture. You will use Internet demographics, both general and industry-specific, to support your plans to create an Internet marketing presence.

The activities in this chapter just might be the icing on the cake when it comes to negotiating for those coveted Internet marketing dollars. You may wish to read this chapter first, before you consider writing a plan at all. Yeah, I know. Now I tell you. Of course, if the facts you gather while completing this chapter don't sway or delay you, then Chapter 3 is appropriately placed.

Section Two: Analyzing Internet Market Statistics

Your Internet marketing plan is best supported by including data that reinforces your decision to market on the Internet. Section Two of your Internet marketing plan may include any combination of the following:

- ◆ References to general Internet studies
- ◆ References to market or industry-specific studies
- ◆ A summary of how market reports advocate Internet marketing for our company

Getting the Most out of This Chapter

The activities in this chapter include examining the different types of Internet statistics being generated by market research firms and consultants. During this process, you will take notes on data that is useful for your company to include in its Internet marketing plan.

You'll notice that some market reports provide general information with little analysis, while others are very detailed in their approach. Some reports contain descriptions of their report methodology, while others would have you believe that all data should be taken at face value. Still others are detailed in their reporting methods, but their methodology may be flawed.

Active versus Passive Internet Marketing

At the end of this chapter, you may be convinced that there isn't anything to gain from actively marketing on the Internet. You may look at the market patterns or the Internet demographics and decide that your company has no place on the Internet . . . at least for now. You'll then pull the plug on all those great Internet marketing ideas, stick your notepad in your desk drawer, and drive home. At that point, you will have become a *passive* Internet marketer.

Here's where I draw a line in the sand. There are two distinct and complementary approaches to a company's Internet marketing activities. I've defined them as *active* and *passive.* One type of Internet marketing won't survive very well without the other.

Active Internet marketing involves the proactive execution of an ongoing program that creates and maintains an online image, for whatever end. *Passive Internet marketing* includes activities that aren't necessarily visible. For example, if you're strictly a passive Internet marketer, your company has no Web site. You have no definable Internet marketing budget. You don't publicize your e-mail address. Maybe you don't even *want* to publicize your e-mail address.

For the sake of those marketers whose companies are not active in creating visibility on the Internet, but who still consider themselves "Internet marketers," I'll expand the *passive* category. Under passive Internet marketing, I'll include keeping up with the information that's out there, as in the phrase "lurker marketing." Maybe your company uses the Internet to perform market research and track editorial coverage for public relations purposes. You're just not publishing or distributing any information of your own online.

You may be convinced that your market isn't big enough to warrant active Internet marketing, and you're convinced it never will be. You're still not off the hook. If you don't handle your Internet marketing presence for your company, someone else just might. Even if you never put up a Web site or answer someone's e-mail inquiry, you'd be courting disaster if you didn't use the Internet to track news and opinion. Do you know what everyone is saying about you, your industry, and your closest competitor? Whether you know it or not, somewhere, someplace on the Internet, your company has been referenced.

For this reason, I'd like to include *reactive* Internet marketing in the passive category. If you don't have a Web page or any kind of original content initiated by your company, you still have an Internet marketing presence, just not a very big or controllable one. You might suddenly find your company listed somewhere as one of the "all-time worst product manufacturers in the history of the world" just because someone felt like it on a Friday afternoon. At this point, you'll probably track down the culprit and ask for some type of retraction, correction, or chance to air your point of view. You're used to doing that . . . after all, you probably called the editor of that trade magazine to amend the incorrect data that appeared in a recent article. If this ever happens to you—for instance, you find something online about your company that makes you cringe—I hope you'll *reactively* evolve into an *active* Internet marketer so it never happens again.

We'll discuss how you can continually monitor online information in Chapters 10 and 11, *Conducting Market Research* and *Executing Public Relations and Promotional Programs.* For now, we want to concentrate on determining if there's enough evidence to support your case that a viable Internet market exists or can be developed for your products or services. This chapter will also help you determine what type of Internet marketer you are going to become.

Gathering and Applying Data

Now you have to do your homework, which means going to these Web sites, reading industry reports, and contacting people to uncover the most up-to-date and applicable trends. In some cases, you will need to spend some of your marketing budget for specialized reports in order to unearth the most valuable data.

A word of advice: If you pick up this book anytime after its first day of publication, the resources listed in this chapter may already be out of date. New companies are emerging and the reports of established companies may have already been challenged and reassessed. I'm only going to make note of the *types* of reports that are being generated now and how to use them in your marketing plan. You probably still have that old article on Internet demographics sitting in your file cabinet that you're hoping to use. If you want to hammer out a quick-and-dirty marketing plan and don't want to spend any additional time and money, don't say I didn't warn you. Now that I've suitably lectured you on the value of obtaining current information, I'll continue.

Fun with Internet Statistics

No other marketing media has generated as much hype as the Internet. Take a look at some of the different numbers on Internet growth. If you're like me, you're already excited about the possibilities for your company and the future of Internet marketing. Just to keep from getting in hot water, here's a disclaimer. I don't endorse any of the Internet research companies or reports mentioned in this chapter. Nor do I impugn any of them. By the time I warn you that company A doesn't know the difference between the Internet and a fishing net, they'll have issued a startling new report that no one dares challenge . . . at least for another three months anyhow.

How applicable are general Internet demographics to your unique situation? Don't assume anything until you see the qualifying description for each report. Look at the facts and how they were gathered; determine who has the best data for your situation; and ask for references in your industry.

"Come on!" you protest. "Who has the best reports now?" I can't tell you that either, mainly because Internet marketing statistics are so subjective and the numbers change so often. However, I will be glad to comment very briefly on information-gathering methodology.

It's most useful to find a research company that surveys individuals both online and off. Telephone calls and mail surveys are not obsolete just because you have a convenient e-mail account and a few thousand e-mail addresses in your database. Any research company that limits itself to surveying only individuals who are willing to answer a question by e-mail risks eliminating data about a major portion of its market. Trying to reach only online users? Well, just because someone has e-mail doesn't mean that e-mail is the most effective way to get answers. Some people are more receptive to a human voice on the telephone than to one more e-mail survey in the in-box.

Misusing Numbers and Other Mistakes

My favorite and most misused Internet estimate is this one, which is quoted at the Anamorph site: "There are 27,000 Web sites, and this number is doubling every 53 days."

Just for fun, and mainly because you might need a break right now, take a look at the Internet Irresponsible Internet Statistics Generator (Figure 3.1) located at Anamorph, http://www.anamorph.com/docs/stats/stats.html. You can use this Web Statistics Generator to make an irresponsible prediction based on the

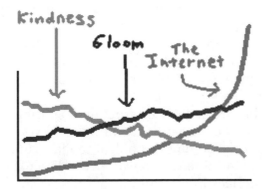

Figure 3.1 Irresponsible Internet statistics. © 1995 by Robert Orenstein, Anamorph, *http://www.anamorph.com/docs/stats/stats.html.*

preceding quote. Simply enter a date in the future and click on the button to compute how many Web sites should be in existence by then. I entered New Year's Day in the year 1998. Here's the ridiculous answer I received:

```
If the number of Web sites were to keep doubling every 53 days, then

On January 1, 1998:

There would be 23,574,707,885 sites on the World Wide Web.

(This represents 3.93 Web sites per person.)
```

Robert Orenstein, creator of the calculator, writes, "Keep in mind that it is impossible for Web growth to continue at this rate." Sun Microsystems Distinguished Engineer Dr. Jakob Nielsen arrived at the original doubling estimate. Dr. Nielsen doesn't "believe the 53-day estimate anymore." He's written an explanation of how he came up with it, how his statement has been misused, and how and why it permeated the industry. His column titled, "Kill the 53-Day Meme" can be found on the Web at the Sun Microsystems site, http://www.sun.com:80/950901/columns/alertbox/index.html. Dr. Nielsen writes, "Of course, growth rates this fast cannot continue indefinitely." His explanation is worth reading, especially to help you put all those exciting and often misquoted Internet statistics in perspective.

Who Cares How Many Web Sites There Are?

What do the number of Web pages or sites have to do with supporting the theory that Internet marketing is a viable option for your company? To use this as a single point in your Internet marketing plan would be like claiming the number of pages in your product catalog is directly proportional to size of your customer base. Showing a growth in Web pages *could* point to some kind of trend. You could claim that the number of Web pages demonstrates an increase in Internet activity and use, which you could extrapolate to mean market acceptance. Does that mean your market or someone else's? Basically, the number of Web pages by itself doesn't demonstrate anything tangible from a marketer's point of view without additional qualifying data. By the way, I'm a big help in adding personal Web pages and sites to the Internet for my friends and family. My miniature dent in somebody's Internet survey statistics doesn't have anything to do with any company's sales except the Internet service provider's. Some Internet statistics are useful. Some are not. And some need a little bit more dissection to be useful. Now that you're ready to take these numbers with a grain of salt, I'm ready to give them to you.

Estimates of Worldwide Users or Hosts

"O'Reilly Survey Sets U.S. Internet Size at 5.8 Million." News release dated October 31, 1995. (*Source:* O'Reilly & Associates, http://www.ora.com/.)

"The Internet has about 26.4 million users as of October 1995, according to a current estimate by Matrix Information and Directory Services." News release dated February 3, 1996. (*Source:* Matrix Information and Directory Services, Inc. (MIDS), http://www.mids.org.)

"Internet Survey Reaches 6.6 Million Internet Host Level— First Half 1995 Growth Is 37 Percent." News release dated August 2, 1995. (*Source:* Internet Society, http://info.isoc .org/infosvc/press/020895press.txt.)

The first thing you'll notice is that no two companies report their statistics in the same way. Until you read the body copy, rather than just the headlines, you're comparing apples to oranges. Are the numbers in one report representative of a subset of another company's report? How does the number of Internet hosts translate into the number of Internet users? Or does it translate at all? How do these different reports complement or contradict each other?

The second thing you'll notice is that not everyone agrees exactly how many users are on the Internet. Let me correct that: Not everyone agrees on *approximately* how many users are on the Internet. As demonstrated by a chart at the CyberAtlas site, http://www.cyberatlas.com/, estimates of the number of U.S. Internet users varies greatly, from a low of 5.8 million to a high of 35 million (Figure 3.2). Why is that so?

It's nearly impossible to know how many people inside an organization have e-mail addresses that are assigned by a specific domain name. A research firm is not going to find that out by counting how many unique names it uncovers in newsgroups. Companies that own multiple domain names account for some of the confusion, as do ghost accounts. I'm referring to those accounts, such as clientservices.pbi@phillips.com, that aren't really created for a specific employee, but rather for a particular function or department, such as customer service.

System administrators and company managers could probably provide us with an idea of how many real human beings in their

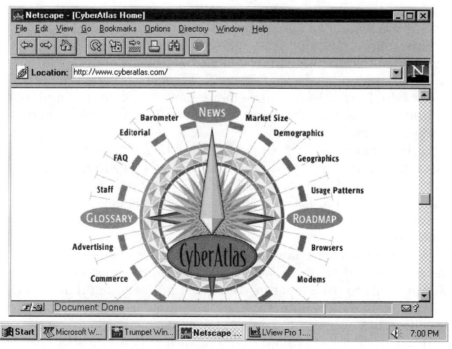

Figure 3.2 CyberAtlas provides summaries of and pointers to a variety of Internet market statistics, including size, demographics, geographics, market research, and growth.

organizations have e-mail addresses. Then there's the daunting
task of contacting the thousands of small businesses around the
world and surveying *their* distribution of account names versus
domain names versus real employees. When market researchers
make these survey telephone calls, sometimes they get an accurate
answer, sometimes a best guess, and sometimes they just get dis-
connected. Sometimes the researcher has had enough on a Friday
afternoon and just wants to go home. Such is life for those hard-
working research folks. That's why you keep hearing references to
"statistical samples." Simply put, it's humanly impossible to survey everybody . . . so there's a whole lotta guessin' goin' on.

Finally, assuming that everybody cooperated with the Internet
surveyers and gave them all the information they needed, you'd
still be in a bind trying to estimate how many unique users are
actually online. Many people in an organization have e-mail
addresses but never use them. Does that make them potential
online customers for your company or not?

Now about those duplicate e-mail addresses. I have several
Internet access accounts, through a combination of independent
ISPs and commercial service providers because of the type of
work I do. Lots of people have more than one e-mail account: one
at home, one at the office, and maybe one at school. How do these
surveys account for that?

Unlike magazine subscription mailing lists where you can weed
out many of the duplicates, the Internet has no central mechanism
for identifying duplicate individuals. At least not currently. Is
Mary Mara from Sausalito, California, the same person as Mary
Mara from Syracuse, New York? Only Mary and her mother know
for sure.

With such a wide span of reported numbers, many being super-
seded on a daily basis by whomever can get the most attention, it
doesn't hurt to dig deeper in your quest for meaningful answers.
That's why you'll need more than the "number of online users" or
the "number of hosts" to support your Internet marketing program. Now that I've said all that, I'll warn you. You'll still hear
some Internet surveyers claim that they can estimate the size of
the Internet. Well, I'm still reserving judgment.

Growth of the Internet

"The Internet is demonstrating significant growth. The number of respondents who had access to the Internet increased 50% between 8/95 and 3/96, with an actual usage growth probably in the same range." (*Source:* CommerceNet, http://www.commerce .net/.)

This measurement of Internet growth has more credibility than the "53-day meme" mentioned earlier. Admirably enough, CommerceNet qualified its statement by declaring that these calculations represent "respondents." The company doesn't try to add to the hype by inflating the significance of its report in the overall scheme of things. As you review the examples you find during your preparation of this section of the plan, keep this in mind.

The number of survey respondents is an important factor in determining whether or not the research company did a thorough job or just went through the motions. Percentages of respondents surveyed are even better. If you know that your market consists of 40,000 professionals, and the research firm has obtained completed surveys from 2,000, you know that they have compiled a report based on 5 percent of your target market. If a certain publication has 35,000 subscribers, and the publishing company has obtained completed surveys from one-twelfth of their entire subscriber base, that gives you something more to go on as well. It's worth asking more questions so you can better interpret the research company's findings.

How Are Growth Statistics Useful?

Showing growth can affect your decision to select a particular media, such as the Internet. If no one in your industry is placing ads on the radio, for example, you're going to look much harder at this choice for your marketing mix. If you regularly review the media kits of trade or business publications during your media planning, then you know the value of showing growth. Publications that can demonstrate additional advertising-page placements can show the media buyer that some type of positive industry activity is occurring to warrant ad placements. You can bet that my nephew Michael isn't skewing these growth statistics unintentionally by placing ads in *Electronic Engineering Times* just to impress his high school friends. Not so with his Web page placement on the Internet.

Print publishers also use growth information to demonstrate that their publication garners more ad pages than the nearest competitor. As a marketer in the computer and electronics industry, I repeatedly heard from competing sales managers about how *EDN* magazine measured up to *Electronic Design.* Editorial content, accuracy in reporting, and the reputations of managing editors and reporters were key factors in determining an engineer's choice of one publication over another. "OK, OK," I'd agree, "You have my attention." For decades, print publications have done an excellent job of showing everyone where the activity lies in their market. They can easily demonstrate where media buyers are putting their dollars and why.

In similar fashion, Internet market researchers mention how many business Web sites exist as proof of the growing Internet business market. Internet service providers, as a subset of the entire Internet service market, mention how many business Web sites reside on their servers.

These Internet growth statistics have some bearing on the growth of Internet marketing, some bearing on the increase in ISP service quality, and some bearing on the development of new technologies and software. General Internet growth statistics, while useful in setting the stage for your plans, are only part of the picture.

If you're going to place an advertisement based on a print publisher's growth statistics, do it because there also exists evidence that you're reaching your target market with that particular publication. Therefore, if you're going to develop a Web site because of Internet growth statistics, do it because the statistics you're using show more growth of Internet users in your market than in the Internet in general.

Revisiting the CommerceNet quote, think about the increasing number of respondents who had access to the Internet. If I'm marketing my products to automobile enthusiasts, the number of wilderness hikers who have access to the Internet doesn't impress me very much . . . unless I can show some correlation between the two. In order for this report to be useful to me, I'm going to have to ask more questions . . . and so will you. Is your product a mainstream, consumer-based product with a diverse customer base? I would say that these general Internet statistics are going to be a lot more useful to you than to the company selling high-end vacation getaway packages to white collar professionals in upper income brackets.

International Reach

Studies on the international reach of the Internet bring us to the question of whether the Internet is truly an international media. For any business that wants to expand its market beyond domestic shores and position itself to compete with multinational corporations and their worldwide sales offices, the answer is a resounding yes. The Internet is, can be, and often should be used as an international media.

What if the international aspects of marketing on the Internet are not as enticing to your company as the national, regional, or even local marketing aspects? Should you consider the Internet if you're not an international company? Again, the answer is yes.

It's a marketing fact of life that local companies bow to the market reach of the regional companies, regional companies to the national ones, and the national to the international. The smaller businesses are and always will be dwarfed in the shadow of the IBMs and the Microsofts of the world. That is, of course, until the smaller companies *become* the next IBM and Microsoft. These are powerful, very successful companies. They have big budgets. They have big staffs. They have lots of money. Maybe you don't. Maybe you're a start-up company. If you're not a start-up, maybe your company is manageable in light of your current business goals. Maybe that's just fine . . . for now.

You're thinking about using the Internet to develop local business and you have no intention of dealing with international prospects any time soon. Is that wise? Sure, why not? Buyers are on the Internet in your hometown. Why should you deny them the convenience of reviewing your product catalog simply because you didn't want to attract a buyer from Brazil? You can always make it clear at your Web site how you define your market geographically. If you get those international inquiries anyway, then build some goodwill by creating a referral network. Who's to say that you won't be able to justify a business expansion if the inquiries become lucrative?

Internet Users by Gender

Statistics that segment by gender can be useful if your product is targeted to a male or female audience. If a well-researched study reveals that there are now more female Internet users on the Internet than ever before, this information can be used to support a reassessment of the marketing mix and a reallocation of advertising dollars. Recently published studies have pointed to this type of trend. As a result, companies who have traditionally courted the female market through television and magazines are now courting the female market through the addition of online services and the Internet.

How Do These Numbers Apply?

As you can see, Internet demographics come in every shape and size. You can justify your Internet marketing plan based on a variety of angles. Figure 3.3 shows a sampling of the different types of Internet surveys being published today and some suggestions for applying them.

Additional Resources

Here is a selected list of resources for Internet demographics, statistics, trends, and surveys:

- ◆ ActivMedia, http://www.activmedia.com/.   Publisher of "Trends in the WWW Marketplace, 1996." This report discusses different product and service types and their

Survey Type	Possible Applications
Overall estimate of worldwide users, host	Starting to justify an Internet marketing program
Growth of Internet use within your industry	Determining expanding market opportunities
Average age of selected users	Marketing to youth, middle-age, and elderly users
Internet users by gender	Marketing products to women versus men
User profiles by education, job titles, and income	Targeting specific online users and industries
Internet business usage trends	Formulating marketing communications strategies
Breakdown of Domain name registrations	Demonstrating an increase in industry users
Impact of the Internet on other media	Supporting the reallocation of marketing dollars
Purchasing behavior and revenue	Proving growth patterns in online commerce
Computer and Internet proficiency among users	Evaluating Internet development options
Browser, platform, and connection speeds	Deciding Web design and navigational issues

Figure 3.3   Applying Internet statistics.

relative success in marketing on the Internet. Activ-Media, Incorporated, was founded in 1994 by professionals from the high-tech community. Its Research Group specializes in quantitative studies of online marketing, augmented by market analysis and case studies.

◆ Advertising, Marketing and Commerce on the Internet, http://www.ntu.ac.sg/ntu/lib/advrtise.htm.   Nanyang Technological University Library Web updates this page regularly with pointers to resources on market research.

◆ CommerceNet, http://www.commerce.net/.   CommerceNet and Nielsen Media Research teamed to conduct the "Internet Demographics Recontact Study" in March/April 1996. The executive summary of their findings is available free on the Internet. It includes an extensive discussion of their survey methodology, with survey highlights and conclusions. CommerceNet is an industry association for Internet commerce. Its membership includes around 150 companies and organizations worldwide. Nielsen Media Research is a provider of broadcast and cable television information services, both nationally and locally.

◆ Coopers & Lybrand, http://www.colybrand.com/. Coopers & Lybrand L.L.P., a leading professional services and consulting firm, serves enterprises in a wide range of industries. Coopers & Lybrand's Media and Entertainment Group recently published the results of a study on the new media industry and its growth in the New York area.

◆ Dataquest, http://www.dataquest.com/. Dataquest is a market intelligence company that can provide research, information, custom consulting, and analysis on the international aspects of new media and the Internet.

◆ FIND/SVP, http://www.findsvp.com/. FIND/SVP's Emerging Technologies Research Group conducts market research on the impact of technological change on consumers and businesses. Its most recent report is "The American Internet User Survey." Search its site for market and industry reports by keyword. FIND/SVP covers a variety of industries, including beverages, biotechnology, chemicals, computers, drugs, financial services, food, health, high-technology, industrial automation, software, plastics, and transportation.

◆ Forrester Research, http://www.forrester.com/. Forrester is working to define the business impact of the Internet and prescribe the right technology strategy for large companies. These efforts span three areas: strategic management research, corporate research, and new media research (Figure 3.4).

◆ Frost & Sullivan, http://www.frost.com/. Frost & Sullivan's Research Publications Group produces market

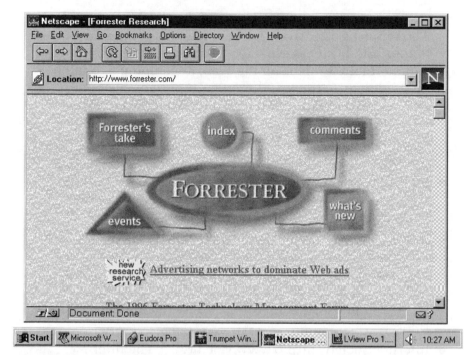

Figure 3.4 Forrester Research believes that the majority of companies marketing on the Web won't realize a return on their investment until the year 2000.

research reports that monitor more than 300 industries. These reports stimulate new ideas, aid business planning, and support investment decisions.

◆ Graphics, Visualization, & Usability Center, http://www .cc.gatech.edu/gvu/user_surveys.   The GVU Center was established by the Georgia Institute of Technology in 1991 in recognition of the central role of Graphics, Visualization, & Usability in the future growth of computing. The GVU Center promotes learning, research, and service by teaching the principles and methods of computer graphics, visualization, user interface software, and usability to members of the academic community.

◆ Hermes, http://www-personal.umich.edu/~sgupta/ hermes/.   University of Michigan's Hermes project researches the commercial uses of the World Wide Web. The project's objectives include understanding why customers and businesses decide to try, use, and provide commercial resources on the Web; developing a reliable methodology to track and predict important customer and corporate trends; and providing useful commerce-related information to the Web community. Hermes' Consumer Survey of WWW Users reports on online information seeking and buying.

◆ IntelliQuest, http://www.intelliquest.com/. IntelliQuest specializes in providing technology companies with survey-based market research information.

◆ International Data Corporation (IDC), http://www .idcresearch.com/. International Data Corporation provides market information and industry analysis on different aspects of information technology, including growth of personal computing and its relationship to the Internet.

◆ Internet Society, http://www.isoc.org/. The Internet Society is an international, individual membership organization for the Internet global cooperation.

◆ Jupiter Communications, http://www.jup.com. Jupiter, a technology consulting company, conducts a variety of studies on Internet growth and demographic trends, including an extensive survey of Yahoo! users.

◆ The Market Research Center, http://www.asiresearch .com. ASI Market Research's site offers market research in the areas of advertising, new media, and entertainment. Articles on market research and free research publications can be found here as well.

◆ Matrix Information and Directory Services, Incorporated (MIDS), http://www.mids.org/. MIDS publishes "Internet Demographics: The MIDS Internet Demographic Surveys." These surveys estimate the demographics of the Internet by surveying organizations connected to the Internet.

- MetaMarketer, http://www.clark.net/pub/granered/ iim.html.   MetaMarketer site contains pointers and discussions of various Internet demographic studies. The site was developed by Erik Granered, granered@clark.net. A section on international Internet demographics contains brief summaries of findings on users, Internet size, and purchasing behavior.

- Network Wizards, http://www.nw.com/.   Network Wizards has been in business since 1990, specializing in products relating to computers and communications. The company designs and sells hardware and software products, both directly and through resellers and OEMs. It is also a consulting company. Its Internet Domain Survey attempts to discover every host on the Internet by doing a complete search of the Domain Name System.

- Nielsen Media Research—Interactive Services, http://www.nielsenmedia.com/.   Nielsen, in cooperation with CommerceNet, publishes the Internet Demographics Study. A free executive summary of the Nielsen results is available on the CommerceNet Web site at http://www.commerce.net, and on Nielsen Media's site at http://www.nielsenmedia.com.

- O'Reilly & Associates, http://www.ora.com/.   O'Reilly & Associates is a publisher of books for UNIX, X, the Internet, and other open systems, and online publishing. Its reports provide demographic information about Internet users and their reasons for using the Internet, Web, or other online services.

- SIMBA Information Incorporated, http://www.simbanet. com/.   SIMBA publishes newsletters, research reports, and directories; it hosts conferences, manages an online information center, and provides consulting services on the global market for information publishing and distribution. Markets and media covered include newspaper, book and directory publishing, online services, multimedia, entertainment, educational publishing, telecommunications and computer publishing and advertising, yellow pages, and television.

Search for additional market research organizations on the Web. Go to Yahoo! at http://www.yahoo.com/ and enter the keywords "Market Research."

Organizations and Associations

Many marketing and industry specific associations offer their members reports, white papers, and research papers on trends in new media for a nominal charge. If you are not a member of a particular organization, you may still be able to purchase some of its reports.

- ◆ American Marketing Association, http://www.ama.org
- ◆ Business Marketing Association, http://www.marketing. org (Figure 3.5)
- ◆ International Association of Business Communicators, http://ccnet.com/~shel/iabc.html
- ◆ Public Relations Society of America, http://www .prsa.org
- ◆ "Associations & Societies: A Useful List" is compiled by Ng Chay Tuan. Go to http://www.ntu.ac.sg/~ctng/ assoc.htm
- ◆ *Encyclopedia of Associations,* Detroit: Gale Research Co., 1961. This multivolume reference is usually found in the reference department of public, academic, or corporate libraries. It contains national, international, regional, state, and local associations of the United States, including trade and professional associations. The encyclopedia is also published on CD-ROM by SilverPlatter, http://sunsite.nus.sg/bibdb/pub/ silverplatter/silverplatter085.html.
- ◆ Search for additional associations on the Web. Go to the NlightN home page, http://www.nlightn.com/ and enter

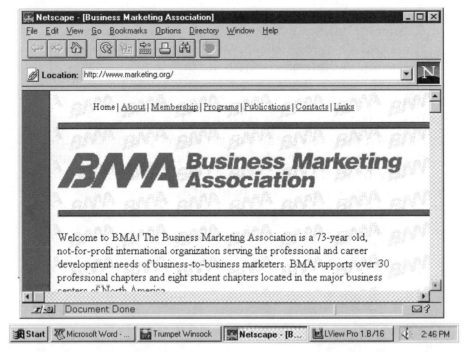

Figure 3.5 The Business Marketing Association offers a variety of publications for sale to both members and nonmembers, including white papers and industry studies.

the keyword "association." You'll find thousands of authoritative entries in information databases, which include directories for a variety of industries.

◆ Go to Yahoo!, http://www.yahoo.com. Search for the keywords "marketing" and "organization."

Trade Magazine Publishing Companies

Many trade publications offer their advertisers surveys, benchmark reports, and studies on trends in new media and marketing. Completing forms such as those illustrated in Figures 3.6 and 3.7 will help you evaluate and apply statistics compiled by companies such as

- Cahners Publishing Company, http://www.cahners.com/. Cahners publishes over 85 business-to-business publications and also provides marketing services and research to various industries. Its Web site provides selected research reports that you can download and use right now.

- Penton Publishing, http://www.penton.com/. Penton has been involved in the study and analysis of industrial and commercial markets for more than 100 years. Penton Research Services offers both primary and secondary research services and has an extensive business and marketing library.

Complete an evaluation form for each report you are interested in using in your Internet marketing plan.

Title of report: _____

Cost of report: $

Organization(s): _____

Contact information for additional questions:

    Person: _____

    Address: _____

        _____

    Telephone: _____

    E-mail: _____ FAX: _____

    Web address: _____

Applicability

This report is (check one):

❑ General to Internet marketing

❑ Industry-specific or contains sections that are industry-specific

❑ Both general and industry-specific information is included

❑ Other. Please specify: _____

Figure 3.6   Evaluating Internet statistics.

Describe the focus of this report. (Include the goals and objectives of this study.)

_____

_____

_____

_____

_____

_____

_____

Briefly list sections of this report that may be applicable to your Internet marketing plan.

_____

_____

_____

_____

_____

_____

Report Dates

When was the survey conducted?

Start (month, year): _____

End (month, year): _____

When was the final report issued? _____

Has this report been updated? If so, when? _____

Is this the most current report available? _____

When will this report be updated? _____

Figure 3.6 (*Continued*)

Respondents

Is the report segmented by job titles or industry? _____

What percentage of respondents are included in your target market? _____

Credibility

This report contains an explanation of its methods for:

❑ Selecting respondents
❑ Distributing surveys
❑ Gathering data
❑ Analyzing data
❑ Other. Please specify: _____

This organization is (check all that apply):

❑ Association (business, trade, industry). If trade or industry, explain:

_____

❑ Commercial online service
❑ Conference, trade show, or seminar organizer
❑ Consulting firm or independent consultant
❑ Educational institution
❑ Industry analyst or market research firm
❑ Internet service provider
❑ Publishing company (business and trade magazines, newspapers, books)
❑ Other. Please specify: _____
Was this survey conducted by my company or an affiliated company?

_____

Figure 3.6   (*Continued*)

Was this report commissioned by another company? If so, by whom?

_____

How many years has this organization been conducting surveys? _____

If this is a new organization, please include any additional information to support its ability to properly conduct this survey. (Name notable staff members, parent companies, etc.)

_____

_____

_____

_____

_____

_____

Name other companies who are currently using data from this report.

_____

_____

_____

_____

Circle the companies listed above that are in your industry.

Describe the reputation of this organization. (Include information from its promotional literature, opinions of sales representatives, editorial opinion, colleagues' and executives' opinions, sales report, and your own assessment.)

_____

_____

_____

_____

_____

_____

_____

Figure 3.6   (*Continued*)

Circle comments listed above that were gathered from the company's promotional literature or sales representatives.

List other similar reports by this organization. (Include dates of issue.)

_____

_____

_____

List any negative comments about this particular report that you may have heard.

_____

_____

_____

Respondents

Estimate of possible respondents in market surveyed: _____

Number of initial contacts made: _____

Number of respondents (included in results): _____

Compute percentage of market actually surveyed: _____

Information Gathering

How were users contacted and interviewed for this survey? Check all that apply.

❑ E-mail
❑ Web site form
❑ Telephone
❑ Fax
❑ Surface mail

Figure 3.6 (*Continued*)

❑ In person (trade show survey, door-to-door, etc.)

❑ Other. Please specify: _____

How were questions asked?

❑ Open-ended (user supplied answers without prompting)

❑ Multiple choice (pick one: *A, B, C*)

❑ *Yes, No,* and *No answer*

❑ Rating scale (points, from 1 to 10, high-low, relevant versus nonrelevant)

❑ Combination of the above

❑ Other. Please specify: _____

Report Findings

Is this report easy to understand? _____

Are unfamiliar terms explained? _____

Are summaries brief and to the point? _____

Can portions of this report be easily used to support your Internet marketing plan? _____

Is any additional interpretation needed in order for this report to be useful? If so, explain:

_____

_____

_____

Your Overall Assessment

Circle one number on each scale.

This report is free of bias or slant.

         Low   **1**   **2**   **3**   **4**   **5**   **6**   **7**   **8**   **9**   **10**   High

Figure 3.6   (*Continued*)

This report is free of information that is ambiguous or contradictory.

        Low   **1**   **2**   **3**   **4**   **5**   **6**   **7**   **8**   **9**   **10**   High

This report is thorough in its findings for its specific purposes.

        Low   **1**   **2**   **3**   **4**   **5**   **6**   **7**   **8**   **9**   **10**   High

This report is relevant to my Internet marketing plan.

        Low   **1**   **2**   **3**   **4**   **5**   **6**   **7**   **8**   **9**   **10**   High

This report is reasonably priced or fits within my budget parameters.

        Low   **1**   **2**   **3**   **4**   **5**   **6**   **7**   **8**   **9**   **10**   High

Total score: _____ (out of a possible 50 points)

Completed by: _____ Date: _____

Figure 3.6 (*Continued*)

1. Which market research reports will you use in your Internet marketing plan?

_____

_____

_____

2. Summarize the number of online users in your market.

_____

_____

_____

_____

_____

_____

3. Summarize the demographic profiles for the users defined in item 2.

_____

_____

_____

_____

_____

_____

_____

_____

_____

_____

_____

_____

_____

_____

Figure 3.7   Applying Internet marketing statistics (Plan Section Two).

4. Do available market reports advocate a move for your company to the Internet? ❑ Yes ❑ No

If yes, briefly explain.

_____

_____

_____

_____

_____

_____

_____

_____

_____

_____

_____

Completed by: _____ Date: _____

Figure 3.7 (*Continued*)

Formulating Marketing Communications Strategies

This chapter defines the "destination" of your Internet marketing presence. Where are you going? If you can't think about the destination, think about the target. What is the ultimate goal of your company's marketing on the Internet? Think about what objectives you wish to accomplish by adding the Internet to your marketing mix. Once you understand your company's objectives in marketing on the Internet, you can begin devising approaches for achieving them.

In Chapter 3, *Analyzing Internet Market Statistics,* you wrote the Section Two of your plan. You reviewed the different types of Internet marketing numbers being tallied today and discovered whether you could use them to support your plan. You uncovered some problems with Internet marketing statistics and became familiar with what to look for. You also told everyone how your company fit into the Internet marketing picture based on the available data.

In Chapter 4, *Formulating Marketing Communications Strategies,* you will complete Section Three of your Internet marketing plan, putting a face on your approach to creating an online presence. Here you'll review some traditional marketing principles that have been reborn as Internet marketing principles. We'll revisit marketing beliefs that permeate the business world regardless of their validity to either new or traditional media.

You will take a look back at our company charter, defined earlier, to determine how you can continue to support your company charter with the introduction of the Internet. Finally, you'll learn how to communicate your Internet marketing objectives and strategies, translating them into tactics for inaugurating your plan.

Section Three: Formulating Marketing Communications Strategies

Your Internet marketing plan is best supported by including data that reinforces your decision to market on the Internet. Section Three of your Internet marketing plan may include any combination of the following:

- ◆ Marketing plan objectives and goals
- ◆ Specific strategies for achieving them
- ◆ A summary of how the use of the Internet will strengthen your overall marketing goals

Getting the Most out of This Chapter

The activities in this chapter include reviewing and comparing examples of marketing strategies. During this process, you will take notes on objectives and strategies that are useful for your company to follow, as well as some that are advisable for your company to ignore. In addition, you'll uncover areas where there are "holes." These holes will be windows of opportunity for your company to shine through.

Some companies are very determined to win and win big with their Internet marketing. Some companies are conservative in their approach, waiting for proof every step of the way before they proceed with another phase. Still others are satisfied with simply "being there," as though they are no longer conspicuous by their absence.

Objectives, Strategies, and Tactics: What's the Difference?

In order to formulate marketing communications strategies, you need to understand what this means. What's the difference between objectives and strategies? How do tactics fit into all of this? Many marketers are confused by these terms, mistakenly using them interchangeably, so here's some help. Let's assume that you want to take a trip. You may know where you're heading, but you may not know how to get there. For example, if you want to get to Denver, you have several choices:

- Drive a car.
- Ride in a bus.
- Take an airplane.
- Walk.

Now suppose you decide to drive a car. You now have your objective (get to Denver) and your tactic (drive a car). What's your strategy? Perhaps you need to get there by a certain time to meet someone. You now have a *revised* objective (get to Denver by five o'clock to meet someone) and a tactic (with your car). You still don't have a strategy. You need a strategy or you won't make it by your designated time. You also need additional information.

If you honor the speed limit on the highway, it'll take you about an hour and a half to drive from Colorado Springs to your destination in Denver, unless you get caught in traffic. Perhaps you need to take into account the traffic flow and possible road construction around the time you plan to travel. Five o'clock is rush hour in most major cities, especially during the week. If you don't leave early and drive at least the posted speed limit, you won't make it to Denver by five o'clock. You don't want to speed, because that would be dangerous. You will also want to consider unforeseen circumstances like running out of gas or having mechanical failure. Here's how it all fits together.

Objectives

Get to Denver.

Meet a business colleague.

Make it there by five o'clock.

Strategies

Arrive in Denver with time to spare.

Avoid rush-hour traffic.

Avoid the road construction near the city of Castle Rock.

Circumvent the roadblocks.

Avoid getting stopped by the highway patrol.

Tactics

Make sure your car is fueled and serviced before leaving.

Bring a map for alternate routes.

Bring your AAA auto club card and your cellular phone for emergencies.

Leave early.

Start your car and drive toward Denver.

Take Highway 87 rather than Interstate 25 to avoid the construction.

Drive the speed limit.

What is an objective?   *A goal you would like to accomplish with your Internet marketing plan.*

What is a strategy?   *An approach to achieving your Internet marketing goals.*

What are tactics?   *Actions you will take during your Internet marketing program implementation.*

Figure 4.1 shows how this translates into Internet marketing objectives, strategies, and tactics. Notice that in the third column, under Tactics, I've included a time frame in the examples. You must include a time frame somewhere in your plans, such as making it to Denver by five o'clock, regardless of your strategies, or you will never achieve your goals.

Traditional Marketing Principles Revised

Now that you have a better grasp of objectives and strategies, let's look at how strategies are formed. Many marketers form strategies based on tried-and-true principles of marketing. These principles are those that they have learned throughout the years, either by formal education or by on-the-job training.

Objectives	Strategies	Tactics
Arrive in Denver to meet a colleague by five o'clock.	Leave early.	Drive the speed limit.
Make direct sales on the Internet.	Shift selected order-processing functions to the Internet.	Install an integrated order-processing function by end of the first quarter.
Increase worldwide product visibility.	Publish product and technical literature on the Web.	Convert all brochures and data sheets to HTML by Comdex Fall.
Build customer goodwill.	Improve customer-service functions.	Train all customer-service staff two weeks in advance of new product releases.

Figure 4.1 Objectives, strategies, and tactics.

By now, you've realized why I chose to emulate a traditional marketing plan in our creation of one for the Internet. Some principles of marketing remain the same, such as step-by-step planning, regardless of the media. By grounding yourself in the basics, you're getting a head start on using the Internet properly.

There are some unique characteristics of the Internet that make it appear somewhat confusing to use. The uniqueness is the area that we'll focus on, and we'll see what the Internet marketer can do to ignore the reasoning that occurs as a result.

Revisiting Old Marketers' Tales

There exist some so-called principles of traditional marketing that businesses have honored through the decades. As a result, some so-called principles of *Internet* marketing have emerged over the past few years as well. These old marketers' tales have these things in common:

- ◆ They are all based on faulty logic.
- ◆ They are all subject to interpretation.

By these varied interpretations, many companies go full speed ahead with their Internet marketing plans, however ill conceived. Let's take a look at some of the false marketing principles that have been reincarnated as Internet marketing principles.

1. If You Have Money, You Can Do Anything

Does this mean that big companies will always have success when marketing on the Internet? Ah, what a superficial view of the world and marketing in general. The person who first correlated this statement to huge budgets probably graduated from the cash-and-flash school of marketing programs. These people believe that anyone with deep pockets will succeed at Internet marketing, especially if they have a good-looking Web site. This half-baked theory doesn't explain why so many well-funded companies with dynamic starts don't survive past their first few years. Furthermore, it doesn't explain why so many companies already marketing on the Internet are quickly outpaced by newcomers.

How about a contrasting marketing principle? On the Internet, successful Web development has no typical dollar amount. Raise your hand if you can tell the difference between a successful $100,000 Web site and a successful $5,000 one. Keep your hand up if you are accurate more than 95 percent of the time.

Now, let's take a look at the flip side. If you believe the dozens of get-rich-quick e-mails that have landed in your in-box lately, you can *make* a fortune marketing on the Internet without *spending* a fortune. Really? So *that's* why so many fledgling companies telephone their interactive marketing consultant and ask what they can get done with $500. Take this test.

Inexpensive Web sites are (check all that apply):

- ❑ Worthy of a cool-site-of-the-day award
- ❑ Merely placeholders for that really big launch later on
- ❑ Able to pay for themselves in a few months
- ❑ An embarrassment to any company that can afford better

❑ A testament to the design-savvy of the Webmaster
❑ Representative of the percentage of budget that went into
   the consultant's pocket
❑ None of the above

There are no absolute answers to the preceding test. Companies can create a dynamic and enticing Internet marketing presence on either a small budget or a large one. It all depends on how well they execute their Internet marketing plan, how well they manage their staff and outside vendors, and how well they meet their original marketing objectives. I'd like to revise this "old marketers' tale" as follows: "If you take the time to plan your Internet marketing program, you will be *more inclined* to succeed, regardless of your budget." All right. So it's not a very snappy rendition. But you get the point.

2. Any Web Site Is Better than None At All

Remember the reason why your company participated in that trade show a few years back? It wasn't because you thought you'd actually get any sales leads out of the event. Someone claimed that if your company wasn't there, you'd be "conspicuous by your absence." Sound familiar? You invested your money, however much it was, to appear at a show, only to find out it was a total waste of your time, or worse, a total waste of your budget. Of course, you *had* to be there. You had no choice, right? The show might have been a great fit, but you fell short somehow. Your company wasn't ready, your product wasn't ready, or your staff wasn't ready to exhibit.

If you're exhibiting on the Internet before you're ready, you risk failure as well. If this type of marketing communications strategy is so advisable, then why is there so much categorizing online and in print for the antithesis of "cool site of the day"? Companies that approach their Internet marketing as little more than an afterthought risk being singled out as below par. Mirsky's Worst of the Web, http://www.mirsky.com (Figure 4.2), is not the type of recognition that your company needs or wants. Pursuing "cool" or "hot" recognition may not be part of your Internet marketing

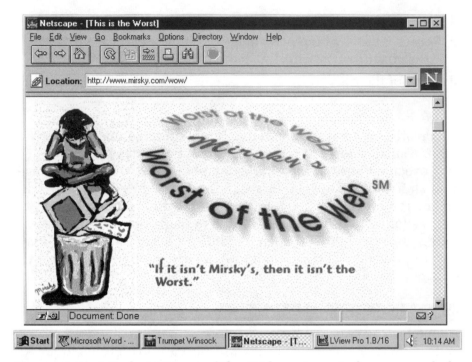

Figure 4.2 Mirsky's Worst of the Web reviews in humorous fashion those sites that exhibit a poorly designed Web presence.

plans, so you may think you have nothing to worry about. Although you're not flirting with these awards, you may still have to deal with their effect.

Let's imagine that you have plans to announce your Web site only after you are absolutely ready and not before. That ought to keep the naysayers at bay. If you don't register your site in an online directory you might think that no one will find you. After all, no *other* pages are indexed at your site. There's really no reason for site robots to come and visit. I've got a surprise for you. Imagine that you are in the process of developing your Web pages. You upload your entire directory and ask for comments from both your onsite and off-site staff. Meanwhile, someone in your industry wonders if you have a Web site yet. Maybe this person indexes sites. He or she opens up his Web browser and enters http://www .your_company.com. Bingo! The searcher has found you. Your company site is now linked to someone else's pages, and you don't even know it. One week later, your URL shows up during a keyword search in Hot Bot, http://www.hotbot.com (Figure 4.3). With over 54,000,000 documents, you're bound to show up eventually, whether you want to or not. Is this a fantasy? No, this happens all the time. Once your site is indexed, you're open for business and subject to review. If your Web site looks sloppy, substandard, amateurish, or flakey, everyone will soon know . . . including your competitors, who would just love to show off how bad your site looks by comparison. Forget about all those comments on how "content rules." If your site is poorly done, what does that say about your company?

3. All Internet Marketing Activities Must Generate Sales

A few years ago, I was asked by a potential client, who was vice president of marketing for his company, if I would be willing to

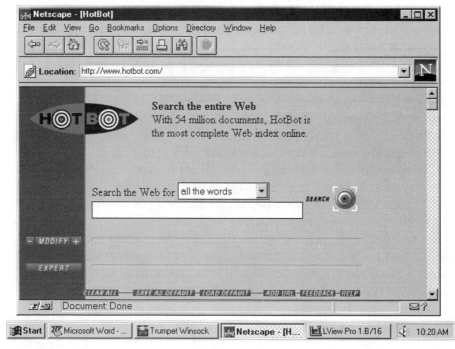

Figure 4.3 Hot Bot attempts to catalog every single document on the World Wide Web, regardless of whether someone has actually registered a page.

manage a public relations account on a contingency basis. The vice president didn't mean that he'd pay me per editorial placement. He meant that he'd pay me a percentage based on sales. I had only to be aggressive in getting his company ink. Being an independent PR practitioner and *not* an employee of his company, I had no influence on inquiry handling, sales-quota management, manufacturing, or even engineering. His customer-service department would somehow track where the leads were coming from and his sales force would close the sales. I would just do a good job, cross my fingers, and hope I got paid.

The vice president had no concept of image-management issues and their long-term influence on decision-making processes. He just wanted to sell product. He had no time for building market awareness, creating goodwill, or establishing a reputation. He had bills to pay. The vice president didn't want to position his company or his executives as authorities in the field. However, he did want the *endorsement* of authorities in the field, as found in the product reviews of trade publications. He wanted ink, he wanted sales, and he wanted them now.

Even if the vice president had a good product, he still wasn't going to succeed. His major lack of foresight lay in his misunderstanding and subsequent discount of the value of a well-planned and -executed media relations program. The vice president's philosophy was simple: No money would be spent on any marketing communications activity unless it could be proven scientifically and measurably that the activity resulted in direct sales. That philosophy also applied to every aspect of public relations and its related activities. Needless to say, he had no public relations program. He didn't see any reason to have one.

Some very successful sites on the Internet are the result of a well-managed public relations campaign. These sites don't take sales. They provide information. They promote goodwill. But somehow, you get the idea that such sites represent companies worthy of your business.

That isn't to say that you can't measure the impact of your PR-oriented Web site on your marketing program. Marketing measurement is a worthwhile endeavor for evaluating the overall effectiveness of your programs, including those on the Internet.

You should definitely measure impact, even if you can't measure sales. A well-managed marketing department can install a measurement system that evaluates different aspects of PR activities and recommends future plans of action. Most of the time, however, analysis and summaries are subjective. Public relations is not an exact science. An exact dollar calculation of the impact of image on income is impossible.

Forget about PR for a moment. Image is one thing; sales are another. If you want to prove your Web site generates sales, you are going to have to track where your leads are coming from. If your Web site is set up to accept orders online, and your customers feel comfortable with the current technology to place those orders, then your objectives to generate sales should work. If your Web site does not accept online orders—that is to say, orders are taken by some other method—you will have to install a procedure for determining where those unidentified leads came from. In the majority of companies, no processes are in place to even take a crack at equating *leads* to sales, which is another marketing communications issue entirely.

Public relations philosophies aside, marketing on the Internet *can* result in increased sales for your company. If your management dictates increased sales as an objective for your Internet marketing plan, then you have your marching orders. However, many companies choose not to formulate strategies based on generating money as a direct result of their Web presence. A sales-generating Internet presence is no more valid than a presence designed from a public relations or even an educational model. It's just different. For example, Corning's Telecommunications Products Division, http://www.usa.net/corning-fiber/ (Figure 4.4), operates a Web site that educates the public, educates the resellers, and doesn't generate a penny through online sales. The Corning Optical Fiber Information Center fulfills its original objectives to provide its market with up-to-date product and technical information, referring interested buyers to the actual companies that sell.

It is perfectly acceptable to establish an Internet marketing program for the sole purpose of building a reputation or enhancing one already established via traditional media. It is also perfectly

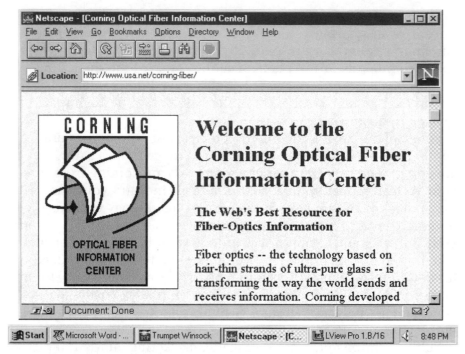

Figure 4.4 The Corning Optical Fiber Information Center offers its visitors the option of receiving literature found at their Web site through a fax-on-demand system.

acceptable to change your objectives once your Internet marketing program gets off the ground.

4. Your Major Internet Marketing Objective Is to Copy Your Competitor's Web Site

I'm somewhat of a risk taker. I like to take chances and make mistakes. I think of Internet marketing as a big adventure. There are still so many uncharted areas to discover. The Internet is so new that many people approach their Web design efforts like homeowners in a town-home development:

◆ Everybody has to have a brown aluminum door on the back porch.

- No one is allowed to put garbage out the night before it's picked up.
- Homeowners may not park more than two automobiles per unit in the common parking area.

These types of rules are fine for maintaining consistent property values for Mr. and Mrs. Cate and their neighbors. The reasoning on which they are based has no real application in Internet marketing. Have you noticed the trends in Web page design? First it was those bulleted lists, then those clunky home page logo banners. Soon everybody started designing those transparent banner images. Now everyone has those colored, left-hand border strips. Too many Webmasters troll the Internet, downloading Web page after Web page to their hard drive. They fully intend to duplicate someone else's page-graphic style, format, and site layout, even down to the colored fonts. So much for establishing a unique online image.

You could certainly include the basic Web design elements by example, but don't stop there. As long as you know your market, your products, and your industry, don't be afraid to come up with your own way of doing things. Your most successful Internet marketing activities just may be those hatched while you were sitting around with your colleagues mocking your competitor's programs. We've all come up with some crazy but exciting ideas when we were "just kidding."

Internet marketing is still young. There are plenty of customers in your market who have an idea of what they'd like to see online, and you have an opportunity to take advantage of those preferences in an innovative way. Don't let your competition dictate the degree of your success by only following in their footsteps.

Of course, you don't want to do *everything* your own way. Why reinvent the wheel? It's not a bad idea to research your competition. Yes, there will be some overlap in the types of activities you engage in. That doesn't make you unoriginal. It just means that you're establishing some programs based on tried-and-true methods. It also means that you are selecting activities that are a fit for your own objectives rather than for everyone else's. If you're looking for tested ideas to help you start creating an Internet marketing program, there are plenty outlined in this book. You'll get a chance to review several dozen for their applicability.

5. If You Know What You're Looking For, You Can Find It Yourself on the Internet

Market research is a very misunderstood activity, as you well know by now. If you have a computer, a modem, and an Internet account, you've been online doing your own brand of market research. Of course, knowing *what* to do is not the same as knowing *how* to do it. Business librarians and other information professionals are skilled at market research. Usually, they've received formalized training in various tools and techniques that make their searches take less time and cost less money. They are in the habit of taking a concept and breaking it down into its logical elements. They use their knowledge to construct effective search strategies. They methodically and thoroughly search appropriate print and online references to uncover the facts. You, on the other hand, have not been trained in computer-assisted retrieval or traditional search techniques. You can surf the Internet with the fortitude of Zeus, but you may only scratch the surface. If you intend to build your market research skills, and your marketing program can survive for now on limited data, you may decide to conduct research in-house. If you don't have a budget for outside talent, that's a reason to do it yourself as well. If you don't have the time, the inclination, or the talent, you're better off hiring a professional.

6. Computing Services Should Be Your Primary Contact for All Internet Development Efforts

Regardless of what some people still believe, Internet marketing is a *marketing* activity. A long time ago, before the arrival of the Internet as a marketing tool, marketers had to bargain their way into hardware configuration, database development, and the like to support their day-to-day marketing functions. Therefore, along this same line of thinking, many companies categorized Internet marketing as a technical development effort. Unfortunately, today, some of these companies still do.

    Notice that this old marketers' tale says "primary" contact. You may think this means "sole" contact. Unfortunately, in some companies it still does. Keep in mind that everyone in your company has a stake in the success of your Internet marketing efforts, some more than others. No one should be burdened, bothered, or beautified with the responsibility of being a primary or sole contact. That doesn't mean you won't have *authorities* on different aspects of Internet marketing development.

The authorities on marketing should be marketers, with input from the technical side. The authorities on Internet access should be computer professionals, with input from the marketing side. There is so much overlap between responsibilities in an Internet marketing program that no one department or person should be the primary anything. Except, of course, for the Internet marketing team manager. With any luck, and with a savvy ability to navigate company politics and personalities, it just might be you.

As a team manager, you will need to direct traffic, and not just the Web kind. Your team will assess what you need done, if it's even possible, how long it will take, and so on. All of the plans, goals, hopes, and dreams for your Internet marketing program must be analyzed in the context of *reality*. You will enlist the aid of the computing services staff in helping your dreams come true. You will tap their knowledge base in hopes of discovering capabilities you didn't even know existed. You will convince them of the importance of meeting marketing milestones and reward them for their involvement. You will respect their opinion. They, in turn, will respect yours.

The success of any marketing effort, whether it involves traditional or new media, lies in the marketer's ability to work from a team approach. If you're a small company, you're not exempt. If you want to launch your Internet presence anytime in the next decade and you want it to be an effective one, enlist the aid of at least one other resource besides yourself to put it all together. You can count this book as one of those resources. See? You're already a team.

7. Internet Marketing Obtains Faster Results than Traditional Marketing

One of the Internet's biggest selling points has been that it is much faster and easier than traditional means of communicating. Any salesperson who's stood for 12 hours in a trade show booth will have a bone to pick with that reasoning. So let's just say that Internet communications are *relatively* fast.

Internet communications are so relatively fast that everyone is bragging about how quickly they've made contact with all their customers. Everyone is excited about how much easier it is to answer inquiries. Their companies are distributing more and more product information on the Internet as time goes by. All this low-cost literature distribution must be a good thing. Eventually, it will result in increased sales.

Some companies are very customer-service-oriented in that they will go out of their way to provide you with non-Internet options for receiving their product information (Figure 4.4). Meanwhile, some companies have already lost track of the impact and subsequent value of these other established forms of communication. Take a look at this face-to-face conversation between Biff (the sales manager) and Kip (the customer).

> Biff (eager): Do you have an e-mail address?
> Kip (nonchalant): Nope. Here's my phone number.
> Biff (insistent): Are you getting an e-mail address soon? It'd be so much easier to send you e-mail.
> Kip (annoyed): No. Just give me a call.
> Biff (clueless): Do you have a fax number?

If your customer doesn't have an e-mail address, you still have to communicate with him or her. When it comes right down to signing on the dotted line, it doesn't matter if you have your entire catalog up on the Internet. It doesn't matter because several of your customers are not surfing the Internet and don't plan to any-time soon. Yet they still manage to do a good job of reviewing purchases for their company and making the right call. They read trade magazines, go to trade shows to say hello to that tired booth staffer, and talk at length to their colleagues. The *speed* of Internet communications has no influence whatsoever. Now let's look at your customers who *are* on the Internet and discuss why the Internet *still* doesn't obtain faster results than traditional marketing.

The Internet *does* expedite the *information-gathering* process. The Internet *does not* always expedite the *decision-making* process. Even if the majority of your customers are on the Internet, you still have to deal with other nontechnical matters . . . human nature, company politics, budgeting issues, and things that have absolutely nothing to do with the way in which you communicate with your market.

Most large companies have a decision-making process in place that involves employees, purchasing agents, cost comparisons, and sometimes an approved vendor list. By providing information to these companies in a timely manner, which may or may not include your company's Internet marketing activities, you are helping that process along. Once you have done your job and stated your case, the rest is up to the buyers. You may not gain any points at all by claiming that they got your information quickly at your Web site.

Your company can continue to help sales along by contacting customers and prospects by telephone, by fax, or in person. You provide product demonstrations. Your executives and technical personnel give speeches and lectures. Your sales force meets customers for lunch. Your customer-service department follows up with telephone calls. Your fax broadcast bureau distributes those technical bulletins in a timely fashion. Internet marketing programs sometimes come in first, second, or even third in the race to build company sales.

There *are* companies that are reaping the benefits of improved communications through use of the Internet. In some cases, these online marketing efforts produce very measurable results. Internet marketing is very tangible to these companies, as evidenced by their increase in direct online sales. As you know by now, all Internet marketing programs are not alike. Therefore, whether your Internet marketing program produces faster results compared to other, more traditional media is relative. Results in your market are primarily a function of how your company, your industry, and your product are purchased.

8. Internet Marketing Should, Can, and Will Replace Traditional Marketing Media

Don't get me started. I hope that's not going to happen anytime soon. I enjoy watching commercials on TV, mainly because some of them are so entertaining that it's relaxing to sit back and just watch. What will I read before bedtime if my favorite magazine goes away? Maybe those ugly highway billboards within the city limits *could* be replaced with something better-looking. Wouldn't it be dangerous to drive around town while looking at the Internet on your laptop instead of listening to music on your car radio? Finally, I think I'd really miss talking to a real customer-service representative on the telephone.

Computers just don't answer questions with the same personality as humans. I cringe when I hear about a company with plans to either bring or force *all* their customers online. Yet I don't want to appear shortsighted. I'll admit that stranger things have happened with technology in a few short years.

Will Internet marketing replace traditional marketing? Radio didn't replace newspapers. TV didn't replace radio. Although in my house, the computer has *displaced* some of the hours we used to spend with TV, but not all. You make the call.

9. Successful Internet Marketing Requires the Use of All Internet Tools, Technologies, and Techniques

My favorite story is about a novice Internet marketer. He was getting his feet wet in the most intense way. Hired just out of college, he had been working for this small company for just a few weeks when he suddenly found himself in charge of planning and executing his company's marketing communications plan. He handled trade shows. He handled PR. He even handled advertising. He was one busy bee. Then came the time to include Internet marketing. Of course, with a small staff (total: one) and an even smaller budget, he couldn't afford to hire anyone. He had to do everything himself. He was determined to impress everyone with his incredible mastery of the online world.

Our novice marketer put up a Web site. He did an excellent job. But he didn't stop there. He opened an FTP site. Of course, this meant that every document prepared for the Web would have to be duplicated in another format for the FTP directory. He was now faced with making sure that updates for all these documents were made in two different places. But he didn't stop there. He soon set up an e-mail autoresponse program designed to automatically fill requests for all of the same information. This meant that, somewhere in between his telephone calls to editors, his ordering of trade show labor, and his scheduling of a sales meeting, he was also managing the Web site, the FTP site, and the autoresponse script. But he didn't stop there. I think you get the picture.

Using every Internet gadget or glitzy trick strictly for innovation's sake is like hyperlinking every word on a Web page just to prove you know how to do it. As with every other marketing media you'll use, select Internet marketing tools, technologies, and techniques because they are *each* a good and proper fit.

Deciding to merge even one Internet tool into your Internet marketing program involves deciding its applicability to the following:

- How your company views its overall Internet marketing objectives and image
- How your product and services are sold and distributed
- How your other marketing programs work together
- How much knowledge and the types of skills your marketing staff possesses
- How much time you want to sleep between midnight and 6:00 A.M.

There are plenty of Web sites that are orderly, well designed, and useful to their customers without incorporating a lot of fuss. There are also plenty of examples of companies that actively use only two or three Internet tools and *still* manage to have an effective Internet marketing presence. Besides, how many different Internet addresses can you crowd on a business card anyway?

10. Traditional Marketing Principles Apply to Internet Marketing

I'll bet you thought this last old marketers' tale would be easy. Maybe. There are a lot of lessons to be learned from companies before the Internet. Which traditional marketing principles apply to the Internet? Let's take a look at a few of them and see what works on the Internet.

"I wish our company could do better at sales, but the competition has beaten us to the punch. Now the only reason they have a big share of the market is because they got there first."   How many times have you heard those comments? In traditional marketing, getting a product to market first can be an important step in gaining a major share of the market. Getting there first can mean many other things as well. Just because you can't be the first in your market doesn't mean you can't be the first at creating something unique. This canon also applies to Internet marketing. The Internet has all kinds of opportunities for "getting there first" because it is so new and users are still discovering it.

The HTMARCOM List (High-Tech Marketing Communications) was *not* the first marketing list or e-mail discussion group on the Internet. It was, however, the first marketing list on the Internet for high-tech marketing communicators in computers and electronics. Sure, you can label anything as the first of its kind if you are willing to add enough qualifiers. Fortunately, there *is* a market for unique marketing discussions on the Internet. In fact, there was, is, and will continue to be a market for unique discussion groups of *any* topic, as evidenced by the thousands now in existance.

> **Marketing principle 1.**   Being first and being unique are equally important. On the Internet, as in the off-line marketing world, plenty of opportunities exist for you to declare your own niche, regardless of the competition.

"It's very frustrating to do business with them. I'd like to take my money elsewhere, but they're the only ones who sell what I need. They don't **have** *to care."*   Did you ever wonder why some people in top positions are very down to earth while others are rude and inconsiderate? Some people let success go to their heads. This is also pretty typical for companies in the business world that have lost site of their objectives as well as common operating procedures like simple business etiquette. At this point, such a company has started saluting a new motto: "We've got it made."

Somewhere in a company meeting, someone proposes a new product that promises to be the *first* of its kind. Weeks, months, or even years later, that strapping new product is introduced. It looks nice. It runs well. No other company has one like it on the market. And best of all, it's easy to use.

Everyone at the company agrees that everyone will want one. Everyone *does* want one. Everyone *buys* one. Everyone at the company agrees that they've cornered the market. And worst of all, everyone agrees that if customers can't figure out how to use it, they must be fairly stupid.

With this attitude in mind, the customer-service department begins answering inquiries. The customer e-mails questions. The questions are basic. The answers are barely useful. The customer has purchased the product but wishes that he or she hadn't. Who wants to do business with a company that isn't very helpful? But who has the choice?

Weeks, months, or even years later a new company comes out with its own version of the product. It looks nice. It runs well. It's easy to use. The first company has one just like it on the market. But best of all, this new company is easier to do business with. And their employees are really personable, too.

> **Marketing principle 2.**   Establish a reputation for good customer service. On the Internet, as in the off-line marketing world, plenty of opportunities exist for you to lose your customers, especially if you let success go to your head.

"I've liked their products in the past, but this one just isn't as good. I think their biggest problem is that they're in over their heads."   I love brainstorming about different ways to expand a product line or service offering. It's fulfilling to find ways to extend a market reach. Of course, some ideas are more feasible than others. The most obvious and most successful augmentation of a company's business lies in what it already markets. The company doesn't have to learn a new trade. The sales force is better able to pitch the new products. The technical service department finds it easier to lend support. The customer expects this from you. The customer *wants* this from you. Take advantage of it.

> **Marketing principle 3.**   Master the obvious first, then master it again. On the Internet, as in the off-line marketing world, plenty of opportunities exist for you to maintain and improve your current market position by marketing what you already know.

"I agree that there's a need for this product, but it has so many problems. I'd rather wait until the next release than deal with installing it now."   Have you ever installed a new software product and wished you hadn't? I look at my computer every day and wonder why a certain piece of software ever made it to market, let alone to my office. Eventually, I'll get around to uninstalling it, since I can't stand to use it anymore. I've heard that the latest version has all of the features the first one didn't have, and it runs better. It has some new features I never even thought of. At this point, my budget is shot and I'm not in the mood to set up the software again. Maybe later, just not now.

Internet marketers are under a lot of pressure. Marketers in general are under a lot of pressure. The competition is fierce out there. The market appears to be moving very fast, hastened by the excitement of the Internet. In high-technology companies, it's a fact of life that products will constantly be released before their time. Management has a vision. Engineers have a mission. Sales has a quota. Marketers have a Rolaid.

> **Marketing principle 4.**   Know when to put on the brakes. On the Internet, as in the off-line marketing world, plenty of opportunities exist for you to rush to market, often before you are ready.

"Well, they used to be a leader in the market, but now they're history. I guess they couldn't or wouldn't adapt."   When my daughter was very little, she was very, very active. Occasionally, she would wriggle out of my arms to get down and then bolt out into the street, without a care in the world. She'd often find herself in the middle of the road staring at the front grill of a car that was screeching to a halt. She didn't know how to respond. Rather than get out of the way, she stood paralyzed, much like a deer caught in the path of bright headlights. Believe me, my heart almost stopped a few times as I sprinted to pull her to safety. Being a parent is not easy. For that matter, neither is being a marketer. As with most growing children, my daughter finally adapted by paying attention to the traffic flow, but not before I taught her a little song: "Stop, look, and listen before you cross the street. Use your eyes, use your ears, then use your feet."

In the business world, customers are very, very demanding. Occasionally, your customers will appear to bolt out and purchase your competitor's product without stopping to look at yours. Sometimes they find themselves with a product that doesn't meet their needs. Many times, however, the purchase was a good decision and you have lost a sale, for whatever reason. Your company doesn't know how to respond. Your company doesn't even know why the customer bought the other product. Rather than finding a way to adapt, you stand paralyzed, much like a deer caught in the path of bright headlights. Your mother or father doesn't come to rescue you, so you get run over. In other words, pay attention to your market. Stop and assess your current position. Look at the market. Listen to your customer. Use the facts. Use your instincts. Use your head.

> **Marketing principle 5.**   Pay attention to your market and learn to adapt appropriately. On the Internet, as in the off-line marketing world, there exist plenty of opportunities for you to suffer setbacks by not recognizing the trends.

Now, if some aspects of these marketing principles appear to contradict each other, you're absolutely right. Marketing is not an exact science. The art in applying traditional marketing tenets to Internet marketing resides in your ability to balance them carefully when formulating your objectives and strategies. That's where we'll go next.

Establishing an Internet Marketing Vision

In this section, you will brainstorm (Figure 4.5). You will think about the trends in your market, what your competitor is doing, and how your company can respond. For this section, it's a good idea to have the following materials ready for reference:

◆ Your traditional marketing plan, if you have one
◆ Competitive literature
◆ A list of your competitors' Web sites
◆ Industry analyst reports
◆ A stack of trade publications to skim through

Instructions
- ◆ Review your company's traditional marketing plan.
- ◆ Review your competitors' literature for an indication of their objectives.
- ◆ Browse your competitors' Web sites to review their About This Company pages.
- ◆ Review industry analysts reports for statements about market trends and case studies.
- ◆ Review trade publications for features on market trends and case studies. Pay particular attention to quotes and interviews by company officials.
- ◆ Review trade publications for features on companies on the Internet. Pay particular attention to quotes and interviews by company officials.
- ◆ Fill in this form using bullets, brief statements, or a combination of the two.
- ◆ Use the answers to draft the next section of your Internet marketing plan.

Name 10 marketing objectives that your competitors hope to accomplish with their marketing programs.

Competitor's Name   **Marketing-Objective Statement**

In the above list, circle all objectives that match your own, whether for traditional or Internet marketing.

Figure 4.5 Phrasing your marketing communications strategies (Plan Section Three).

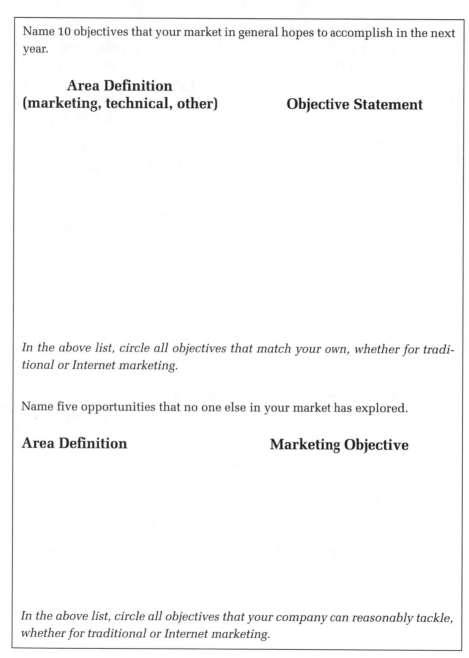

Name 10 objectives that your market in general hopes to accomplish in the next year.

**Area Definition
(marketing, technical, other)**   **Objective Statement**

In the above list, circle all objectives that match your own, whether for traditional or Internet marketing.

Name five opportunities that no one else in your market has explored.

Area Definition   **Marketing Objective**

In the above list, circle all objectives that your company can reasonably tackle, whether for traditional or Internet marketing.

Figure 4.5   (*Continued*)

Check off all the objectives you circled that your company can reasonably achieve this year, whether for traditional or Internet marketing. Now think about how you can modify these objectives to create your own unique image online. Draft a succinct paragraph that explains your company's objectives for its Internet marketing program.

_____

_____

_____

_____

_____

_____

_____

_____

_____

_____

_____

Briefly state your strategies for achieving the above objectives.

_____

_____

_____

_____

_____

_____

_____

_____

_____

_____

Figure 4.5 (*Continued*)

Summarize how the use of the Internet will strengthen your overall marketing goals.

_____

_____

_____

_____

_____

_____

_____

_____

_____

_____

Completed by: _____ Date: _____

Figure 4.5 (*Continued*)

Additional Resources

Here are some additional resources for assistance in formulating this section of your Internet marketing plan.

Studies

Marketing case studies can be found through marketing associations, government agencies, colleges and universities, market research firms, and possibly through surveying your own customer base. Here are a few resources:

American Marketing Association
250 South Wacker Drive, Suite 200
Chicago, IL 60606
Toll-free (800) AMA-1150
Tel. (312) 648-0536
Fax (312) 993-7542

http://www.ama.org/
info@ama.org

Business Marketing Association
150 North Wacker Drive, Suite 1760
Chicago, IL 60606
Toll-free (800) 664-4BMA,
Tel. (312) 409-4262
Fax (312) 409-4266
bma@marketing.org.
McGraw-Hill Business Information Bureau

Cahners Advertising Research Reports
Cahners Publishing Company
A division of Reed Elsevier Inc.
275 Washington Street
Newton, MA 02158-1630
Tel. (617) 964-3030
Fax toll-free (800) 497-5448
marketaccess@cahners.com

Publications

If you are looking for case studies on companies marketing on the Internet, these stories appear in just about every type of publication on the newstands today. Rather than attempt to list every relevant publication, I recommend that you check out your public or academic business library for most business marketing and Internet magazines, such as *Advertising Age, Business Marketing,* and *Internet World.*

A list of these publications appears in Appendix C.

chapter five

Planning Your Internet Marketing Budget

This chapter will help you become familiar with budgeting for activities associated with bringing your company online. Before you start saying that you don't need, use, or even want a budget, remember that marketing on the Internet is not as cheap as "they" say. In order to keep these costs from getting away from you, you must at least define the initial financial parameters for creating your Internet marketing presence. This chapter contains a brief overview of the options, along with tips for developing your budget.

As part of your budget responsibilities, you may need to include preliminary estimates for new or upgraded computer equipment and software. If you are in charge of actually purchasing and configuring your own Web server, there is a wealth of books on the market to help you. This isn't one of them. For marketers, the less time spent on assuming the role of a systems operator, LAN administrator, or MIS manager, the better.

You'll notice that I've placed the chapter on budget planning activities after the chapter on strategy formulation. That isn't necessarily a definitive statement of priority. Budgeting could just as easily come at the end of your entire Internet marketing plan. You may not know what the numbers are until you read the other chapters. Completing this chapter will not give you all the numbers you need on which to base an Internet marketing decision. Other chapters in this book will provide you with additional insight into the costs involved, for example,

Chapter 6, *Forming the Internet Marketing Task Force.* Whether you hire an outside agency, in-house staff, or just do it yourself, you will need to know how this impacts your Internet marketing budget.

Chapters 7 through 13 discuss implementation of the Internet marketing plan and contain individual marketing communications activities that may or may not affect the bottom line.

Chapter 15, *Measuring Internet Marketing Results,* discusses how to track results effectively. If you plan to demonstrate how well your Web site performed, you will need to implement some type of measurement program. It may include downloading and installing a shareware program that measures Web traffic or hiring an outside agency to design a customer package that meets your needs.

In Chapter 4, *Formulating Marketing Communications Strategies,* you reviewed some traditional marketing principles and their application to Internet marketing. In addition, you brainstormed on possible objectives and strategies for your company's Internet marketing presence.

Section Four: Planning Your Internet Marketing Budget

Your Internet marketing plan is best supported by including data that reinforces your decision to market on the Internet. Section Four of your Internet marketing plan may include any combination of the following:

- ◆ Estimates on Internet service and development costs, including upgrade expenses
- ◆ Estimates of purchasing, configuring, and operating an in-house server
- ◆ A budget spreadsheet with cost breakouts for each Internet marketing plan element
- ◆ An assessment of the impact of your Internet marketing program on other traditional media expenditures

Why You Need an Internet Marketing Budget

Management likes to know where it has spent its money. It's just that simple. Of course, *needing* an Internet marketing budget and *getting* one are two different things. How do you allocate or obtain funds for your program? Three possible choices are as follows:

- Wait for your company to come around and provide you with working funds.
- Pick a number out of the air.
- Drive that action right now by gathering, analyzing, and presenting the facts.

Ways to Determine a Budget: A Look at Methods

You never have enough money to do everything you'd like to do when it comes to marketing. The Internet is no exception. If you don't have an endless supply of funds, you'll have to come up with an approach. Of course, management may just walk up to you and say, "Here. What can you do with this?" You may just look at the current balance in your company checkbook and decide from there. In which case you have to employ the best methods you can for the money you have. Yeah, I know. That's pretty much an intangible and useless guideline.

   By the end of this book, you will have quite a bit of ammunition needed to win those coveted Internet marketing budget dollars. That doesn't mean that you'll get what you ask for, but it's certainly worth a try. You can improve your chances if you understand a little bit about how companies determine budgets. If you're not part of that peculiar decision-making process in your organization, it can sometimes appear to be magical and mysterious. Some companies are better at budgeting decisions than others. Let's look at some of the options.

The Internet Marketing Budget Is Based on Last Year's Internet Marketing Budget

Of course, I'm assuming that you've already developed an Internet marketing presence and you are reading this book to help you refine it, or at least you already have a history on which to base your budget. Assume you kept track of where your company spent the money, what worked, and what didn't. Now you have an even better concept of how to use your budget this year. When creating your budget, be sure to consider how costs have changed since the previous year, and whether any of your objectives include increasing your online visibility. In this case, you will need to propose an increase in budget to cover the additional programs you hope to implement.

The Internet Marketing Budget Is Based on a Percentage of Company Sales

When it comes to marketing, I believe in the separation of church and state. Editorial and advertising departments of reputable trade publications operate independently. Company marketing and sales departments should operate independently also—related only in that most marketing activities will hopefully bring in more revenue. It may take sales revenues several months to catch up with your Internet marketing efforts. If you look *only* to your sales dollars for guidance in determining marketing dollars, your programs could suffer. If it doesn't bother you that this sounds like the tail wagging the dog, then you could use this approach until you've proven the worthiness of your Internet marketing program.

What should the percentage be? That's not an easy question to answer, but there are helpful resources out there if the decision is yours. Look for industry-specific almanacs, such as *The Computer Industry Almanac* by Karen Petska Juliussen and Egil Juliussen, that contain information on the marketplace, trends, and market forecasts. You can use these guides as a beginning for determining a reasonable percentage. Industry market and financial almanacs will also be useful for gathering facts on which to base Internet marketing strategies and for Internet marketing plan data that supports your market analysis.

Under this method, your budget may not necessarily remain a fixed dollar amount. You may or may not be able to count on it from one sales period to the next. In which case you will want to make an effort to show a direct return on your investment upon which the company can base future budgeting decisions. If allocating a percentage of sales is your only choice, you can still work with it, just not as effectively.

The Internet Marketing Budget Is Based on a Percentage of the Total Marketing Budget

This approach assumes that Internet marketing is not a complementary or equal partner in the marketing mix. It is merely a subset. That's the bad news. In many companies, Internet marketing is merely the icing on the cake. The company has already established a very strong presence independent of online media. That's the good news. With this type of budget, you appropriate new dollars. You will be able to continue other established marketing programs without a financial impact.

The Internet Marketing Budget Is Based on a Reallocation of Marketing Dollars

This approach assumes that you will either decrease or eliminate certain activities in traditional media, while Internet marketing takes up the slack. If you already know that some programs aren't working and you are eliminating them in favor of the Internet, then you're shifting dollars to more effective marketing tools. That's perfectly acceptable.

If you reallocate marketing dollars because you hope that your Internet marketing presence will automatically decrease a need for other media, then you're shifting dollars away from tried-and-true methods in favor of something new. This approach is extremely risky. If your Internet marketing program fails to meet projections, then you have lost on two fronts: on the Internet and in the programs where you have siphoned funds.

The Internet Marketing Budget Is Based on What Other Companies in Your Industry Are Spending

In traditional marketing, companies such as AdScope report on advertising-dollar expenditures by industry and company (Figure 5.1). Reports are emerging on estimated Web expenditures, but not nearly enough to cover every industry and possible configuration. On the Internet, it's nearly impossible to make these guesses by yourself. There are just too many variables for this method to be 100 percent accurate, including the costs of Web development and Internet access, which appear to change regularly.

Let's suppose for a moment that you have the information you need. You know exactly how much your competitor spent to put together its Web site. Your competitor is spending a relative for-

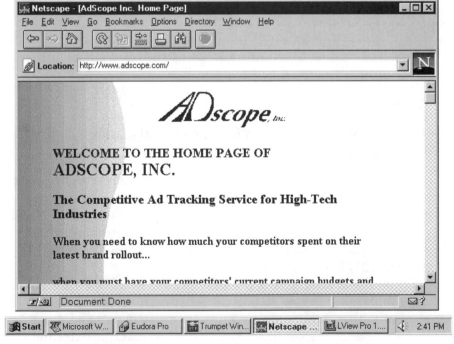

Figure 5.1 AdScope, Inc., provides a competitive ad-tracking service for high-tech industries on what competitors are spending on their latest brand rollouts.

tune to make itself known online. You would like to position your company in the same manner. Yet you have decided to create an effective marketing presence without selling the farm. Good for you.

Take a good look at the objectives of your competitor's Internet marketing presence before you assume that you have to up the ante. If your competitor uses its Web site only for public relations purposes, and you plan to take orders online, then your approaches to allocating budget dollars are driven by different objectives.

The Internet Marketing Budget Is Based on Creating an Effective Online Presence

How much does it cost you to get what you need? This is the best approach to creating an Internet marketing budget. This type of budgeting method looks at the actual activities associated with creating an Internet marketing presence. It allocates the funds accordingly. The primary focus of your Internet marketing program is to meet the company's marketing needs. This budgeting method is also the one used least often, especially by those companies that need it the most.

The Internet Marketing Budget Is Based on a Graduated Plan Tied into Measurable Results

This budgeting method assumes that you will continue to operate your program from year to year. Of course, this budgeting method also assumes that you will be able to continually demonstrate either a return on your investment or some type of positive effect. Provided you allocate enough time for measurement, this is one good approach to budget planning for Internet marketing.

If your Web site takes direct orders online, then you have little to worry about . . . at least as far as total sales dollars generated. If your site has been established for other reasons, including those related to image management, then you will have to apply more stringent formulas for demonstrating success.

The Internet Marketing Budget Is Based on a Combination of Several Factors

In many ways, both traditional and new media marketing success is so intangible that you can't rely on just one approach to budgeting. How should you present your Internet marketing plan budget? The best approach may include a combination of all the previously mentioned methods. If part of your Internet marketing proposal includes asking for new dollars to implement it, you will want to provide management with some options.

- Prepare three budgets—one low, one medium, and one high—in terms of total program dollars.
- Include whatever information you have to support each of these approaches, such as the following:
    — Competitive advertising expenditures, if you are able to obtain this elusive cost data
    — Highlights of budget changes from one version to the next
    — A subjective assessment of how each budget version may impact your overall marketing program

By being fully prepared, you will be more effective in influencing managerial decisions. At the very least, you will have provided your executives with additional insight into what they can reasonably expect for the available dollars.

Dialing for Dollars: How Much Does Everything Cost?

Now that you've become familiar with the reasoning behind budget allocations, it's time to start evaluating the size of the budget we are talking about. Here are just a few of the areas that you will need to cover in your Internet marketing plan.

Internet Service Options (ISPs)

Chances are that you already have access to the Internet. If so, and if you work for a big company, discuss options with your computing services department for upgrading your existing account to meet Internet marketing goals. This may include finding a better or bigger service provider (Figure 5.2). Even though these costs may come out of the computing services budget, it's still a good idea to include this information in any Internet marketing budget request (Figure 5.3).

Internet Service Options: In-House Web Servers

If you anticipate that the user traffic to your Web site will either drain current in-house system resources or substantially increase costs for operation on your ISP's host machine, consider the purchase of an in-house Web server (Figure 5.4). Remember that the decision to install an in-house server will demand that someone be responsible for its 24-hour operation. System outages are intolerable on a round-the-clock network like the Internet's World

Figure 5.2   Mecklermedia's List catalogs rates and services for and provides links to Internet service providers around the world.

Instructions

- ◆ Ask your computing services department for details on the current configuration and costs for your company's Internet account.
- ◆ Ask for computing services' assistance in completing this form, if possible.
- ◆ Visit various ISP Web sites for preliminary information on costs and services.
- ◆ E-mail the Internet service provider for additional information.
- ◆ E-mail or telephone the ISP's customer-service department for additional clarification.
- ◆ Duplicate this form as needed for each Internet service provider.
- ◆ Check off choices and fill in the blanks with costs where applicable.

Name of Internet service provider: _____

Contact person: _____

Telephone or e-mail: _____

1. Account setup or activation fee _____

2. Monthly service plan or usage cost estimate

   _____

   a. Dial-up access _____

   b. High-speed access _____

3. Software (check one): ❑ Included ❑ Optional ❑ Not available

   a. Bundled Internet startup package _____

   b. Browser upgrade _____

Figure 5.3 Internet service costs worksheet (Plan Section Four).

4. Upgrades in access

    a. Dedicated/leased line _____

        (1) Number of additional company users _____

        (2) Estimated Web site traffic volume _____

    b. Toll-free line usage _____

    c. Wireless access _____

    d. Training (check one): ❑ Included   ❑ Optional   ❑ Not available

        (1) Classes _____

        (2) Manuals _____

5. Miscellaneous Internet services

    a. Listserv operation (check one): ❑ Included   ❑ Optional   ❑ Not available

        (1) List setup fee

        (2) Monthly maintenance and operation fees

    b. Anonymous FTP area (check one): ❑ Included   ❑ Optional   ❑ Not available

    c. Gopher area (check one): ❑ Included   ❑ Optional ❑ Not available

    d. Newsgroup creation (check one): ❑ Included   ❑ Optional   ❑ Not available

6. Web access (check one): ❑ Included   ❑ Optional   ❑ Not available

    a. Hosting services

        (1) Basic _____

        (2) Premium _____

    b. Disk storage charges (check one): ❑ Included   ❑ Extra _____ per _____ megabyte

    c. Domain name aliasing (check one): ❑ Included   ❑ Extra _____ per _____

Figure 5.3 (*Continued*)

d. Web log analysis (check one): ❑ Included
   ❑ Extra _____ per _____

e. HTML-to-mail function (check one): ❑ Included
   ❑ Extra _____ per _____

f. CGI scripting (check one): ❑ Included
   ❑ Extra _____ per _____

7. Telephone company service (check one):
   ❑ Not needed   ❑ Needed

   a. Installation of additional telephone lines _____

   b. Upgrade to better line _____

Figure 5.3   (*Continued*)

Wide Web. If you do not have the personnel to assume dedicated responsibility for your server's operation, you're better off leaving your pages on an outside host.

Web Design Services

Many Internet service providers offer package services that include access, hosting, Web design, and maintenance services. For example, CommInt, http://www.commint.com/ (Figure 5.5), is an example of those ISPs that provide both Web design and hosting services. The Web Factory, http://www.twf.com/, is one of many Web design boutiques that offer Web design packages for different budgets and needs.

Whether you decide to have your Web pages designed in-house or outside, your budget will include costs associated with Web site design and development (Figure 5.6).

Additional Resources

For comparisons of pricing and services for international Internet service providers, hardware options for internal Internet Web servers, and Web hosting services, visit these sites.

Instructions

- Ask your computing services department for details on the current configuration and costs for operating your company's Web servers, if applicable.
- Ask for computing services' assistance in completing this form, if possible.
- Visit various computer hardware Web sites for preliminary information on servers.
- E-mail individual Internet service providers for additional information.
- E-mail or telephone a local computer dealer for additional clarification.
- Contact your ISP for hardware advice on taking your Web pages in-house.
- Duplicate this form as needed.
- Check off choices and fill in the blanks with costs where applicable.

1. Hardware

   a. Additional workstations (check one): ❑ Not needed ❑ Needed
      _____

   b. Upgrade in hard-disk capacity (check one):
      ❑ Not needed   ❑ Needed _____

   c. Increased memory (check one): ❑ Not needed
      ❑ Needed _____

   d. Higher-speed modems (check one): ❑ Not needed ❑ Needed
      _____

   e. Upgrade to 256-color monitor (check one):
      ❑ Not needed   ❑ Needed _____

   f. CD-ROM drives (check one): ❑ Not needed
      ❑ Needed _____

Figure 5.4   Web server cost worksheet (Plan Section Four).

g. Other (specify)

_____

Cost: _____

2. Software

a. Web server (check one): ❑ Not needed
❑ Needed _____

b. List manager (check one): ❑ Not needed
❑ Needed _____

3. Additional personnel

a. Is someone in your company on call in case computer systems go down? ❑ Yes ❑ No

b. Do you have in-house technical personnel who can be dedicated to a Web server? ❑ Yes ❑ No

c. If no, do you plan to hire someone? ❑ Yes ❑ No
If yes, when? _____

4. Telephone company service (check one):
❑ Not needed ❑ Needed _____

a. Installation of additional telephone lines

_____

b. Upgrade to better line _____

Completed by: _____ Date: _____

Figure 5.4 (*Continued*)

Internet Service Providers

- Mecklermedia's The List (of Internet service providers), http://thelist.iworld.com/
- ISP Comparison Chart for Basic Business Web Hosting Service, http://www.qfsys.com/ispchart.htm
- Internet Service and Marketing Provider Comparison, http://www.buffnet.net/~frisbee/work/in2.htm

Figure 5.5   CommInt offers both managed and unmanaged hosting services for companies desiring a turnkey solution to their Web presence.

- ◆ Comparison of Internet Service Provider Prices, http://www.europa.com/~jra/pcw/surfcost.htm

Computer Systems

- ◆ The Internet Hardware Review, http://www.frugal.com/~danielf
- ◆ Hardware and Software Reviews, http://www.andamo.com/

Both of these sites contain opinions on the various types of hardware associated with setting up an Internet presence, including modems, servers, CD-ROM drives, controllers, and backup systems. Useful for small companies that need help in selecting the best products on the market.

Instructions

- Visit various Web designer sites for preliminary information on services and costs.
- E-mail individual Internet service providers for additional information.
- E-mail or telephone a local Web designer for additional clarification.
- Contact your ISP for hardware advice on having your pages designed.
- Duplicate this form as needed.
- Check off choices and fill in the blanks with costs where applicable.

1. In-house development

   a. Staff hiring or training

      (1) Use current employee (check one): ❑ Yes ❑ No ❑ Undecided

         (a) Wage or salary _____

         (b) Hours per week needed _____

      (2) Hire part-time employee (check one): ❑ Yes ❑ No ❑ Undecided

         (a) Wage or salary _____

         (b) Hours per week needed _____

      (3) Hire full-time employee (check one): ❑ Yes ❑ No ❑ Undecided

         (a) Wage or salary _____

         (b) Hours per week needed _____

   b. Hardware

      (1) Additional workstations (check one): ❑ Not needed ❑ Needed _____

Figure 5.6 Web Site design worksheet (Plan Section Four).

(2) Upgrade in hard-disk capacity (check one):
❑ Not needed   ❑ Needed _____

(3) Increased memory (check one): ❑ Not needed ❑ Needed
_____

(4) Higher-speed modems (check one):
❑ Not needed   ❑ Needed _____

(5) Upgrade to 256-color monitor (check one):
❑ Not needed   ❑ Needed _____

(6) CD-ROM drives (check one): ❑ Not needed
❑ Needed _____

(7) Other (specify)

_____

Cost: _____

c. Software

(1) HTML editor (check one): ❑ Not needed
❑ Needed _____

(2) Graphics suites (check one): ❑ Not needed
❑ Needed _____

2. Interactive agencies and boutiques

a. Turnkey site design packages (check one): ❑ Yes
❑ No   ❑ Undecided

(1) Option A (attach description)

_____

(2) Option B (attach description)

_____

(3) Option C (attach description)

_____

b. À la carte design (check one): ❑ Yes   ❑ No
❑ Undecided

(1) ASCII-to-HTML conversion services _____

Figure 5.6   (*Continued*)

(2) Custom graphics _____

(3) Home page banners _____

(4) Icons _____

(5) Image mapping _____

(6) Audio-clip conversation _____

(7) Video-clip conversation _____

(8) Image scanning _____

Completed by: _____ Date: _____

Figure 5.6   (*Continued*)

- ◆ SBA * Consulting's Guide to Computer Vendors,
  http://guide.sbanetweb.com/

Lists over 2,000 hardware vendors, software vendors, and value-added resellers.

Web Hosting Services

- ◆ Budget Web, http://budgetweb.com/budgetweb/

This growing list of low-cost Web services provides pointers to a variety of Web development resources.

chapter six

Forming the Internet Marketing Task Force

This chapter discusses the various aspects of evaluating potential participants and forming your Internet marketing task force or team. This chapter does not assume that you are a big company. It does not assume that you are a small one, either. Regardless of your company's size, there are various options open to you. My only presumption is that you will need *some* type of assistance, be it technical or Internet marketing, whether you are a one-person shop or a large corporation.

In Chapter 5, *Planning Your Internet Marketing Budget,* you started to collect budgeting information for your written Internet marketing plan.

In Chapter 6, *Forming the Internet Marketing Task Force,* you will become familiar with the capabilities of your in-house staff and outside services. After evaluation, you will be better equipped to make recommendations on the composition of your Internet marketing task force (Figure 6.5). This chapter will make up Section Five of your Internet marketing plan.

Section Five: Forming the Internet Marketing Task Force

Your Internet marketing plan is best supported by including data that reinforces your decision to market on the Internet. Section Five of your Internet marketing plan may include any combination of the following:

- ◆ Recommendations on task force leadership
- ◆ Suggestions for different staffing options
- ◆ Capability statements and bids from outside vendors and service agencies

Getting the Most out of This Chapter

The activities in this chapter include reviewing and comparing one or more options for Internet marketing program implementation. Review these options with your colleagues, coworkers, human resources department, personnel administrator, and/or upper management. There may be some individuals currently employed within your company who have the skills needed to assist you in your program. If not, start gathering recommendations on interactive agencies, Web design boutiques, computer consultants, and so forth. You can also search the Internet for presence providers, visit their Web sites, see samples of work, and obtain bids via e-mail.

Do We Want to Farm This Out or Not?

Why would you want to use employees to implement your Internet marketing plan? For many small companies, this question has already been answered. There are no funds to hire outside help, so you'll *have* to do everything in-house. That's not necessarily a bad thing. In fact, even if you're a large company, you might want to consider keeping *some* Internet marketing projects in-house. There are internal personnel issues such as career opportunities, existing skill sets, and interest at stake here.

Why would you want to use an outside service to implement your Internet marketing plan? That's the $64,000 question in many circles: to outsource or not to outsource. It takes a lot of dedication to get an Internet marketing presence off the ground. You need to explore what all these different Internet presence providers can offer.

Before you decide one way or the other, ask yourself these questions.

- Do you personally have the time to develop Web pages, monitor online discussions and news, and so on?
- How do these activities fit in with your current workload, interests, career goals, or skills?
- Does anyone on your marketing staff or in your company have the time?
- How do these activities fit in with *their* current workload, interests, career goals, or skills?
- Is there anyone else in another company department who could assist you, even temporarily?
- How do these activities fit in with his or her current workload, interests, career goals, or skills?
- How does this employee's supervisor feel about loaning or transferring this employee?
- What is your company policy for hiring now employees, temporary personnel, or outside vendors?
- Is your computing services department experienced in configuring Internet server software?
- Does your computing services department have the time to maintain an in-house Web server?
- How reliable is your computing services department when it comes to system outages?

If you're in charge of proposing whether or not to hire additional staff and/or outside services, you'll need to know both sides of the argument. We'll presume that you're considering hiring someone or some agency to handle the marketing part of Internet marketing. I'll be glad to shoulder the role of devil's advocate as we look at this issue from both sides of the fence (Figure 6.1).

As you can see, everybody has an opinion about whether you should assign your Internet marketing responsibilities to an employee or an outside specialist. Your best choice is to evaluate the options and propose your best plan of action, which may be a combination of the two. You may decide that only certain activities should be hired out. Outsourcing is rarely an all-or-nothing proposition.

In Favor of In-House Development	In Favor of Outsourcing
On-site employees are easier to manage.	*Outside agencies require less supervision.*
Outside agencies cost money.	*Employees have other responsibilities.*
Outside agencies have no respect for budget.	*Employees have no concept of cost overruns.*
The company doesn't have a big budget.	*The agency is willing to negotiate.*
Using current employees will save money.	*Using outside agencies will save time.*
Employee salaries and wages are already a given.	*Agencies use fewer people for the same work.*
Employees already know the company and products.	*Outside agencies already have the skill set.*
The market is full of HTML editing tools.	*A software package doesn't make you a designer.*
Employees can be trained in HTML.	*Novices can make embarrassing mistakes.*
In-house employees are more trustworthy.	*In-house employees never meet deadlines.*
Management wants us to hire and promote within.	*Outside consultants can offer on-site training.*
If anything goes wrong, the agency's to blame.	*If anything goes wrong, the employee's to blame.*
If anything goes wrong, marketing's to blame.	*If anything goes wrong, the agency's to blame.*
Hiring a vendor requires bids and paperwork.	*Using an in-house employee requires staff hours.*

Figure 6.1 In-house versus outsourcing—comments we've all heard.

In Favor of In-House Development	In Favor of Outsourcing
Our last outsourcing project was a disaster.	*You hired the wrong agency or consultant.*
Employees respect the chain of command.	*Agencies know whom to talk to to get things done.*
Temporary personnel services can solve this.	*All the best people are already employed.*
Outsourcing makes the marketing staff obsolete.	*Outsourcing makes the marketing staff look good.*

Figure 6.1 (*Continued*)

If you manage a marketing staff, discuss your Internet marketing plan with them in great detail. Don't forget to mention that some or all implementation activities *can* occur in-house if interest, skills, and time are on your side. Take a good long look at the job descriptions or hobbies of your marketing employees.

If marketing has experienced layoffs recently, now might not be a good time to suggest additional projects. Don't overlook skilled employees in other parts of the company who are interested in changing jobs or taking on additional responsibilities (Figure 6.2).

Hiring Staff Members

If you are responsible for creating a job description for the new Internet marketing–specialist position you plan to fill, first do some research. You can start by browsing through the various newsgroups dedicated to job listings. Go to DejaNews, http:// www.dejanews.com/, and search with the keywords "Internet," "marketing," and "job posting." You'll find out which skill sets are usually specified for Internet marketing staff members.

You can also construct a basic job description by using the Dictionary of Occupational Titles (DOT) Index, http://www.wave .net/upg/immigration/dot_index.html. The DOT Web site con-

Which functions are handled by your marketing communications department? (Check all that apply.)

❑ Advertising   ❑ AV production   ❑ Collateral materials
❑ Co-op programs   ❑ Corporate identity   ❑ Direct mail
❑ Public relations   ❑ Sales support   ❑ Trade shows
❑ Other: _____   _____   _____

_____ _____   _____

_____ _____   _____

_____ _____   _____

How many hours per week does your average marketing employee work?
_____

How many hours per week can your department devote to Internet marketing activities? _____

Can you devote enough time with current personnel to complete major portions of your Internet marketing program within a reasonable period of time?
❑ Yes   ❑ No   ❑ Unsure

Has your company or department been downsized lately?   ❑ Yes   ❑ No

If yes, how has that affected your department's mood, enthusiasm, or workload?

_____

_____

_____

How will employees react to added responsibilities in Internet marketing?

_____

_____

_____

Figure 6.2   Evaluating in-house resources.

Does anyone in your company have any Internet marketing–related skills that you can tap?

❑ Yes ❑   No   ❑ Unsure   This can be further answered by: _____

_____

If yes, list these company employees.

Employee name   Internet marketing–related skill or activity

_____   _____

_____   _____

_____   _____

_____   _____

_____   _____

Circle all employees above who are in your marketing department.

Check off all Internet marketing–related activity *not* covered by the above employee review.

❑ Audio conversion   ❑ CGI scripting   ❑ Copywriting
❑ Domain name selection   ❑ Forms design   ❑ Graphic design
❑ HTML   ❑ Java scripting   ❑ Literature conversion
❑ Plan development   ❑ Market research   ❑ Promotion
❑ Scanning services   ❑ Server installation   ❑ Site hosting
❑ Staff training   ❑ Video conversion   ❑ VRML
❑ Web design   ❑ Other (list below): _____

_____   _____   _____

_____   _____   _____

_____   _____   _____

Circle all the above functions that can be implemented in-house with the proper training.

Figure 6.2   (*Continued*)

What training or educational options are needed to keep these activities in-house?

Function	Training or education	Provided by	Training cost
_____	_____	_____	_____
_____	_____	_____	_____
_____	_____	_____	_____
_____	_____	_____	_____
_____	_____	_____	_____
_____	_____	_____	_____
_____	_____	_____	_____
_____	_____	_____	_____

Incorporate this additional cost information into your Internet marketing budget.

Completed by: _____ Date: _____

Figure 6.2   (*Continued*)

tains an alphabetical index to the Dictionary of Occupational Titles (DOT), revised fourth edition, 1991, as supplied in electronic format by the North Carolina Occupational Analysis Field Center. It is the latest edition of the DOT now available. You won't find *exactly* what you need in the DOT, but you can use it to adapt and combine job descriptions from various disciplines, such as marketing, advertising, public relations, and computing.

Evaluating Outside Vendors and Services

Before you begin looking for outside services, be very clear about exactly what services you need. Here is a selected list of common Internet marketing services that are performed either in-house or by outside agencies.

Internet Marketing Services

- Audio conversion
- CGI scripting
- Copywriting
- Domain name selection
- Forms design
- Graphic design
- HTML programming
- Java scripting
- Literature conversion to HTML
- Marketing plan development
- Online market research
- Online promotion
- Scanning services
- Server installation
- Site hosting
- Staff training
- Video conversion
- VRML programming
- Web design

Several Internet resources, including your Internet service provider, can provide you with leads for Web presence developers. The International Directory of Women Web Designers, http://www.primenet.com/~shauna/women.html, is a directory of Web design and Internet consultancy firms owned and operated by women. Web Consultants Showcase, http://infotique.lm.com/cgi-bin/phpl.cgi?webcon.html, is a developing directory of Web publishing companies and consultants. Listings are currently alphabetical, but they are planning a geographical listing to be implemented soon. Delta Business Directory, http://www.delta-design.com/softad/, is searchable by keyword. Enter the word "Internet" and you'll be presented with a selection of applicable links. The Pagefolio Consultants Directory, http://www.pagefolio

.com/, is another developing directory of consultants segmented by discipline, including the Internet, advertising, marketing, and public relations. After you select your area of interest, click on the links by state.

Working with Computing Services

If you are a marketer without much experience in the technical aspects of the Internet, or even computers in general, you may feel somewhat intimidated when it comes to discussing your program with your company's computing services personnel. Perhaps you feel that they really don't understand what you are trying to accomplish. Or you feel that you won't understand them.

I'm not going to guess what type of relationship you have with these technical colleagues, but I do believe that the proper attitude goes a long way in enlisting their support. Perhaps part of this concern is due to an issue of authority. Perhaps company management has decided that computing services will be your primary contact for all Internet marketing development projects.

Here's some advice on working with MIS, LAN support, database development, or other computing services departments. If you treat computing services as the ultimate authority in deciding how to approach your marketing program, then you might as well go into another line of work. On the other hand, if you tell computing services that you want this form, that programming, this capability, and that server, without regard for their expertise, work flow, and other responsibilities, take a number. If you treat computing services staff members as know-nothing outsiders who just fill your order, then you *will* have a primary contact . . . for failure. And I won't blame them one bit.

So just in case the hair on the back of your neck is standing up at the thought of working with those same people who helped you recover that file last month, here are two tips:

- ◆ Don't discount the unlimited amount of knowledge these midnight engineers have amassed over the years.
- ◆ Don't let them discount yours.

Evaluating Internet Service Providers

If you find that in-house computing services personnel are unable to meet your needs for Internet marketing, you may have to look elsewhere for technical support. This quest may include evaluating and selecting an Internet service provider (Figure 6.3). If you haven't yet read Chapter 5, *Planning Your Internet Marketing Budget,* cost analysis forms for ISPs are included there.

The Business Card Litmus Test

By now, almost every ad agency and consultant in America has hung out a shingle announcing Internet marketing services. There you sit, not knowing the difference between FTP and STP (one goes in your car). You know you need help, but how do you separate true Internet marketers from Internet marketer wanna-bes? Here's a quick and easy way to uncover fakers at your next business social. Fade in to a COMDEX cocktail party. Sounds of happy conventioneers and loud rock music is heard from a nearby hospitality suite.

Tom:	We've been advising our clients in Internet marketing.
Kaitlyn:	Really? Do you have a business card? [*She takes card.*] Where's your e-mail address?
Tom:	Uh . . . my new cards are being reprinted as we speak.
Kaitlyn:	So, you just started doing Internet marketing?
Tom:	Oh, no. We've been online for years. It just hasn't been an issue until now.
Kaitlyn:	Then what's your e-mail address?
Tom:	Tom999@aol.com.
Kaitlyn:	You're using an AOL address? How much direct Internet marketing tools experience do you have?
Tom (*shaky voice*):	Oh, we've used all the Internet tools. I thought my AOL address would be easier to

Instructions

- ◆ Contact individual service providers and/or your colleagues to complete this form. The more viewpoints the better.
- ◆ Copy this form for each ISP you wish to review.
- ◆ Complete more than one evaluation per ISP and average the results.

Name of Internet service provider _____

Web URL: _____ E-mail address: _____

List the services this Internet service provider offers:

_____ _____ _____ _____

_____ _____ _____ _____

_____ _____ _____ _____

_____ _____ _____ _____

_____ _____ _____ _____

_____ _____ _____ _____

Rate each of the following:

Customer-service responsiveness

        Low   **1**   **2**   **3**   **4**   **5**   **6**   **7**   **8**   **9**   **10**   High

Customer-to-staff ratio

        Low   **1**   **2**   **3**   **4**   **5**   **6**   **7**   **8**   **9**   **10**   High

Downtime and outages

        Low   **1**   **2**   **3**   **4**   **5**   **6**   **7**   **8**   **9**   **10**   High

Experience level

        Low   **1**   **2**   **3**   **4**   **5**   **6**   **7**   **8**   **9**   **10**   High

Figure 6.3   Internet service provider evaluation.

Features and services
        Low   **1**   **2**   **3**   **4**   **5**   **6**   **7**   **8**   **9**   **10**   High

Pricing
        Low   **1**   **2**   **3**   **4**   **5**   **6**   **7**   **8**   **9**   **10**   High

Speed and connections
        Low   **1**   **2**   **3**   **4**   **5**   **6**   **7**   **8**   **9**   **10**   High

Technical support
        Low   **1**   **2**   **3**   **4**   **5**   **6**   **7**   **8**   **9**   **10**   High

List hours: _____ A.M. to _____ P.M.

Circle days that you can reach a human by phone:
        Sun.   Mon.   Tues.   Wed.   Thurs.   Fri.   Sat.

Other (specify):
        Low   **1**   **2**   **3**   **4**   **5**   **6**   **7**   **8**   **9**   **10**   High

Other (specify): _____
        Low   **1**   **2**   **3**   **4**   **5**   **6**   **7**   **8**   **9**   **10**   High

Other (specify): _____
        Low   **1**   **2**   **3**   **4**   **5**   **6**   **7**   **8**   **9**   **10**   High

Other (specify): _____
        Low   **1**   **2**   **3**   **4**   **5**   **6**   **7**   **8**   **9**   **10**   High

Other (specify): _____
        Low   **1**   **2**   **3**   **4**   **5**   **6**   **7**   **8**   **9**   **10**   High

Overall quality of this ISP (this answer is an average of the above answers):
        Low   **1**   **2**   **3**   **4**   **5**   **6**   **7**   **8**   **9**   **10**   High

Completed by: _____ Date: _____

Figure 6.3   (*Continued*)

remember. Here, let me write down my Internet address for you. [*He writes Tom@faker
.bogus.alter.net.*]

Kaitlyn: Hmmm . . . alter.net. This is your service
provider's address?

Tom: Yes, they've been very helpful in providing
support to our clients.

Kaitlyn: How long have you had an Internet account?

Tom: Two years.

Kaitlyn (*gasps*):   And in all that time, you never registered
your own domain name—for example,
agency.com? And you want to counsel me on
using the Internet for marketing?

Anything less than a couple of years with direct, hands-on Internet access for someone claiming to be an expert in this field is
unacceptable. Keep in mind that no one becomes an expert overnight, or even by association. Furthermore, an Internet marketing
consultant who doesn't have his or her own domain name isn't
worth the paper his or her business card is printed on. Period. And
any Internet marketing expert who flaunts a hard-to-remember,
multidigit, CompuServe address is too absurd to even acknowledge.

Online tools have been a strategic part of marketing research
and communications for years. Consequently, online experts have
a history of working in this medium long before Internet surfing
was in vogue. Ask your consultant-to-be how long he or she has
been using online tools, what kind, and for what propose.

Be wary of the Internet access provider who's suddenly moon-
lighting as a marketing specialist. Access providers are mainly in
the business of selling Internet connect time, leased lines, and
associated services; they are not in the business of providing marketing advice.

Internet marketing consultants should have a background that
includes a balance of Internet and marketing communications
experiences. Quiz your consultant on the differences between
using traditional and online media. This critical conversation
should reveal a mastery of the Internet, marketing strategies and
tactics, and how the two fit together.

In any industry, experts make their mark by publishing. Has your consultant been published in the area of Internet marketing? Look for a byline on a magazine article or book. Experts can also be found speaking at seminars and meetings.

Hiring an Internet marketing expert and accompanying help translates to the bottom line: Can you trust this professional to meet your needs in the most efficient way possible?

> Adapted from an article by Kim Bayne that originally appeared in *Business Marketing* magazine, Insight section, Dec. 15, 1994, vol. 79, no. 12, p. 9 (1). Reprinted with written permission.

For a directory of consultants, go to ConsultantSee Network, http://www.consultnet.com/. This site helps hiring managers locate independent consultants, freelance professionals, and small businesses. There are 60 professional-specialty categories into which they have placed résumés and capability statements, including computers, graphic artists, and marketing.

Selecting an Internet Marketing Agency

If you've decided that you need a turnkey operation for your Internet program, you may be ready to evaluate an Internet marketing agency (Figure 6.4). There are just a few ground rules to consider:

- Know exactly what you want and what you're going to get *before* you sign on the dotted line.
- Make sure both your company and your agency agree on the deadlines.
- Get plenty of recommendations and see plenty of examples of the agency's work.

Hiring a Web Boutique

In the last chapter we discussed how some aspects of your budget will be affected by whom you hire, if anyone, to assist you in completing your Web design. Before you decide *whom* to hire,

Instructions

Interview your professional colleagues and the Internet marketing agency's client contacts to complete this form. The more viewpoints the better.

Copy this form for each Internet marketing agency you wish to review.

If you are missing information, contact the agency directly to fill in the gaps. Ask them for additional references.

Complete more than one evaluation per Internet marketing agency and average the results.

This form may also be used to evaluate independent consultants and Web design boutiques.

Internet marketing agency: _____

Contact information: _____

Person being interviewed: _____

What percentage of your company's Internet marketing activities are handled in-house or outsourced?

_____ % in-house   _____ % outsourced

How long have you been working with this Internet marketing agency?

Weeks _____ Months _____ Years _____

Were you the person responsible for selecting this Internet marketing agency?

❑ Yes, by myself.   ❑ Yes, as part of a team.

❑ No, I inherited this agency.   ❑ No, someone else hired them.

How many other Internet marketing agencies did you or your company interview before you hired this one? _____   ❑ None, they were the only one contacted.

Figure 6.4   Evaluating an Internet marketing agency.

How long has this agency been:

In business? _____

On the Internet? _____

Does this agency have its own e-mail address?

❑ Yes, it is: _____   ❑ No

Does this agency have their own Web site?

❑ Yes, it is: _____   ❑ No

What is the mix of technical to marketing expertise at this agency?

_____ % technical background   _____ % marketing background

Would you consider this a good balance?   ❑ Yes ❑ No

If no, why not? _____

_____

Respondent: Rate these statements on a scale of 1 to 10, with 10 being the highest. Do you highly agree or highly disagree with each of these statements regarding your Internet marketing agency?

This agency has a lot of experience in my industry.
 Strongly disagree **1   2   3   4   5   6   7   8   9   10** Strongly agree

This agency is very careful about not taking on competitive accounts and would not design a Web site for a competitor of mine while working on my account.
 Strongly disagree **1   2   3   4   5   6   7   8   9   10** Strongly agree

They know what I'm trying to accomplish on the Internet and work well within those parameters.
 Strongly disagree **1   2   3   4   5   6   7   8   9   10** Strongly agree

They have a diverse and impressive roster of currently satisfied clients.
 Strongly disagree **1   2   3   4   5   6   7   8   9   10** Strongly agree

Figure 6.4 (*Continued*)

They are able to adapt to any style on the Internet, as shown by examples of their work, in order to meet my needs or corporate personality.
Strongly disagree **1 2 3 4 5 6 7 8 9 10** Strongly agree

They provided me with several client referrals whom I was able to contact and interview to help support my hiring decision.
Strongly disagree **1 2 3 4 5 6 7 8 9 10** Strongly agree

They have both the ability and the interest to service any size account, big or small.
Strongly disagree **1 2 3 4 5 6 7 8 9 10** Strongly agree

They exhibit an equal degree of professionalism, regardless of the account size.
Strongly disagree **1 2 3 4 5 6 7 8 9 10** Strongly agree

This agency always completes my projects on time.
Strongly disagree **1 2 3 4 5 6 7 8 9 10** Strongly agree

Account executives warn me well in advance of any deadline problems so that I can make other arrangements.
Strongly disagree **1 2 3 4 5 6 7 8 9 10** Strongly agree

This agency respects my expertise and never tries to make me feel that I don't understand marketing.
Strongly disagree **1 2 3 4 5 6 7 8 9 10** Strongly agree

I rarely, if ever, have any miscommunications or misunderstandings with this agency's staff.
Strongly disagree **1 2 3 4 5 6 7 8 9 10** Strongly agree

This Internet marketing agency currently offers all the services any company would need to implement an Internet marketing program.
Strongly disagree **1 2 3 4 5 6 7 8 9 10** Strongly agree

The agency rarely outsources projects or portions of projects to other agencies or consultants.
Strongly disagree **1 2 3 4 5 6 7 8 9 10** Strongly agree

Figure 6.4 (*Continued*)

This Internet marketing agency has a strong staff with excellent skills and experience.
 Strongly disagree **1** **2** **3** **4** **5** **6** **7** **8** **9** **10** Strongly agree

This Internet marketing agency has retained a loyal staff and they do not experience much turnover.
 Strongly disagree **1** **2** **3** **4** **5** **6** **7** **8** **9** **10** Strongly agree

This Internet marketing agency has account executives that are always available whenever I need assistance.
 Strongly disagree **1** **2** **3** **4** **5** **6** **7** **8** **9** **10** Strongly agree

My opinion of this agency's account executives is that they are courteous, helpful, and resourceful.
 Strongly disagree **1** **2** **3** **4** **5** **6** **7** **8** **9** **10** Strongly agree

This Internet marketing agency prices its services fairly, competitively, and consistently from project to project.
 Strongly disagree **1** **2** **3** **4** **5** **6** **7** **8** **9** **10** Strongly agree

This Internet marketing agency doesn't low-ball bids to land projects or accounts and rarely has cost overruns as a result.
 Strongly disagree **1** **2** **3** **4** **5** **6** **7** **8** **9** **10** Strongly agree

This Internet marketing agency came highly recommended by a personal colleague of mine.
 Strongly disagree **1** **2** **3** **4** **5** **6** **7** **8** **9** **10** Strongly agree

Overall reputation of this Internet marketing agency (this answer is the average of the above answers):
   Low **1** **2** **3** **4** **5** **6** **7** **8** **9** **10** High

Completed by: _____ Date: _____

Figure 6.4   (*Continued*)

you should decide *what* you're hiring them for. If you've already identified Web page development as one of the services you plan to outsource, use the agency evaluation form (Figure 6.4) to evaluate a Web design boutique or similar service firm.

Once you've selected a Web boutique, start requesting bids on services. Before you can get bids, understand what you need or want for your Web site. If you are undecided, here are some Web design-package suggestions from The Web Factory, http://www.twf.com/, to get you started.

- ◆ *Plan A: Presence Page.*　The Presence Page is perfect for the company or individual who wants to express its message in the most cost-effective way. This plan allows the Internaut to access your information and interactively respond to you by filling out an on-screen form, which is then sent directly to your e-mail address.

  One page with graphics and links.

- ◆ *Plan B: Small Business Plan.*　Have a small business? Want to test the waters marketing a product or service on the Internet? Do you have product updates or other information you would like to make available? Then this is the plan for you! Internauts can explore your area, then interactively place an order, download a file, or rocket off to other areas of the world, right from your page.

  Home page and 10 to 20 secondary and third-level pages.

  Graphics and links.

- ◆ *Plan C: Virtual Catalog.*　This plan expands on the Small Business Plan. It is designed for the company that wants to offer a number of products and/or services to the Internet community.

  Homepage 30 to 40 product/service pages.

  Graphics and links.

- ◆ *Plan D: Corporate Plan.*　Designed with the medium-to-large businesses in mind, the Corporate Plan offers a complete solution for moving into the information age.

Imagine the benefits of a secure link, available only to employees, where information can be distributed instantly to all locations on a companywide basis. You can form your own interactive HyperNews discussion groups to gain direct feedback from customers and/or employees. Working with Oracle-Web interfaces, Java, Director-Web, and other tools, we can take *your* World Wide Web site into the next century. (Wow.)

> Homepage and 20 to 60 secondary and third-level pages.
>
> Graphics and links.

Source: Dave Faulkner, davef@twf.com, The Web Factory, http://www.twf.com/, 6547 N. Academy Blvd., Suite 416, Colorado Springs, CO 80918. Tel. (719) 535-0731 or (800) 980-1100.

Hiring a Graphic Artist

If you need only some graphics designed for your Web site, you could hire out this portion of your program to a graphic artist. It helps if that artist has the following qualifications:

- ◆ Knowledge of various file formats
- ◆ Ability to create simple as well as detailed graphic banners for your Web site needs
- ◆ Equipment resources, such as scanners for flat artwork, photos, slides, and transparencies
- ◆ Connection to the Internet
- ◆ Willingness to do work for hire

If you don't know what *work for hire* means, you're in for a big shock. A work-for-hire agreement means you had a job, you bid it out, and the person you hired completed the work on your behalf. As long as you pay your bill, you have met your obligation. Copyright ownership of the work is now yours. You may reproduce it and modify it at will.

Some graphic artists and photographers require you to sign a copyright statement up front stating that you have only initial rights to the art or photos. Subsequent reproductions or use requires additional fees. If you're purchasing one-time reproduction rights from a photographer or stock photo agency, this situation is totally understandable and acceptable. After all, you're asking to use work that was previously produced for another purpose.

However, if you own the logo they're incorporating into your Web design, if you plan to supervise the development of new graphics for your site, or if you own the product they're photographing, you have a right to demand a work-for-hire agreement. There are just too many hungry artists and photographers out there who can do a good job and are willing to let you own what you pay for.

The Internet marketing task force will be managed by (list in order of authority):

_____

_____

_____

Do you plan to hire additional employees?　❑ Yes　❑ No

Our company/department will:

Hire (number) _____ of permanent employees

Job title: _____ Salary/wage/hours: _____

Job title: _____ Salary/wage/hours: _____

Job title: _____ Salary/wage/hours: _____

Job title: _____ Salary/wage/hours: _____

(For hourly employees, estimate the total number of hours per week dedicated to Internet marketing.)

Figure 6.5　Forming the Internet marketing task force.

Hire (number) _____ of temporary employees

Job title: _____ Salary/wage/hours: _____

Job title: _____ Salary/wage/hours: _____

Job title: _____ Salary/wage/hours: _____

Job title: _____ Salary/wage/hours: _____

(For hourly employees, estimate the total number of hours per week dedicated to Internet marketing.)

Use current employees only.

List company employees who will be included on the Internet marketing task force. (Include all marketing and technical personnel, as well as those individuals who will join your team from other company departments.)

Name	Department	Internet Marketing Responsibility
_____	_____	_____
_____	_____	_____
_____	_____	_____
_____	_____	_____
_____	_____	_____
_____	_____	_____

Completed by: _____ Date: _____

Figure 6.5 *(Continued)*

PART TWO

Implementation: Fitting the Internet into Your Marketing Communication Mix

chapter seven

Designing Advertising and Direct-Mail Campaigns

In Part 1 of the Internet marketing plan, *Creation: Building Your Internet Marketing Plan,* you developed Sections One through Five of your Internet marketing plan.

In Chapter 2, *Preparing the Business Overview and Executive Summary,* you created Section One, an introduction that set the stage for your program.

In Chapter 3, *Analyzing Internet Market Statistics,* you created Section Two by reviewing different Internet marketing demographics and surveys, selecting applicable statistics, and applying them to your company's target market.

In Chapter 4, *Formulating Marketing Communications Strategies,* you discovered why your company wants to market online and determined your strategies. You added Section Three to your plan.

In Chapter 5, *Planning Your Internet Marketing Budget,* you began the process of compiling costs on the different expenditures associated with your plan. You summarized your budget and included this synopsis in your plan's Section Four. This chapter was only the beginning of your budget planning.

In Chapter 6, *Forming the Internet Marketing Task Force,* you made managerial decisions regarding the composition of your Internet marketing team and wrote an assessment of your team's organization for Section Five of the plan.

Introduction to Part 2: Implementation

In Part 2 of the Internet marketing plan, *Implementation: Fitting the Internet into Your Marketing Communications Mix,* you will continue to write your Internet marketing plan. You will also keep track of additional expenses to include in your budget.

In Part 2, we will discuss the different opportunities available for fitting the Internet into your marketing communications mix. The programs you select in Chapters 7 through 14 will comprise Section Six of your Internet marketing plan.

Chapters in this section include the following:

- Chapter 7.   Designing Advertising and Direct-Mail Campaigns
- Chapter 8.   Utilizing Collateral Materials/Sales Literature
- Chapter 9.   Developing a Corporate Identity
- Chapter 10.   Conducting Market Research
- Chapter 11.   Executing Public Relations and Promotional Programs
- Chapter 12.   Incorporating Sales Support Functions
- Chapter 13.   Planning Trade Shows
- Chapter 14.   Launching Your Internet Marketing Program

Internet and Traditional Marketing: The Perfect Marriage

There are two main ways to marry your traditional marketing to the Internet:

- Integrate the Internet into your marketing communications mix.
- Integrate your marketing communications mix into the Internet.

What exactly does this involve?

Reminders of the Blatantly Obvious

"Advertise that you're advertising," that's what I always say. Reproduce your e-mail address and Web URL on every traditional marketing communications vehicle you are now using. This includes every piece of paper, every scrap of cloth, every photograph, every audio or video production, and every physical object within your reach. You might even consider a tattoo on your forearm if your company name is Harley-Davidson. Still not sure what I mean? You'll get plenty of help in Part 2.

Suggestions on the Not-So-Obvious

In support of your marketing communications program, you may have relied strictly on resources that were available only in print. Now you can reduce your marketing budget in selected areas simply by taking advantage of the wealth of free information found on the Internet. Throughout Part 2, you will find out about some of these resources designed to make your traditional marketing communications life much easier.

Find new places and ways to publicize your Internet presence that you haven't included in your marketing communications program until now. This could mean developing and distributing an interactive software program on disk that just happens to promote your Internet presence while it's introducing a new product. Or it could mean something entirely different. Still not sure what I mean? You'll get plenty of help in Part 2.

Uncover ways to enhance your traditional marketing communications program by using the Internet as an automated partner. This could mean offer a scheduling function on the Web to editors whom you might meet in person at a conference. Or it could mean something entirely different. Still not sure what I mean? You'll get plenty of help in Part 2.

Think about how you can use the Internet to point to your traditional marketing communications activities. This could mean posting your trade show schedule at your Web site as a reminder that you will be exhibiting in various locations. Or it could mean something entirely different. Am I being a bit vague? Keep reading.

Section Six: Internet Marketing Program Implementation (Chapters 7 through 14)

Chapter 7, *Designing Advertising and Direct-Mail Campaigns,* begins Part 2 of the Internet marketing plan, the segment on implementation. Here is where we get down to brass tacks about how to use the Internet and advertising together. As part of your advertising responsibilities, get ready to select which activities to include in your Internet marketing plan. Include costs associated with each activity in your budget. If you are in charge of actually purchasing different types of media for your company's advertising program, then you are already familiar with the duties associated with advertising planning and placement. This chapter will contain some review material for you. If you have never placed advertisements for your company before, you will begin to develop a basic understanding of traditional print advertising.

In Chapter 7 you will become familiar with different aspects of advertising and direct mail as it appears on the Internet (Figure 7.3). Advertising, being a subset of Internet marketing, assumes many different forms. You can pay for placement of a graphical ad banner at someone's Web site, you can sell advertising on your pages, and you can pay for a brief text-based message to be included at the beginning of a mailing list digest, to name just a few. There are even opportunities for you to advertise on the Internet without spending any money at all. This chapter contains a brief overview of these options, along with tips for developing Section Six of your Internet marketing plan.

What This Section of Your Plan Might Include

Your Internet marketing plan is best supported by including all data that reinforces your decision to market on the Internet. This next section of your plan may include any combination of the following:

- Brief paragraphs on each advertising expenditure
- Your rationale for selection of advertising programs
- A discussion of how each activity complements your overall program
- An assessment of the impact of your Internet advertising on your traditional advertising

Media Planning with Internet Resources

If you're responsible for media planning, your library or office probably contains the following:

- Bulging files of advertising media kits
- Rat-torn, thick volumes of Standard Rate and Data Service
- Sample issues of your favorite publications
- A disk and/or print subscription to your favorite media directory

You gathered these resources by the following methods:

- Telephone calls or faxes to a publication's regional advertising manager
- Postcards sent in from direct-mail postcard decks
- Luncheon meetings sponsored in your city by the publishing company
- Subscriptions purchased with marketing communications funds
- Materials brought in from your home or your previous job
- Former advertising left in your office by manager before he or she took that promotion

Nothing replaces having your own finely tuned media list, whether you use it for advertising, public relations, or both. Today you can enhance your advertising planning activities by using the Internet to create a new media list or to enhance one already in use. The result may be a cost savings in the traditional advertising portion of your budget.

The American Newspaper Network, http://www.amnewsnet.com/, offers downloadable planning software to facilitate the planning process: a newspaper rates and data database of U.S. dailies that you can search by circulation and state, online media kits, and an ad placement service that allows you to submit both insertion orders and materials on the Internet.

Magazinedata, http://plaza.interport.net/magazinedata/, contains a media-kit library for major consumer magazines. The Web directory also includes telephone and fax numbers, e-mail links to ad sales departments, and links to available online media kits. This Web site is targeted at advertising placements for consumer magazines.

If you are interested in finding out about additional media planning resources on the Internet, try subscribing to a free e-zine, or electronic magazine, on media planning. One such e-zine is Media Professional, a free monthly newsletter covering print and online media. Subscribers include publishers, marketers, advertisers, and ad agencies. Back issues are located on http://www.accessabc.com/ ympc/ympmedia.html. To subscribe, e-mail MediaProfl@aol.com.

Traditional Advertising and the Internet

How is advertising on the Internet different from traditional advertising? Furthermore, how is it similar? Webmasters are usually referred to as Internet publishers mainly because it's a text-based medium. There are video and audio capabilities on the Internet, but the current technology doesn't support their transmission as well as broadcast media does (i.e., television and radio). Therefore, I've limited my comparison of the Internet to print media. Take a look at how print is compared to two of its online cousins: mailing lists and Web pages (Figure 7.1).

Print	Internet
Subscriptions and Circulation Records	
Subscriptions are ordered by mail, direct mail, association memberships, publisher's reps, and telephone calls to toll-free numbers, accompanied by a delay in receiving first issues; individual copies are regularly purchased from newsstands and at checkout lanes; local newspapers are delivered in person by newspaper carriers.	Subscriptions are ordered to mailing lists by sending an e-mail message to the list server; subscriptions or registrations at Web sites are usually instantaneous, with forms completed and submitted on the spot for subscriber access.
Circulation lists include subscriber names and addresses, with city, state, and country; circulation lists are used frequently for direct-mail purposes without subscriber's direct consent.	Mailing lists include subscriber e-mail addresses and sometimes subscriber names; lists are rarely used for commercial purposes without subscriber's consent; Web sites that require registration frequently compile e-mail addresses for bulk e-mail activities.
May be distributed free, via controlled circulation, or by paid subscription.	The majority of mailing lists are distributed free of charge; selected electronic newsletters have subscription fees; electronic versions of print editions vary in price; the majority of Web sites are free to visit, some Web sites limit free access to registered visitors.

Figure 7.1   Print advertising versus the Internet.

Controlled circulation publications prequalify and regularly requalify free circulation lists via reader surveys or qualification cards; readers who do not provide complete data risk being deleted from the publication's subscriber list.

Mailing lists usually do not prequalify or renew readers; multiple bounced messages should trigger removal of subscribers from distribution list; the majority of Web sites do not requalify their visitors or require registration to continue access; requalification of a sort may occur through user-transparent software.

Market Demographics

Outside service bureaus, such as the Audit Bureau of Circulation, verify actual subscriber numbers for many magazines; subscriber audit reports for these types of publications include breakdowns in job titles and other demographics.

Outside service bureaus rarely audit mailing list demographics; outside service bureaus, such as the Internet Audit Bureau, may audit hits, clickstreams, and other aspects of Web site visitors; a variety of server-side software packages audit Web sites as well.

Editorial Calendars

Editorial calendars are usually planned and printed in advance to aid the placement of ads in special or focused issues as well as public relations efforts.

Editorial calendars do not exist for the majority of mailing lists, electronic newsletters, or Web sites; those resembling an off-line print edition are the exception.

Figure 7.1 (*Continued*)

Readership Surveys: Retention and Interest

Publishers do not know exactly which articles have been read and which ads have been seen unless they survey the readers immediately after the issue has been distributed; readers may not always remember exact details.

Webmasters can find out exactly which pages users visited, how long they stayed, which pages they clicked in which order; where they came from before visiting the site, which ad banners they clicked on, and so forth; all of these options require prior system installation of some type of clickstream log-analysis tool.

Advertising Insertions and Premium Positions

Premium ad positions may include front cover, back cover, spine, bellyband, or special sections; page positions may include upper right-hand corner, lower right-hand corner, etc.

Premium ad positions for mailing lists are limited to headers and footers; Web sites may offer special positions on selected pages but limit graphics to tops and bottoms of page.

Specially printed inserts, such as business reply cards, may be bound or included in issues.

Web sites are linked to ad banners; files can be attached to mailing lists, but are rarely included.

Insertion-order closing dates coincide with publication schedules, such as a few days, weeks, or even months prior to the date of issue.

Advertisements are usually accepted anytime and can be run immediately if space is available.

Figure 7.1   (*Continued*)

Mechanical Specifications

Mechanical specifications for ads may include printed copies of ads, pasted-up layouts, film negatives; some publishers accept file formats.

Mechanical specifications for Web ads include graphical file format; list messages are usually text, sent to the list owner by e-mail.

Materials for advertisements may be black and white or color; preprinted advertiser inserts allow even more leeway.

Materials for advertisements are not color-based for mailing lists; materials for Web site ads may be as high as 256-color.

Consecutive ad-page placements are common; full-page ads and fractional ads may be placed.

Consecutive page placements are encumbered by the visitor's choice of links; only the Internet equivalent of "fractionals," a portion of a page or a header, are available; by definition, on the Internet a full-page ad is your own home page.

Artwork is usually sent to the publisher via mail or overnight courier; publishers accepting file formats allow the advertiser to upload files to an FTP directory or deliver it on disk, but they must usually follow up with a print of the advertisement by regular mail or courier.

Artwork is usually uploaded to an FTP directory or sent to the Web site attached to an e-mail message.

Figure 7.1 (*Continued*)

Advertising Sales

Recognized ad agencies may take a 15 percent commission on placements; in-house agencies deduct 15 percent from the ad space costs.	Ad agencies, whether independent or in-house, may still have to negotiate for commissions with most Webmasters and list owners.
Advertising sales offices for national publications are sometimes located worldwide.	Advertising sales office is usually located in the same city as the Webmaster or list owner; Internet ad brokers may serve as sales brokers for placements; geographically diverse sales offices are unnecessary on the Internet.

Reader Service Inquiries

Reader service inquiries are forwarded to the advertiser.	Visitor inquiries culminate in a mouse click and a transfer directly to the advertiser's Web site.
Advertisers know from which magazine their reader service labels came; incoming telephone inquires and trade show booth visits require human intervention to determine the source.	Log-analysis tools, such as referral logs, identify the domain name of the visiting user; cookies can identify even more; Web sites that require passwords know exactly who is visiting.

Figure 7.1   (*Continued*)

Now for a Few Definitions

If you're not familiar with advertising on the Internet, here are some definitions to get you started.

Ad Banners

Banners are those small graphical rectangular elements placed on Web pages (Figure 7.2). Banners may appear on either the top or bottom of the page, or both. Usually, the Webmaster who accepts an ad banner placement will include some wording near the graphic to encourage visitors to "click here" or "visit our sponsor." Additionally, Webmasters will include an alternate description in the HTML code for those users who either do not have graphic capabilities or have deselected the image-loading function of their browser.

Webmasters usually wish to retain a consistent look throughout their sites, so they will usually provide some parameters for banner specifications. Some sites are very particular about specifying their banner sizes, while others allow some leeway for individual variations. The size of an ad banner will vary with the Web site it's placed on. Some typical banner dimensions, in pixels, are as follows:

- 400 × 40
- 460 × 55
- 468 × 60
- 230 × 33

The Internet Link Exchange, http://www.linkexchange.com/, restricts banner dimensions to 400 × 40 in order to guarantee both a uniformity of sizes among members and to leave room for the attachment of the ILE logo on every banner placed through their site. ILE also restricts file sizes in order to minimize download time. Some sites will put restrictions on the number of colors (64 or 256), as well.

Figure 7.2   The American Cancer Society banner uses a clean layout with a boldly colored URL.

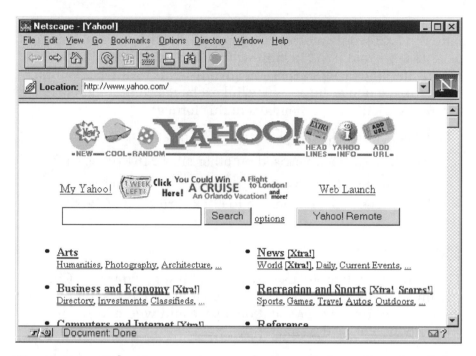

Figure 7.3 Yahoo! generates ample income from its advertising sales activities.

Hyperlinked Banner

The majority of banners placed on Web pages contain a link to the advertiser's Web site for additional information. This link is actually HTML code within the document. The code allows the user to jump to another Web location by clicking on the linked banner. The ability to transport to the advertiser's Web site is the primary advantage of ad banners and links over other forms of advertising. Webmasters have the option of putting a border around the banner by specifying this preference in the Web page code. The appearance of a border outline could affect your rate of clickthroughs from your ad.

Clickthrough Ratios

This represents the number of times a user has actually clicked on your ad banner to visit your site. Some sponsorable sites report this as a percentage of total appearances of the banner. A clickthrough ratio of 12:43 would mean that 12 people clicked on the banner out of 43 that viewed it. A clickthrough ratio of 24:43 would show better results, since your purpose in advertising is to attract visitors. The Link Exchange, http://www.linkexchange.com/, reports click-through statistics to its members in this format:

We have registered 4322 visits to your site.

You have been advertised on other sites 2161 times so far.

You have received 31 visits through your banner.

This gives you an exposure to click-thru ratio of 69.7:1.

Clickstreams

This is the path that the user has taken through your site. Click-stream analysis can contain any number of variations, including the length of time a user spent on a page and where he or she went upon leaving the site.

Headers

This term can refer to a mailing list, also known as an e-mail-driven discussion group. Lists are e-mail-based. In reading the multiple messages distributed by lists, subscribers use different systems and e-mail programs. As a result, graphics are not usually attached to or included in the messages distributed by lists. While this may change in the future, currently a list advertiser places text for an ad.

The amount of text available for a message varies with the list. Sometimes a paragraph of up to 10 lines is available to the advertiser for an advertising message (Figure 7.4). Usually, this paragraph is attached to the beginning or end of the list digest. A digest can be a consolidation of all the single messages posted to the list over a predetermined period. Advertisements placed on digest headers receive a lower frequency than those ads placed on single messages. However, ads on single messages are usually shorter.

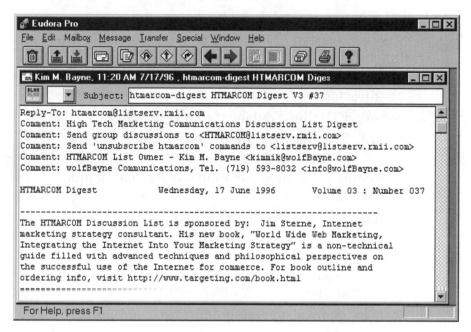

Figure 7.4 Jim Sterne, noted Internet marketing expert, placed a sponsorship message in the header of the HTMARCOM list digest.

As demonstrated, advertisements on the Internet consist primarily of two main types:

1. Text-based advertising
2. Graphics-based advertising

Text-based advertisements take copywriting skill; however, they are the fastest to implement. They can be created by rewriting or repurposing content from preexisting advertisements and changing the writing style or length to fit the Internet audience. Enhance the copy with a "grabber" or headline to get the reader's attention if the Webmaster or list owner allows it.

Text-based advertising can consist of any of these possibilities:

1. E-mail messages containing advertising copy
   a. Messages created in response to a request for informa-
      tion
      (1) ASCII-based text files stored in an online
          directory
          (a) FTP files available for downloading
          (b) Text inserted automatically into a response
              generated by a mailbot script or program
      (2) Manually created e-mail messages that include
          the following:
          (a) Reused boilerplates from other text files
          (b) Customized sections of the message to per-
              sonalize it
          (c) Personalized responses created entirely from
              scratch
   b. Posts to appropriate newsgroups, lists, and forums
   c. Signature blocks within e-mail messages
   d. Sponsorship sentences or paragraphs placed in the
      headers or footers of a mailing list
2. Descriptions of your site on other Web sites, with or
   without hypertext links
3. Hypertext links on other Web sites, with or without
   graphics
4. Content at your own Web site in various forms
   a. Documents converted to HTML
   b. Text-only files linked to your Web pages, such as list
      digests
   c. Scrolling text displayed through Java script on a
      browser bottom

Graphics-based advertising can consist of any of these possibilities:

1. Graphics files attached to e-mail messages

2. Graphics files incorporated into a downloadable software product or demo disk
3. Graphics files on Web sites
   a. Logos or icons on other Web sites with hypertext links
   b. Banners on other Web sites with hypertext links
4. Banners at your own Web site in various forms
   a. Logos or icons within your site directing visitors to other parts of your site
   b. Advertising banners within your site directing visitors to other parts of your site

Whether the online advertisement you place resides on a page or a list, on your company's site or another's, Internet advertisements usually serve three purposes:

◆ Attract the user to a Web site (yours or someone else's)
◆ Coax the user through the different pages of the Web site
◆ Can encourage the user to return to the Web site . . . often

As part of your Internet marketing program you can choose any combination of advertising activities to supplement your traditional advertising program. These include free advertising, fee-based advertising, and revenue-generating options.

Budget Considerations

Free or low-cost online advertising options will have little or no impact on your Internet marketing budget, other than saving funds that you can use on other programs. Free Internet advertising options can include the following:

◆ Creating an informational file in ASCII text for use by a mailbot or e-mail autoresponse program

- Contacting Webmasters and offering to exchange hyper-text links
- Placing sponsorships or advertisements on other mailing lists managed by your company
- Exchanging reciprocal links with other sites by contacting their Webmasters or registering in a link or banner exchange directory
- Exchanging sponsorships or advertising space with partner companies
- Including ads at your own site, such as banners and scrolling browser text

On the other hand, fee-based online advertising options will have to be tallied for inclusion in your budget. These can include the following:

- Costs to create an ad banner for placement opportunities
- Placing sponsorships or advertisements on other mailing lists at other companies
- Placing sponsorships or advertisements on other web sites within your company
- Creating and distributing software or disks for promotion of your Web site

The Reality of Internet Advertising

Advertising on the Internet is now a reality. Have users accepted it? That's debatable. For example, either out of respect for the Internet's former "no advertising" policy or merely as a euphemistic approach to selling space, some Internet marketers will refer to Internet advertising as "sponsorship." Sugar-coated politically correct label or not, it is clear that Internet advertising has stimulated a lot more than just income.

Littering the Information Superhighway

Some Internet users believe that the cost of online services and information retrieval will increase if companies are not allowed to recover their expenses for Internet marketing development. In some cases, advertising sales generate enough revenue to not only offset the costs of a Web site's operation, but also surpass it.

Meanwhile, other users believe that advertising online is a nuisance—a modern canker sore on the Internet that they once knew and loved. To some extent, these users are right. Along with the thousands of companies who respect the culture of the online world, there are thousands of companies who feel that any visibility is good visibility, Internet etiquette be damned. These so-called Internet marketers bombard individuals with countless untargeted e-mails. They place the responsibility on the user to request removal from their database. They claim that the Internet is a public thoroughfare, free of speed limits. They challenge anyone who would deny them the right to use it as they see fit. In any society, there exist a few rogues whose sole purpose lies in taking advantage of a situation. The Internet is certainly no exception. Fortunately, the industry is comprised of conscientious individuals who self-police and educate in an effort to maintain the quality of life in our online community. With a vigilant Internet marketing cooperative effort and any luck, the responsible marketers will triumph over the irresponsible ones in the long run.

Acceptable Online Advertising

There are acceptable and unacceptable methods of advertising online. As young as the Internet is, there are already some established norms for advertising online. Unsolicited advertising is still met with opposition. Recipients go out of their way to punish inconsiderate e-mailers with flames or notices to their Internet service provider. On the other hand, discreet and well-crafted signature blocks, those brief paragraphs or favorite sayings found at the end of e-mail messages, appear to have reached total acceptance by the online community.

Graphical ad banners are still receiving mixed reviews. Some users like seeing these colorful ad banners. They serve as reminders that there are other exciting places to visit online. Some users feel that advertising, in its various forms has littered the Internet and downgraded its quality. If you're interested in exploring this point of view, you might read an opposing view on the advertising efforts of the Internet Link Exchange, a free ad banner registry and service. The commentary is available on the Web at http://weber.u.washington.edu/~jgurney/peeves/.

Rather than submitting themselves to an advertiser's message, users choose to change the options on their Web browsers so that graphics do not load automatically. This change allows users to view only the Web page text. Webmasters, having adapted to that last tactic, include descriptions in the HTML source code, known as ALT tags (Figure 7.5). The advertiser's message or company

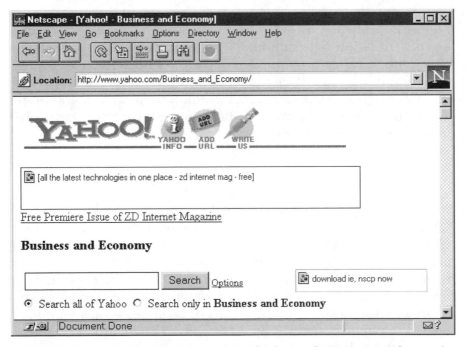

Figure 7.5   Yahoo!'s Webmaster includes a descriptive phrase for users who, for some reason, cannot see an advertiser's banner.

name still appears on the page, but in text. So much for circumventing an ambitious advertiser's intentions.

Advertisers Prevail

All that is Internet advertising is not bad. Naysayers of all types of Internet advertising, regardless of content, have forgotten one thing. Where there is advertising, there is operating revenue. It is the successful development of the Internet economy that will either make or break the Internet. Without some type of ongoing subsistence, the Internet will cease to exist. It does not appear that advertising on the Internet will go away soon. There are too many financial issues at stake and too many interested individuals to let that happen. When there's money involved, businesses have been known to defend their territory with a vengeance. Internet advertisers will not give up without a fight.

Internet Advertising Is Not Alone

The growth in advertising is certainly not unique to the Internet. The last several years have witnessed a tremendous expansion in advertising in many different forms. It's not enough for companies to place a yellow-pages ad, a spot on the radio or television, or even run a series of ads in consecutive Sunday newspapers. Telephone and utility companies now include advertising inserts with their monthly bills. Dairies accept advertising placements on the sides of their milk cartons. Elementary schools send home flyers advertising a "back-to-school" skating night at a local roller rink. School districts and airline companies accept ads to be painted on the sides of their buses and airplanes. Marketers say, "Where there's a space, there's an ad." The Internet is only one small part of this trend.

Advertising Management Firms Abound

Companies have emerged to capitalize even more on the advent of Internet advertising. Web sites, such as CyberGold, Inc., http://www.cybergold.com/ (Figure 7.6), offer Internet users payment for viewing advertisements. SoCoOL Network Advertising,

Figure 7.6 CyberGold and its customers reward users who choose to read advertisements.

http://www.socool.com/socool/net_ads.html, entices Webmasters to place banners at their sites in exchange for financial incentives. For Webmasters who are trying to increase revenue possibilities at their sites, AdJuggler, http://www.adjuggler.com/, can allow placement of more than one ad per Web page (Figure 7.7).

Creating Your Own Ads

If you choose to create your own advertisement in-house, you have several options. You can repurpose or rewrite content from a company brochure or news release for an Internet ad. You can write entirely new copy. Whatever your approach, avoid hackneyed headlines. Internet users will tune you out. Empty self-praise, such as "we're number one," has little meaning for the customer. Declar-

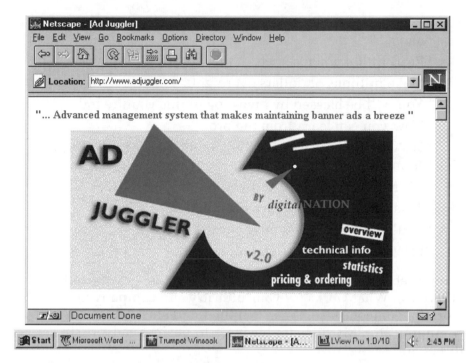

Figure 7.7 Ad Juggler is a Web tool designed to randomly rotate and display hyperlinked banner ads.

ing that you're the "number one" anything is more self-serving than it is customer-oriented. Maybe you're number one because you're good at fooling people until they open the package.

I lean toward those short statements that tell me how I will benefit by visiting a Web site and buying. But I'm also attracted to ads with personality—not the obnoxious "operators are standing by" approach, but the clever ones based on humor. Do these preferences conflict? Maybe. Your experience and industry may differ. Here's a list of advertising copy ideas that don't work when they're directed at me.

Kim Bayne's Personal List of Really Rotten Internet Advertising Lines

"It's the most exciting and ingenious product around."

"Never before has anyone ever had it so easy."

"Advertise to over 100,000 people for only your connect-time charges."

"Read little-known secrets of the world's millionaires."

"Make millions of dollars overnight."

"You will be blessed by investing in this venture today."

"Now you can learn from the pros."

"We've sold more cars than any other dealer in the Rocky Mountains."

"We're making history and you can be part of it!"

"This is the answer you've been waiting for."

"You'll be sorry if you miss out."

"Prices will never be this low again."

Internet copywriting is a style issue. Don't let anyone tell you otherwise. What works for your industry and company may not work for someone else. I'm a computer and electronics marketing communicator. My rules for business-to-business advertising are threefold:

1. Know your audience.
2. Emphasize features and benefits.
3. Inject a little personality.

Look less like an online carnival barker and more like a class act. Skillfully brag about your company, products, and services in terms that fit well within your market. Take advantage of the Internet by encouraging users to ask for additional information.

I used to take the wimpy approach to Internet copywriting by eschewing personality. I counseled marketers to tone down copy for the Internet by stripping out anything that even vaguely resembled advertising. I felt that a straight-as-an-arrow slant was more acceptable. At the time, this advice suited the educational aspects of the Internet's history. Advertising on the Internet hadn't been accepted yet. It certainly wasn't as far-reaching as it is today. Fortunately, I've evolved, and so has the Internet.

Recently, I read an article written by Ivan Levison in *The Levison Letter.*

A lot of Internet gurus are giving out lousy advice about writing Web sites.

Believe me, if you're selling software on the Internet, the last thing you want to do is sound like the new cure for insomnia.

O.K. I agree that you shouldn't sound like you're selling Ginsu knives, but let's get real! As I mentioned before in my newsletter, the Web today is a text-based medium and you've got to quickly capture the reader's interest and attention. In other words, as always, you have to establish a relationship with the reader and therefore write with energy, enthusiasm, and personality.

If you don't, you may wind up sounding like...flatter-than-a-pancake Web copy.

Source: The Levison Letter: Ideas for Better Direct Mail & Advertising, September 1996 issue, Ivan Levison & Associates, Marketing Communications, 14 Los Cerros Dr., Greenbrae, CA 94904. Tel. (415) 461-0672, fax 415-461-7738, ivan@levison.com, http://www.levison.com. Reprinted with written permission.

To paraphrase the author: Balance is the key. If you're a business marketer, you don't want to develop an image more fitting for a late-night infomercial. However, you do want to stand out in a crowd. Still too vague for you? Honestly, copywriting is an art, not a science. If you can't write balanced, professional, Internet copy that grabs your audience, hire a skilled copywriter. It's just that simple.

Banner Design Services

If you include Web advertising placement in your Internet marketing plan you need to design, or have someone design, a banner. If you are trying to keep costs to a minimum, you can use some tools on the Internet for generating the graphics yourself (Figure 7.8). If you decide to have your Web advertising banner created by an

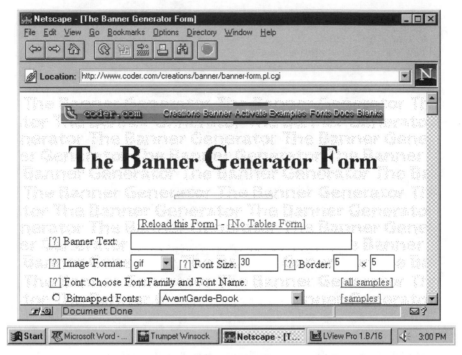

Figure 7.8   The Banner Generator helps Internet marketers with step-by-step instructions for creating a simple but attractive ad banner.

outside firm, your budget will include these costs. Check with your Web design firm for additional charges.

Placing Advertising on the Web

Several market research firms have predicted that advertising placement on the Internet will be the primary Internet revenue-generating force by the year 2000. If you haven't taken a look at these studies yet, go to Chapter 3, *Analyzing Internet Market Statistics,* for some excellent resources in this area. For a quick pointer to many of these reports, go to CyberAtlas, http://www.cyberatlas.com, which summarizes and provides links to each of the research firms mentioned.

Where are the resources for placing advertisements on the Internet? If you have seen an ad at a favorite Web site or on a list, you already know at least one contact point. However, if you're interested in analyzing several different Internet properties at the same time, compare rates at an Internet advertising rates' directory, such as WebTrack's Ad Space Locator, http://www.webtrack.com/sponsors/sponsors.html (Figure 7.9), or SI Software, http://www.sisoftware.com/.

Selling Advertising on the Web

Before you decide to offer your site for sponsorship, think about what the advertiser has to gain by advertising at your site. Once you've decided that your site is a worthwhile Internet property,

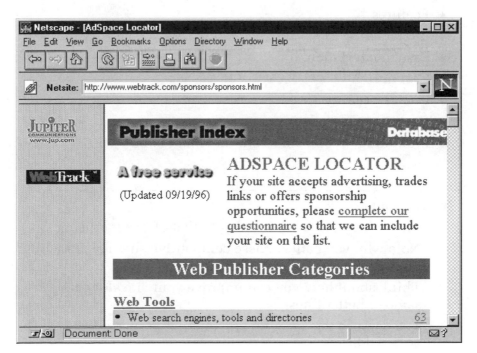

Figure 7.9 WebTrack helps companies who wish to advertise and those who wish to sell advertising.

start gathering data for your advertising rate card. A rate card tells the prospective advertiser what it costs to place an ad (Figure 7.10), among other things. By addressing this issue, you will also determine whether it is worth it to you to take on this responsibility.

Attracting and Retaining Advertisers

In order to attract advertisers, your site must fulfill certain criteria. Your site must be targeted to a specific audience; that is, your site attracts members of this audience and they return often. How do you know if your site meets this standard? If you haven't defined your audience, you have a problem. If you don't know who your audience is, then neither will potential advertisers. Compare your site to other sites in your industry that also offer sponsorship for the following key points:

- Features
- Interactivity
- Ease of navigation
- Graphics
- Content quality
- Frequency of updating
- Promotion on other sites and in other media

Instructions

Visit other sites in your industry that offer advertising.

Note why you believe these competitive sites are attracting advertisers.

Think about how you can improve your site along the same or better lines.

You can use this form for any Internet property that will accept ads.

Figure 7.10   Offering advertising on the Internet.

Internet Marketing Goals Review

Why do you want to accept Internet marketing, and how do your overall Internet marketing goals support this activity?

_____

_____

_____

_____

_____

Competitive Analysis

Who are your competitors in offering advertising on the Internet?

_____

_____

_____

_____

_____

What do your competitors' sites offer? (Check all that apply.)

❑ Large customer base

Unimportant   **1**   **2**   **3**   **4**   **5**   **6**   **7**   **8**   **9**   **10**   Important

❑ Highly targeted customer base

Unimportant   **1**   **2**   **3**   **4**   **5**   **6**   **7**   **8**   **9**   **10**   Important

❑ Audio   Specify: _____

❑ Video   Specify: _____

❑ Java   Specify: _____

❑ VRML   Specify: _____

❑ Searches   Specify: _____

❑ Other   Specify: _____

❑ Other   Specify: _____

In the above list, circle all the features your site provides.

Figure 7.10   (_Continued_)

Drawbacks to Accepting Advertising

How much time per week do you want to devote to integrating ads into your Web site?

_____

How much time per week do you want to devote to billing activities?

_____

How much time per week do you want to devote to site maintenance issues, such as content and improvements?

_____

Current Site Value

Publishing frequency: How often do you update your site?

_____

How does your site compare to other advertising sites on the Internet?

_____
_____
_____
_____

Why would someone want to advertise at your site compared to your competitors'?

_____
_____
_____
_____
_____

Figure 7.10 (_Continued_)

Based on your answers to this point, how likely is it that you will offer advertising at your site?

Highly unlikely   **1 2 3 4 5 6 7 8 9 10**   Highly likely

If you selected a rating of 5 or less, stop right now. You are not ready to accept advertising.

If you selected a rating of more than 5, you are ready to accept advertising. Continue this form.

Sponsorship Information for the Media Buyer

Rate card: What would you charge for an ad?

Compare your site with others in your industry and determine a competitive rate.

Adjust your rate up or down depending on your site's competitive position.

Fixed fee rates are based on (check all that apply):

❑ Impressions (number of audited hits per ad)

Insert guaranteed minimum number of impressions per ad: _____

❑ The period the ad will run:

Insert rates per week _____ Month _____ Other term _____

❑ The position of the ad in the Web site or on the list:

Insert rates per position standard _____ Premium _____

Other position _____

❑ Frequency discounts

Figure 7.10   (*Continued*)

Please describe: _____
_____
_____

The variable rate is based on (compare your site with others in your industry and determine a competitive rate):

❑ Impressions (number of hits per page)

Insert anticipated impressions per ad: _____

❑ Clickthroughs (number of users clicking on the advertiser's ad)

Insert anticipated clickthroughs per ad: _____

Will you pay a commission to a recognized placement agency?   ❑ Yes   ❑ No

If yes, typical commissions for advertising agencies are 15 percent if paid within 30 days.

Circulation demographics (traffic)

Note: You must have analysis software or an auditing bureau in place before you can answer this question.

How many unique users visit your site?

_____ per _____ ❑ day ❑ week ❑ month

Circulation demographics (audience)

Describe the type of your targeted audience, readership, subscribers, or visitors.

_____
_____
_____
_____
_____

Figure 7.10   (*Continued*)

Who actually visits your site?

Visitor Description	Visitors per Time Period	Percentage of Total Visitors
_____	_____ per _____	_____ %
_____	_____ per _____	_____ %
_____	_____ per _____	_____ %
_____	_____ per _____	_____ %
_____	_____ per _____	_____ %

Is your site audited? ❑ Yes ❑ No

If no, stop right now. If advertisers cannot verify your claims, you may not be able to convince them to buy.

If yes, continue.

How will you manage ad placements at your site? (Check all that apply.)

❑ Accept and manage ad placements entirely in-house.

❑ Hire an outside firm to advertise or list my site. Cost to add to budget: _____

❑ Hire an outside firm to manage billing and invoices. Cost to add to budget: _____

❑ Hire an outside firm to manage site content and maintenance. Cost to add to budget: _____

❑ Install a feature to rotate advertising banners. Cost to add to budget: _____

❑ Limit banner dimensions and file sizes.

Specify: Dimensions _____ by _____ File size _____

❑ Limit placement of the ad throughout the site.

Figure 7.10 (*Continued*)

Specify: ☐ Top of page ☐ Bottom of page ☐ Other _____

State your policy for accepting or rejecting advertisements.

_____

_____

_____

_____

_____

_____

_____

_____

_____

_____

Income Potential

Keep in mind that your site may not sell ads immediately or fill all available ad space 100 percent of the time.

Number of Web pages available for ad placement _____

Multiply by number of ads rotated per page   × _____

Multiply by average price per ad   × _____

Estimate maximum gross advertising revenue _____ per _____ (period)

Minus expenses to upgrade or operate site   − _____

Estimate maximum net advertising revenue _____ per _____ (period)

What is your target or goal for advertising sales in the following time periods?

The next month _____

The next two months _____

The next three months _____

Figure 7.10   (*Continued*)

Why Should You Place Advertising on the Internet?

From a marketer's viewpoint, analyzing why, where, and how to place an advertisement on the Internet requires reviewing your objectives and comparing them to several other factors unique to your organization. Before you decide to purchase Internet advertising space, ask yourself several questions (Figure 7.11). Review the various options of Internet advertising and determine which activities would be the best fit (Figure 7.12). Try to anticipate any biases that others in your company might have to this particular Internet marketing activity. If you are convinced that Internet advertising would be a beneficial program for your Internet marketing plan, you must be prepared to defend your position.

Selecting a site to sponsor involves the following steps:

- Visiting sponsorable sites in your industry
- Comparing various sites for audience, demographics, site statistics, and pricing
- Being realistic about what you hope to accomplish

Instructions

Complete each question as briefly as possible, using bulleted and concise statements.

If you are unable to answer a question, brainstorm with others in your organization.

Excerpt portions of this form for use in evaluating multiple options.

Use the statements from this form to draft supporting or opposing paragraphs on Internet advertising for your Internet marketing plan.

Figure 7.11   Placing Internet advertising.

Why Do You Want to Advertise?

List five overall marketing benefits that you will realize from placing advertisements on the Internet.

_____

_____

_____

_____

_____

Based on these benefits, list five company-specific reasons why you should place advertisements.

_____

_____

_____

_____

_____

List five overall marketing risks that you might take from placing advertisements on the Internet.

_____

_____

_____

_____

_____

List five company-specific reasons why you should not place advertisements on the Internet.

_____

_____

_____

_____

_____

Figure 7.11 (_Continued_)

Take a look at the answers given in the previous question. Are any of the following reasons related to (check all that apply):

❑ Lack of budget   ❑ Reputation   ❑ Competitive influences

❑ Staff capabilities ❑ Management resistance ❑ Marketing plan objectives

❑ Traditional media ❑ Past experience ❑ Other _____

Do you believe any of these risks are insurmountable? ❑ Yes ❑ No ❑ Unsure

If you answered yes, stop right now. Come back to this form after you have completed evaluations of other Internet marketing activities.

If you answered no, continue.

How would you counter or challenge each of the above objectives to Internet advertising?

_____

_____

_____

_____

_____

Based on your answers, how likely is it that you will place advertisements on the Internet?

Low probability **1 2 3 4 5 6 7 8 9 10** High probability

If you selected a rating of 5 or less, stop right now. You are not ready to advertise.

If you selected a rating of more than 5, continue.

Figure 7.11 (*Continued*)

Ad Positioning

Who do you want to target with your Internet marketing ad? (Be specific.)

_____

_____

_____

Have you identified your online market?   ❑ Yes   ❑ No

If no, stop right now and research this question.

If yes, continue.

Have you identified specific Internet properties for ad placement?   ❑ Yes   ❑ No

Selecting a Site to Sponsor

Which of the following Internet advertising activities are you considering?

❑ Web site ad banners   ❑ Signature blocks   ❑ Link exchanges

❑ Banner exchanges   ❑ List messages   ❑ Other _____

❑ Other _____

❑ Other _____

If you narrowed down your selection, complete this portion of the form for all sites under consideration. What does this Internet property offer? (Check all that apply.) Rate their importance to your industry.

❑ Large customer base
Unimportant   1   2   3   4   5   6   7   8   9   10   Important
❑ Highly targeted customer base
Unimportant   1   2   3   4   5   6   7   8   9   10   Important
❑ Audio
Unimportant   1   2   3   4   5   6   7   8   9   10   Important
❑ Video
Unimportant   1   2   3   4   5   6   7   8   9   10   Important

Figure 7.11   (*Continued*)

❑ Java
Unimportant   **1   2   3   4   5   6   7   8   9   10**   Important
❑ VRML
Unimportant   **1   2   3   4   5   6   7   8   9   10**   Important
❑ Searches
Unimportant   **1   2   3   4   5   6   7   8   9   10**   Important
❑ Other
Unimportant   **1   2   3   4   5   6   7   8   9   10**   Important
❑ Other
Unimportant   **1   2   3   4   5   6   7   8   9   10**   Important

Statistics Reporting

Is this site audited?   ❑ Yes   ❑ No

If yes, explain: _____

How are statistics at this site reported to the advertiser?

_____

_____

_____

_____

_____

Based on this information, how likely is it that you will advertise at this site?
Highly unlikely   **1   2   3   4   5   6   7   8   9   10**   Highly likely

If you selected a rating of 5 or less, stop right now. Evaluate another site.

If you selected a rating of more than 5, put this site in your plan. Complete this portion of the form for any additional sites. Continue this form.

Figure 7.11   (*Continued*)

Designing Your Advertisement

Using features and benefits, state how you will differentiate your products and services from those of your competitor.

_____

_____

_____

Using your previous answer as a reference point, what do you want your ad to emphasize?

_____

_____

_____

Is price important to your customer?　❑ Yes　❑ No

If yes, how much does this product or service cost?

_____

Do you have any photography or illustrations that you can incorporate into a banner?　❑ Yes　❑ No

If you are placing a graphical banner and you answered no, consider ordering product photography and/or graphic design services.

Completed by: _____ Date: _____

Figure 7.11　(_Continued_)

Instructions

Review your company's Internet marketing plan objectives.

Evaluate all Internet advertising activities listed below that support these objectives.

Evaluate all Internet advertising implementation activities that complement or enhance your traditional marketing plan.

Prioritize these selected Internet advertising activities in the order in which they will be the easiest for you to implement. Start with number one (1) for the activity that you can implement immediately with the least amount of preparation and cost.

If you choose to place fee-based advertisements, start collecting rates and other information.

If you choose to offer fee-based advertisements, start estimating anticipated revenue from selling sponsorships to other companies.

Prepare an estimate of your Internet advertising expenditures and income.

Add this cost information to your Internet marketing budget.

Summarize these advertising activities for your Internet marketing plan.

Free Internet Advertising Options

❑ Creating companywide standard for signature blocks to appear on all outgoing e-mail messages

❑ Creating an informational file in ASCII text for use by a mailbot or e-mail autoresponse program

❑ Placing sponsorships or advertisements on other mailing lists managed by your company

Figure 7.12 Fitting Internet advertising into your marketing communications mix.

❑ Exchanging reciprocal links with other sites

❑ Exchanging sponsorships or advertising space with partner companies

❑ Other _____

❑ Other _____

Fee-Based Internet Advertising Options

❑ Place sponsorships or advertisements on other mailing lists at other companies

❑ Place sponsorships or advertisements on other Web sites within your company

❑ Place sponsorships or advertisements on other Web sites at other companies

❑ Other _____

❑ Other _____

Revenue-Generating Advertising Options

❑ Offer fee-based sponsorship or advertising space on your company's mailing list

❑ Offer fee-based sponsorship or advertising space on your company's Web site

❑ Other _____

❑ Other _____

Figure 7.12 *(Continued)*

Advertising Specialties

Using the Internet in your advertising program includes publicizing its presence in the physical world. Leveraging established marketing programs for your Internet advertising is a good way to stretch your budget. When using imprinted specialty items for customer gifts and incentives, include your Internet addresses (Figures 7.13). Functional items have a longer shelf life than cute gadgets. If you're using ad premiums as a trade show booth giveaway, you may want to consider having your visitor "earn" the gift by sitting through a presentation or completing a qualification form.

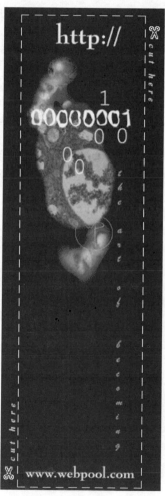

Figure 7.13 WebPool reproduces its URL on a traditional bookmark. Courtesy of The WebPool Syndicate Inc., 2-1070 West Pender Street, Vancouver, British Columbia, Canada V6E 2N7. Tel. (604) 685-3197, fax 604-685-8977, www.webpool.com.

Give very important customers something functional and wearable . . . a watch. Whenever they check the time, they'll be reminded of your Internet presence (Figure 7.14).

Direct Mail and How to Make Online Enemies

Well there's egg and bacon; egg, sausage, and bacon; egg and spam; bacon and spam; egg, bacon, sausage, and spam; spam, bacon, sausage, and spam; spam, egg, spam, spam, bacon, and spam; spam, spam, spam, egg, and spam; spam, spam, spam, spam, spam, spam, baked beans, spam, spam, spam, and spam; or lobster thermidor aux crevettes with a mornay sauce garnished with truffle pâté, brandy, and a fried egg on top of spam.

Excerpt from a skit by the comedy troupe Monty Python's Flying Circus (as it appeared in the Roadmap Workshop Distribution List operated by Patrick Douglas Crispen, Tue., Oct. 18, 1994).

Figure 7.14 Wondering what time it is? It's time for the Internet. Photo courtesy of Lynx Marketing Corporation, http://www .logotime.com/ and The Tenagra Corporation http://arganet.tenagra .com/.

If you're ever wondered why unsolicited e-mail is referred to as "spam," well, now you know. There's nothing more annoying than being continually bombarded with either an unwanted menu choice or unwanted electronic mail. Yet some advertisers on the Internet have justified to themselves that it's open season on everyone who has an e-mail address. If you have ever posted a message to a newsgroup or joined a mailing list, you are now fair game in their eyes.

Compare this to the e-mail you may have received as a result of signing up for a discussion list. You started a subscription to a list for the purposes of networking with your peers by discussing marketing communications issues. Now every list broker that retrieves that list of e-mail addresses from the list server will assume that anything that has to do with marketing will appeal to you.

American Express regularly sends out notices to its card holders allowing them the option of being removed from mailing lists. They screen advertisers and accept only those that they believe offer a product that would appeal to their customer base. Unfortunately, anyone can request the e-mail addresses from a public mailing list on a public server without authorization from the list owner. No one is screening its use. When a direct e-mail broker assumes you want to receive his or her customer's mailings, the broker is making an assumption that doesn't necessarily ring true on the Internet.

Three Cheers for AOL

Commercial service providers are beginning to wake up to the customer inconvenience caused by these e-mail marauders. In 1996, America Online took a stand against unsolicited e-mail. A letter from Steve Case was issued on September 4 with this position statement.

Excerpt from an Online Letter by Steve Case to AOL's Concerned Subscribers

```
In my August letter, I addressed the issue of reducing junk e-mail.
Unfortunately, a growing number of upstarts are attempting to bypass our
quality controls by creating unauthorized mailing lists of AOL members, and
sending some of our members junk e-mail. This is often called "spamming" on
```

the Internet, and it's a growing problem. Our Terms of Service and Rules
of the Road have always prohibited this sort of junk mail, and now also
prohibit collecting AOL screen names to create these mailing lists.

We have now contacted junk e-mailers and their service providers and have
asked them to stop sending such solicitations to our members. Several junk
e-mailers refused to work with AOL to limit junk e-mail or did not respond
to our inquiries at all. We have denied access to a handful of these junk
e-mailers from sending spam mail to AOL members. These sites include:
cyberpromo.com, honeys.com, answerme.com, netfree.com and servint.com.

Let me make it clear—AOL has only denied access to a handful of the most
abusive junk e-mailers who have generated numerous member complaints.

Later this month, we will introduce a new feature that members can use to
refuse mass mailings by blocking specific addresses.

A September 1996 newspaper story reported that AOL was
ordered to cease blocking the transmission of e-mail messages by
Cyber Promotions Inc. Cyber Promotions, as one of those companies trafficking in unsolicited electronic mail, feels that the time
has come to open up the floodgates and allow companies to
advertise as they please. I disagree.

Internet users are now receiving more and more unsolicited
e-mail advertisements than ever before. In most of these cases, the
sender offers to do the same thing for the recipient that he just did
to the recipient, clog up a mailbox (Figure 7.15).

The Impact of Unsolicited E-mail

Although direct mail campaigns are essentially "unsolicited mail"
the impact on the user is not the same. Traditional direct mailers
cost the advertiser money. The advertiser must pay for printing
and pay for postage. As a result, advertisers can be very picky
about which lists they purchase. Under pressure from the paying
customer, direct-mail list brokers can be very picky about which
lists they offer for sale. Many list brokers offer customer rebates
when obsolete mailing addresses are found. This allows them to
keep their lists as clean as possible, but it also costs them money.

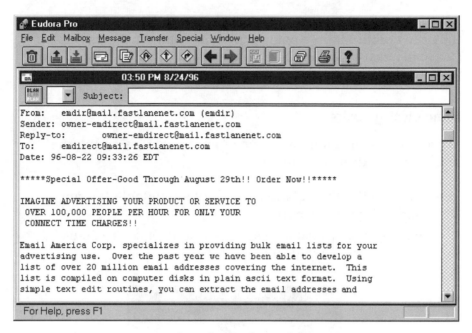

Figure 7.15 Direct mail and unsolicited e-mail are not the same animal.

Due to the low cost of e-mail distribution and the technology used to gather these lists of names, bulk e-mail houses are not as picky about the addresses they gather and sell. The method by which they sell them is questionable, as is the quality of many of these lists. Furthermore, unsolicited e-mail can cost the recipient online time charges and can impact workflow.

Deciding to Use Bulk E-mail Lists

If you choose to use bulk e-mail addresses, determine how the list was compiled. If it was compiled from the names of users who specifically asked to receive more information on a certain topic, you have a better chance that your message will not offend. For example, PostMaster Direct, http://www.netcreations.com/postdirect/, offers direct e-mail only to interested recipients. Users have signed up for this service voluntarily and therefore know what to expect.

Direct mail and the Internet are the most compatible when they are combined in a complementary manner. Gates Rubber Company mails customers a postcard citing its Web page URL (Figure 7.16).

Some Closing Advice

My advice to marketers who wish to use e-mail as an Internet marketing medium is simple:

- ◆ Build individual relationships and a reputable Internet marketing presence first.
- ◆ Inquire about a customer's contact preference (e.g., e-mail, mail, fax, telephone) and honor it.

Figure 7.16 Gates Rubber Company announces its Web page with a simple card mailed to established customers. *Source:* Gates Rubber Company, PO Box 5887, Denver, CO 80217, www.gates.com/gates/.

- Ask customers to voluntarily provide e-mail addresses. Provide an incentive such as product giveaways or access to a password-protected portion of your Web site.
- Always keep initial e-mail messages as brief as possible.
- Do not automatically add a user to a list just because they requested information.
- Offer the recipient a choice to retrieve additional information.
- Do not automatically place the burden of being removed from a list on the user. If a user has voluntarily subscribed to your distribution list, remind that person of the options for removal.
- Do not give away, trade, or sell a user's e-mail address without explicit permission.

Resources

Here are selected resources to assist you in planning the advertising portion of your Internet marketing plan.

Advertising Placement and Sales

- Ad Exchange Co-Op, http://www.webcom.com/key/adex
- Ad-Net, http://www.ad-network.com/what.htm
- AdMaster, http://www.ad-network.com/ad-master
- Commonwealth Network, http://commonwealth .riddler.com/
- Directrix Advertising, http://www.directrix.com/
- DoubleClick, http://www.doubleclick.net/
- Internet Banner Network, http://www.banner-net.com/
- Internet Link Exchange, http://www.linkexchange.com/
- Reciprocal Link Exchange, http://www.reciprocal.com/

- The Internet Billboard Company, http://adboard.com/
- The Web Ad Space Registry, http://www.fwy.com/

Direct Mail

- National Mail Order Association, http://www.nmoa.org
- The Direct Marketing Association, http://www .the-dma.org

chapter eight

Utilizing Collateral Materials/Sales Literature

This chapter will discuss collateral materials or company sales literature as related to Internet marketing. To get the most out of your collateral material, you must decide how to leverage it for the Internet. You will inventory all documents in your sales literature library and determine which pieces, if any, will be included in your online library. You will provide your online customers with options for obtaining your product literature in a variety of forms. You'll think about how to make your literature interactive, possibly by adding demonstration capabilities on the Web through the use of audio and video tools.

Using the Internet in your collateral programs may involve little more than adding an action item or two to the list of activities. You will simply change a few production choices when working with the various suppliers, printers, illustrators, and photographers who produce your printed pieces. A few activities will involve an investment in order to update your literature for use on the Web. Remember to obtain costs for any additional services or equipment for your Internet marketing budget.

In Chapter 7, *Designing Advertising and Direct-Mail Campaigns*, you evaluated a variety of advertising-related activities. You determined whether or not you would place advertising on the Web, or if you would generate income for your company by accepting advertising yourself. You reviewed the differences between traditional advertising and Internet advertising, and became familiar with related terminology. You even learned about some Internet tools designed to make your traditional media planning activities easier.

In Chapter 8, *Utilizing Collateral Materials/Sales Literature,* you will learn how to issue your sales literature or collateral materials on the Internet. Company literature, commonly referred to as *publishing* on the Web, assumes many different forms. You can convert individual documents files to HTML. You can publish an entire searchable database on the Web. There are even opportunities for you to publish on the Internet without spending any money at all. This chapter contains a brief overview of some of these options.

Effective Supporting Materials for the Plan

Your Internet marketing plan is best supported by including data that reinforces your decision to market on the Internet. Section Six of your Internet marketing plan can be expanded by including any combination of the following:

◆ Plan of action for converting selected collateral materials to the Internet

◆ Suggestions for incorporating Internet addresses into your literature

◆ Ideas for transforming your literature into more than just HTML

◆ A summary of how incorporating the Internet into literature activities will improve your marketing communications program

Integrate the Internet into Your Collateral Materials

In Chapter 7, I talked about blatantly obvious ways to include the Internet in your traditional marketing communications program. Basically, if you forget to take advantage of these opportunities, you're missing out on "a whole lotta" free advertising for your Internet presence. There are plenty of good examples of this principle in action. If you advertise your toll-free and fax numbers on your literature, there's no reason you can't do the same for your Web address. Customers will be glad to find your product information on the Web, especially if you link your catalog to a nice interactive feature, such as automated order processing. Any piece of paper that you use to promote your company is fair game when it comes to getting the word out and leveraging your printed matter for the Internet.

Integrate Your Collateral Materials into the Internet

Webmasters are sometimes referred to as *Internet publishers,* mainly because the Internet is a content-based medium. You include graphics at your Web site, just as you do in your printed sales literature, and the major portion of your Web document is in text. The major difference between the physical world and the Internet is the absence of paper from online literature. Well, there's *supposed* to be an absence of paper. People *will* print out your data sheet to show someone else.

There are other differences between the two media as well. This is where many novice Internet marketers get into trouble. They expect to be able to take that data sheet and duplicate it exactly on the Web. There are some aspects of printed literature you will give up when you convert to online. There are also some nice features of the Internet that printed literature doesn't have (Figure 8.1).

In traditional printing, what you envision from the start is pretty close to what you get for the final result. On the Internet, what you see is not always what you get. If anything can go wrong or can be changed by the Internet or the user, it most certainly will be. If anything controllable does go wrong, such as a mistake in HTML coding, it's your responsibility to correct it immediately.

Why Put Your Literature on the Web?

Here are some reasons you would want to duplicate your literature on the Internet:

Printed Literature	Online Literature
Colors and Inks	
Printing processes include black and white, two-color, three-color, four-color; identical colors, even when specified by exact PMS number, can appear different on various papers; anything printed on paper can appear in color; during the prepress stage, colors may be separated into plates; printers can compensate for color imbalances before producing the final printed piece; subsequent print runs may not always match ink color.	Browsers can display most colors, but variations in browsers and incompatible TSR software on the user's computer will cause color shifts; users can set browser preferences to override Webmaster's choices; HTML allows some color specifications, including fonts, backgrounds, frames, and links; color imbalances can occur; subsequent downloads can match in color due to page caching.
Format	
Margins and layout are predetermined by a graphic artist and executed by the printer; software programs can be set to specify page layout, including columns, page sizes, pagination, etc.; print jobs are run vertically and horizontally; paper can be folded and opened by the reader to view text.	Margins and layouts are predetermined by a Webmaster; Web authoring tools can be used to create layouts that are close to print; pagination is not an internal document issue; browsers can scroll to view both vertical and horizontal formats; vertical formats are preferred on the Web because browsers open to a default setting that most users do not change; documents that overextend monitor dimensions simply frustrate users as they scroll left and right to read.

Figure 8.1   Print collateral versus the Internet.

Art

Materials can include typesetting, photography, and illustrations combined into a "comp"; negatives and transparencies are converted to film and stripped in place; printers can accept comps on disk, such as a PageMaker or PostScript file, but may still convert to plates for printing presses.

Materials can include photography and other illustrations; art appears on the Internet in a variety of graphical file formats, however *.GIF is the most commonly used one for the Web; documents are converted into text, HTML, or other formats and uploaded; photography and illustrations are converted to file formats and uploaded into place.

Typography and Copy

Graphic artists or designers specify the typeface and fit the copy before printing; there are thousands of typefaces a designer can choose from.

Webmasters can specify the typeface, but the user has the final say; copyfitting is not a problem for plain HTML; some Web page layouts, including tables and frames, may require copyfitting corrections; there are several fonts a Webmaster can choose from, but the user has the final say by setting browser options.

Binding and Pages

Multipage documents are usually printed in even numbers (such as four-page, eight-page) due to signature or page-group binding; full-color literature is run in quantities of a few thousand or more.

Multipage documents can be any length; long documents take time to download and are best viewed when broken into several files; literature appears in quantity one on the Web.

Figure 8.1 (*Continued*)

Paper

Papers come in a variety of stock: coated, uncoated, recycled, laser-compatible, etc.

Paper is an issue only when the user prints your Web page or text for viewing off-line, but the Webmaster has absolutely no control over paper.

Size

Standard paper sizes for individual sheets are 8½ by 11 inches, 8½ by 14 inches, 8 by 5 inches.

Standard page sizes for the Web are equivalent to a screen, with multiple screens making up a document.

Special

Spot varnish, metallic colors, die cutting, inserts, foldouts, embossing, scoring, perforations, binding, deckled edges, fluorescent inks, watermarks.

Not currently transferable to the Internet, there are some HTML and graphics features which can simulate special effects, such as animated and transparent *.GIFs and wallpapers.

Prepress Proofs

Graphic artist, agency, and/or customer must sign off on inspection sheets, such as bluelines and color keys, before print job is run; mistakes must be corrected before production; mistakes noticed after production are tolerated until the next print run.

Webmaster should view the finished page off-line with a browser before uploading; HTML, typographical, or other mistakes noticed after publishing can be corrected immediately; publishing can be corrected immediately; Internet users are not very forgiving when mistakes remain online.

Figure 8.1   (*Continued*)

- Reduced print costs
- Reduced literature-fulfillment costs
- Wider geographical distribution
- Added search capabilities
- Expanded site content
- Included product demonstrations

Publishing your documents on the Web because you wish to reduce printing costs is one consideration for converting your library of documents. You probably won't realize a cost savings immediately, and you may not realize a cost savings at all. In some cases, your literature distribution costs will increase, since more people will have access to your literature, and more people will want your literature in their hands. Reducing literature distribution costs can make a big difference in your budget, especially when you take into account the costs of literature storage and fulfillment.

More people worldwide are accessing your literature than ever before. That may or may not be a good thing. For those individuals who are conducting research on the Internet and have no intention of purchasing your product, you have avoided the costs of mailing to an international destination. Customers you don't know about are able to locate your materials on the Web immediately. This may mean that you are attracting more inquiries from around the world.

Large data books, such as those distributed by computer and electronic companies, are bulky, difficult to ship, and expensive to print. By converting your data books to the Web, you are able to reduce the number of people who receive your printed data book to only the most serious buyer. Searching for the right product in your data book may be a time-consuming job. By installing a search capability and/or an index at your Web site, you allow users to search your literature library by keyword or concept. They locate product information faster, and many times without the help of your customer-service personnel (Figure 8.2).

Many technology product manufacturers include the following at their Web sites, linked directly from the individual product literature pages:

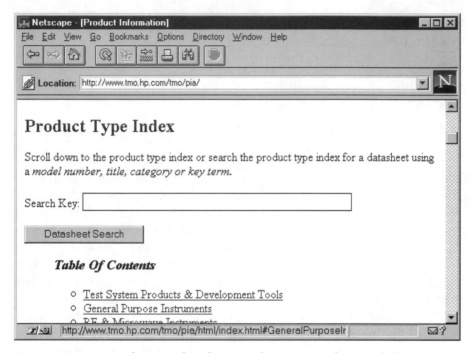

Figure 8.2   Hewlett-Packard provides a search capability to an extensive cache of product sheets.

- ◆ Downloadable software demos
- ◆ Screen captures of software, configured as clickable images (Figure 8.3)
- ◆ Slide show simulations of product features
- ◆ Online contests to test visitor's product knowledge

What Should You Publish on the Web?

Think of the Internet as an adjunct to your literature printing and distribution activities. If your goals include increasing literature distribution and reducing printing costs, consider converting any or all of the following print documents:

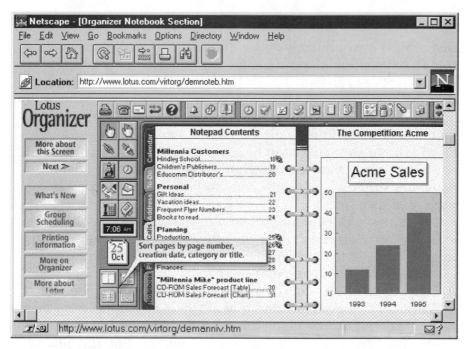

Figure 8.3   Features of Lotus Organizer, http://www.lotus.com/
virtorg/demnoteb.htm, are demonstrated through a screen shot
hyperlinked to product information.

- Annual reports
- Application notes
- Brochures
- Company brochures
- Data books
- Data sheets
- Product catalogs

Some of these documents will be easy to adapt, while others, such
as large catalogs, will be cumbersome. You may decide to either
divide your document into manageable files or publish it in a
form other than HTML.

Document Formats

Documents are published on the Internet in ASCII (plain text), HTML (HyperText Markup Language), PDF (Portable Document Format), SGML, and so on. The most recognized format on the World Wide Web is HTML. If you're interested in exploring other options, go to Common Internet File Formats, http://www.matisse .net/files/formats.htm. The page includes an index compiled by Eric Perlman and Ian Kallen for Internet Literacy Consultants. It contains a chart showing descriptions of the different Web formats, file suffixes, and compatible software options, complete with reference links.

The Portable Document Format allows hypertext features to be added to PostScript documents. Web documents using PDF require the user to download additional software before viewing text. To read PDF documents, you need a reader, such as Adobe Acrobat Reader, http://www.adobe.com/Software/Acrobat/.

While readily available and downloadable from the Web, these readers are not experiencing the same widespread use as browsers among Internet users. This fact is not a reflection on the quality or features of these different products. The decision to use one format over another is a variation on the old "VCR versus Beta tape" debate. If you produce videotapes in a format that's incompatible with the majority of players in use, you risk losing sales. If you publish your Web documents in formats other than HTML, you currently risk losing your audience to sites with browser-compatible literature.

One advantage to using these nonstandard publishing tools is that they can maintain the look of your original document. Maintaining a consistent layout is important to the marketer concerned with corporate identity issues. It is less important to the user. Given the choice, Internet citizens will take the easy route, perhaps by passing your site altogether. Downloading and installing one more piece of software to view documents on the Internet is also a matter of available hard-disk space and priorities. If you decide to publish your company literature in a format that may not be accessible by the majority of visitors, provide additional formats, such as HTML or plain text, as well.

Annual Reports and Other Financial Data

An April 3, 1995 issue of the newsletter *PR News* included a story, titled "Annual Reports: Experts Cite Trends, Tips for Success," that discussed the growing trend in publishing annual reports on the Internet. Back then, publishing annual reports on the Internet was under consideration by many companies and was starting to gain momentum. In spite of this trend, federal law still requires that print versions of these reports remain available. Restricting publication of your company's annual report to only the Internet doesn't fulfill that requirement.

Companies are still not taking advantage of the Internet for publicizing this portion of their Web sites. Considering the millions of Web documents in place, a recent search of the Web using the keywords "annual report," "quarterly report," "financial report," "10-K," "10-Q," "offering," and "prospectus" produced negligible results. Companies such as StreetNet at http://www.streetnet .com/, Investor Relations Information Network at http:// www.irin.com/, and Prospects Unlimited at http://www .prospectsunlimited.com/ (Figure 8.4) assist companies in publishing their annual reports online. In addition, they provide needed visibility by cataloging these reports at their sites, making it easier for online investors to locate information.

Marketers who have taken their annual reports to the Web use just as many variations as they do for their other Web pages. Baxter International Inc., http://www.baxter.com/, allows its visitors to search their annual reports by keyword through the last few years (Figure 8.5). Systems & Computer Technology (SCT), http://www.sctcorp.com/annualover.html, indexes its annual report with hypertext links to its different sections (Figure 8.6). GE includes all of the sections of a typical standard report, with simple graphics and an easy-to-navigate look (Figure 8.7).

Equipment Needs

If you're converting any of your documents in-house, regardless of the format, you'll need to incorporate existing artwork. A scanner

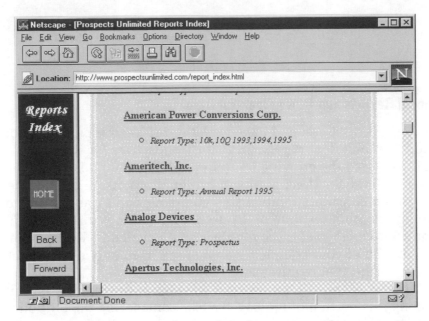

Figure 8.4 Prospects Unlimited indexes annual reports in one central location on the Web.

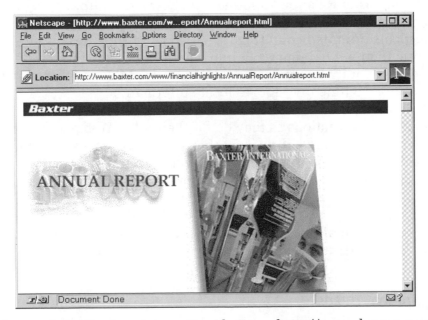

Figure 8.5 Baxter International Inc., http://www.baxter.com/, allows its visitors to search their annual reports by keyword through the last few years.

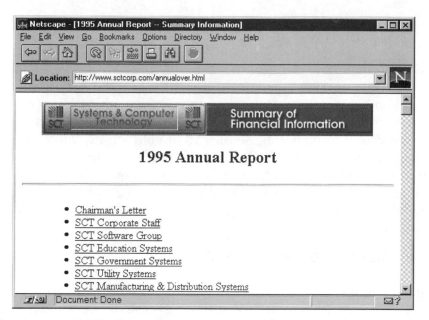

Figure 8.6 SCT allows its users to complete an HTML–to–e-mail form to request a printed copy of the report.

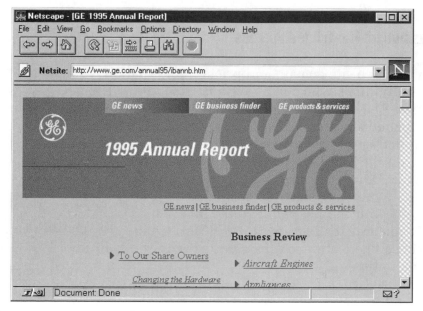

Figure 8.7 GE supplements its annual report by providing a link to its current stock quote.

would be helpful, unless you plan to rely on your interactive agency or an outside service bureau. Start comparing costs for services versus equipment. Inventory all of your slides, photographs, transparencies, and other illustrative materials to see which scanner would be best for your needs. Consider standardizing the final format for future photo sessions if you plan to purchase only one type of scanner.

How Much Are You Going to Put Online?

Before you get started, make a master document list of your company literature (Figure 8.8). You'll need these details so you can get accurate bids from outside services. If you don't use an outside firm, you'll still want to know how much work you're considering. Don't forget to keep track of where the files reside, in both off-line and online form, even after you upload them to the Internet.

Password-Restricted Access

If your Web site contains proprietary information, you risk access by individuals who don't have a need to know. The news is full of stories of companies who have had their security compromised. It happened simply because they underestimated the skills of a disgruntled employee, a competitor, or just some kids out for a fun ride on the Net. If it's on the Internet, it's open season. A word of advice: Don't publish anything on the Internet you don't want seen. If you distribute it to customers in print, it's probably safe to assume you can publish it on the Internet.

If you are creating a password-restricted area on the Web, you can use this feature to offer selected access to your library by one or more types of visitors:

◆ Editors and reporters
◆ Very important customers

- Registered visitors
- Your friends at the Pentagon

Password-protected sites evoke different responses from Internet users. Password-protected sites with easy entry gained through a simple registration procedure can be viewed as a bonus to the registrant, especially when the content is unique or helpful. Password-protected sites can also be viewed as intimidating, annoying, and downright rude. There are still plenty of people who feel that information on the Internet should be free. "Free" means I don't have to provide you with my identity, either.

Your choice to create this type of site may include a need to track exactly who is reading your online literature. Many users will reregister at a Web site several times using an assumed name, thereby skewing your results. This happens often, especially when there are so many password protected sites around. Users just can't keep track of all the different user names and passwords (Figure 8.9).

Another consideration for password-protected literature is cost. If you are a publisher who regularly charges for copies of your magazine or newspaper, you may not want to freely publish all of your documents on the Web. Web publishing may reduce the income you receive from selling copies of the printed work. You may choose to excerpt portions of your documents. You may wish to discuss your strategy for re-creating sales literature online beforehand. Creating a password-protected site is big business. It may involve additional computing services costs you didn't consider. Obtain these cost estimates for your budget beforehand.

Different traditional print publishers have different strategies when it comes to republishing their print editions online. *TV Guide,* http://www.tvguide.com, decided to offer practically all of its print editions on its Web site for free. Considering that they are a predominant publisher of TV listings in the United States, this is a big decision that could either positively or negatively impact their sales. Working in their favor is the belief that most people will still prefer to have the print edition in their hands while surfing TV channels.

Document Title	Description	Authoring Choice	Total Text Pages	Graphics No., Types, Sizes	Estimated Conversion Costs	Enhancements
Background Music Catalog	Artist and title, artists' photos, album covers	HTML— Web; ASCII text—FTP and mailbot	16 pages plus insert	2—35mm slides 4—4×5 transp 8—color 8×10 photos	(16 pages × $25) + (14 scans × $12) = $568.00	Add selected audio and video clips of artists linked to their names

Figure 8.8 Master Document List

Enhancement Costs	Archive Location	Online Location	Assignments	Uploaded	Updated	Initials
(7 audio clips × $35) + (3 video clips × $65) = $440.00	c:\nash\music.htm plus disk #24	../nash/music.htm	Kim Bayne—HTML and graphic conversion; Bruce Bayne—file upload	7/25/96	8/25/96	

Figure 8.8 (*Continued*)

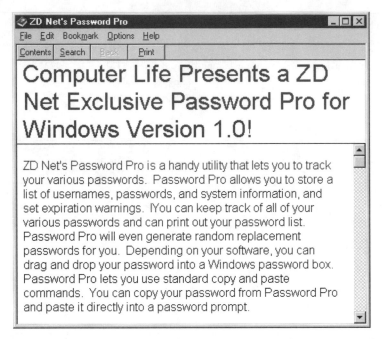

Figure 8.9 ZDNet provides free, downloadable, password management software for individual users.

The Web Demands More

After you decide on your strategy for converting or republishing your company literature on the Internet, ask yourself again whether or not the Internet has added anything to the mix. If you are limiting your conversion of documents to a few HTML lines of code and several linked graphics, then your product literature will remain static in an interactive environment. Investigate how you can use hyperlinked screen shots, video clips, VRML, Java, or something else to invigorate your literature and demonstrate product features. Involve your visitor instead of adding more links to other documents. Take advantage of the unique properties of the Internet, and you'll improve your overall product literature presentation.

chapter nine

Developing a Corporate Identity

This chapter discusses establishing guidelines for developing a consistent corporate identity for your Internet presence both on- and off-line. Consistently applying identity standards to your Internet marketing program will ensure that you are clearly communicating to your market in a manner that encourages recollection of your company, its products, and its image.

The true measure of a company's market identification is in its recognition. Few companies command it without some type of consistent message, whether it includes a company name or nickname, a corporate logo or identifiable graphics, a slogan, or simply a clearly defined communication style. That's why it is so essential to apply the principles of corporate identity to your Internet marketing presence.

In Chapter 8, *Utilizing Collateral Materials/Sales Literature,* you reviewed your sales literature, such as corporate brochures, product catalogs, folders, and data sheets for content that could be repurposed and enhanced for the Internet. You also reviewed examples of how other companies were re-creating their literature library.

In Chapter 9, *Developing a Corporate Identity,* you will continue to strengthen your marketing mix by adding Internet elements into your corporate identity. This chapter will contribute to the further development of Section Six of your Internet marketing plan.

Effective Supporting Materials for the Plan

Your Internet marketing plan is best supported by including data that reinforces your decision to market on the Internet. Section Six of your Internet marketing plan can be expanded by including any combination of the following:

- ◆ Plan of action for teaming portions of selected corporate identity activities with Internet activities
- ◆ A preliminary draft of your corporate Internet style manual
- ◆ A summary of how incorporating the Internet into the corporate identity function will improve your marketing communications program efficiency

Getting the Most out of This Chapter

The activities in this chapter include reviewing and comparing one or more options for enhancing your corporate identity activities. If you have a traditional corporate identity style manual, now is the time to dig it out. It will contain practical information on guidelines you have already applied for the consistent use of your company logo. It will be useful to you for incorporating some of your company's style methods into your Internet marketing. It will also keep you from overlooking anything that may create a problem later on. Finally, you should include any Internet marketing guidelines that you have developed as an addendum to your corporate identity manual. That way, you can be sure that it gets the attention it deserves.

Applying the Internet to Your Corporate Identity

Part of the fun in developing a company image lies in watching that image take on a life of its own. How many times have you glanced at the logo of a nationally known company and recognized it immediately, even without the company name nearby? Do you ever refer to one company's name as similar to another's? The companies that have earned your recognition did so for the following reasons:

- ◆ They uniformly applied their identity to their marketing communications programs.
- ◆ They regularly reviewed its application.
- ◆ They updated its use to suit the times.

In applying corporate identity principles to the Internet, do not establish rigid guidelines that require the use of a ruler, a magnifying glass, or some other type of exacting physical measurement. On the Internet, many of the guidelines you are used to working with, such as color selection and typeface specifications, are a lost cause. You can attempt to duplicate these elements on the Internet, but the ultimate decision maker on some of these choices may turn out to be your users.

Many marketers, accustomed to unbending adherence to identity guidelines, experience culture shock when they enter cyberspace. Corporate identity guidelines are just that . . . *guidelines.* They are not a doctor's prescription that must be filled precisely. Corporate identity guidelines are a blueprint. They help you maintain a certain look and feel in the marketplace—one that can't or won't be confused with any other company. Corporate identity guidelines shouldn't be used as a ruler to slap the hands of creative marketers. Corporate identity guidelines shouldn't be used to force a size 8 foot into a size 5 shoe. In many cases, the Internet *is* that "size 5 shoe."

How Corporate Identity Guidelines Change Online

Application of your established corporate identity program to your Internet programs is hampered by several factors. These factors are a combination of the technological restrictions, the culture, and online management issues. If you become better aware of them, you can best address how you are going to circumvent corporate identity issues online.

The majority of documents on the World Wide Web are formatted in HTML. HTML approximates formats found in print documents, but currently cannot duplicate them exactly. For text, the range of colors, font types, and sizes is comparatively limited. If your company has a specific corporate typeface and PMS (ink) color, you may have to accept some substitutions during your Internet development. Decide on which substitutions will be made and include this information in your Internet style manual.

The ability to create special effects in HTML, such as those afforded by the use of wallpapers, may create readability or recognition problems when used alongside your company logo or wordmark. Your traditional corporate identity manual may specify restrictions on the types of paper or paper color on which you are allowed to reproduce your company logo. Make note of this and reference a similar policy for the Internet. At the end of this chapter, you will draft your Internet style manual.

Take Advantage of Your Identity

If you are in charge of applying your corporate identity guidelines to marketing communications, such as advertising, sales literature, packaging, or trade shows, then you are well aware of the importance of your logo or company name in the physical world. Companies who are marketing on the Internet have already taken the obvious approach in applying the Internet to their traditional marketing materials, such as stationery and business cards. Some companies incorporate their addresses into company letterhead with a unique flair for Internet style (Figure 9.1). Some marketers find a way to take a standard corporate identity vehicle, such as the business card, and give it an entirely new look and usefulness (Figure 9.2). Still other corporate identity administrators, fully aware of the Internet's influence, allow it to drive their entire off-line image.

Now why is it so important to watch your identity on the Internet? After all, you don't use your company logo in your e-mail messages. That Web site you're designing is the only place you'll be reproducing your graphics. You're controlling how it's being created, right?

FIRE **FG** GIRL

FireGirl Promotion Options

Graphical Link in FireGirl Fairgrounds and Travel Guide
$299 per year*

Reach the 25,000+ visitors who come to FireGirl every month. Your web site will be linked to a 2.5" x 2.5" graphic in two of FireGirl's most popular sections, the FireGirl Fairgrounds, and the FireGirl Travel Guide.

Graphical Link in The FireGirl Fairgrounds only
$199 per year*

Designed for hot sauce manufacturers who don't have a physical place to visit, but who still want to reach the hot food lovers from over 30 different countries who come through the FireGirl doors every month. Your web site will be linked to a 2.5" x 2.5" graphic from inside the FireGirl Fairgrounds.

Non-linked graphic in FireGirl Travel Guide
$199 per year*

So, you're not on the Internet yet. Don't worry. People are still traveling, and once they get to your city, you will want to stand out from the other hot spots. A 2.5" x 2.5" non-linked graphic will promote your company 24 hours a day, everyday in the FireGirl Travel Guide.

* Graphics must be web-ready. Include an additional $15 if your graphics need to be made web-ready.

RR 4, Box 4970, Sidney, Maine, USA 04330
207.465.9536
email: info@firegirl.com

HTTP://WWW.FIREGIRL.COM

Figure 9.1   FireGirl's unique typeface, chosen to display a Web page address, makes a bold statement on company stationery. Fire-Girl, RR 4, Box 4970, Sidney, MA 04330. info@firegirl.com.

Figure 9.2 Omaha Truck Center, the first freightliner dealer in the United States to establish a presence on the Web, hands out business cards to promote its Web site. *Source:* Omaha Truck Center, 10710 I Street, PO Box 27379, Omaha, NE 68127, www .omahatruck.com.

Well, the Internet is a public thoroughfare. You may put up a sign that says NO SPITTING, but sometimes it just doesn't do any good. The Internet continues to grow at a tremendous rate. As with most growing entities, there are growing pains. The users are testing the Internet's limits, again and again. The users are also testing the limits of the companies who are marketing online. That's why it's not only important for your company to apply its corporate identity to the Internet consistently, but also to monitor its application.

Domain Name Ownership and Trademark Issues

One of the biggest areas of corporate identity confusion on the Internet is in the area of domain names. Recently, university administrators were upset about a domain name service offering e-mail accounts resembling the names of universities, and rightfully so. While it may have appeared as a prank to some, domain name confusion can be the source of lost revenue or a damaged reputation for many businesses and organizations.

Compare these different domain names and the list of owners and see if you can match them up correctly. Look at the domain name on the left and find the correct company name on the right. They are *not* matched correctly as shown here. (By the way, it's not fair to look up the registrants online first.)

Domain Name	Registered to
SHOE.COM	Shoebox Inc.
SHOES.COM	Shoe Boxes for Shoes, Inc.
SHOE.ORG	Future Industries
SHOES.ORG	Alan's Shoes
SHOEBOX.COM	Footwear Retailers & Distributors Association
SHOE-BOX.COM	InterNetWorx, Inc.

Interested in checking out your answers? Go to InterNIC, http://rs.internic.net/, and look up the domain names and/or company names with the Web Interface to Whois. You can also find the answers at the end of this chapter.

Now imagine how confusing this must be to the customer. Alan's Shoes routinely receives e-mail addressed to postmaster @shoes.com or webmaster@shoes.com, rather than the address it publicizes. Sometimes it's very obvious that the user is looking for another company. Sometimes it's not. Some of these messages *could* be intended for shoe retailers in other cities. There's no way to know, so all responses contain a standard .signature block with company name, street address, and telephone number, just in case there's any confusion.

What does Internet domain name confusion have to do with the bottom line? New customers in Oregon who want to buy Birkenstock shoes on the Internet don't really care if they reach the right shoe store in Tucson or not, just as long as the selection exists, the price is reasonable, and the order is filled promptly. Wouldn't this problem be eliminated if Internet users were more careful? Internet users are as careful as the technology helps them to be.

Why Can't the Federal Government Do Something?

In a July 29, 1996, issue of *PC Week,* executive editor Linda Bridges posed the question, "What's in a name and who owns it?"

Her editorial discusses the need for federal laws to extend trademark protection to Internet domain names. Let's examine this idea further. If the federal government eventually extends its protection to domain names, the problem still isn't solved.

If you have a company or product name that you'd like to register, you can apply for a registered trademark with the federal government. In the off-line world, trademark registration is but one formal solution to protecting your identity. You may think this is foolproof, but it's not. A company called Travel Bug located in New York can still register its trade name with the state. Across the country, another Travel Bug in Colorado can register that same name there. Are these companies related? It doesn't matter. If neither of them engages in interstate commerce, then no one will be financially harmed by the duplication.

In anticipation of an expanded market, many business owners choose to register a trade name that doesn't conflict with either federal or state registrations. They hire a trademark lawyer who determines if and where an identity conflict can occur.

Take the case of the product name Independence. I once worked for a company that was interested in trademarking this product name for one of its tape drives. Having had experience in online databases, I conducted a trademark search for this name in anticipation of my employer's registration of it. I limited my search to the federal records, and yet I came up with 34 different products named Independence. I wonder what I would have found had I researched further? Most of the products named Independence were in different industries. A few, however, were in the computer industry. Eventually, after consulting a trademark lawyer, company management decided against attempting to register the name.

How Did Everything Get So Messed Up?

Certain Internet users, who saw the wave in domain name registrations coming, took advantage of the situation. They registered names as fast as possible in order to scalp potential registrants. If that problem wasn't enough, the variations in domain name extensions (for example, *.us, *.com, *.org, *.edu, *.gov) made it impossible to stop anyone from registering any name they chose.

With enough creativity and some Internet gymnastics, your competitor can wear an Internet name similar to your own. The result is equivalent to having directory assistance operators point your customers to someone else.

The situation for domain name registrations *has* improved. InterNIC, tired of the problems associated with domain name issues, established a dispute policy to help manage the situation. The policy is posted at InterNIC's Web site. Why wasn't the domain name policy clearer before? Up until the past few years, there really wasn't any need to address these Internet identity issues. Besides, domain name issues became domain name disputes *because of* marketing on the Internet. And nothing's worse than a whiner, especially an Internet marketing whiner.

Whose Responsibility Is Your Identity, Anyway?

When it comes to locating you on the Internet, it's not the customers' responsibility to make sure they reached the right store. It's really the responsibility of the company to make sure the path to its door is easy to find. Having the right domain name, such as one closely related to your company's trademark, will help a lot. But it's better not to rely exclusively on that avenue for securing your place on the Internet.

No matter what, the government, the courts, and even the domain name registries won't help if you don't take preventive steps. Unscrupulous individuals will always find a way to take advantage of your conscientious efforts to establish or maintain a market identity, whether it's on the Internet or not. The courts and lawyer's offices are full of business owners who are trying to stop someone else from intentionally capitalizing on their previously established name.

If you're hoping someone else, like InterNIC or the federal government, will solve your Internet identity problems for you, you're going to be waiting a long time. You can complain all you want about things you have no direct control over, such as company or product name confusion, intentional or otherwise. You can complain about the thousands of duplicate company names in the world. You can gripe about the way domain names are issued.

You can blame any of a number of different governing agencies for this mess. It doesn't really solve anything. You have a job to do. You have to get the word out that you're on the Internet. It's time to take some action.

Action Item 1

If you're going to establish an Internet presence, you need to create your own domain name (Figure 9.3). A company-specific domain name is portable. You can take it with you regardless of where your Internet access originates. A company-specific domain name says you are serious about your Internet presence. If you are marketing on the Internet for the long term, you'll want your customers to find you easily.

Internet marketers without a domain name send a different message to the marketplace. For example, think about the message a company like UPS would send if it had its customer packages delivered by the post office. If you are in a company that is prominent in the market or one that would like to be, you don't want to do anything online that detracts from your image. A company that uses its access provider's address on company literature makes a nice statement . . . for the service provider. As a marketer, you want to promote *your* company's presence, *not* someone else's.

The most obvious choice for your domain name is your company name. You may decide not to register your company name due to preexisting Internet conflicts, whether they are by accident or intentional. You may not be able to register your company name as a domain name because it may already be taken by someone else.

Many large companies have circumvented the problem by registering as many variations on their company name as possible. By doing so, they shut out all other companies who may have a legitimate claim to a variation. Domain name registration isn't free anymore. It costs money now. Multiple registrations are an option that are feasible only for the large company. Meanwhile, the opportunity takes advantage of the small company. There are some domain registry restrictions that will limit your ability to register multiple domains, even if they resemble your company name, by requiring a separate server for each.

Instructions

- ◆ Review Chapter 2, *Preparing the Business Overview and Executive Summary,* for examples of companies and their domain name choices.

- ◆ You may choose to complete this form with full sentences, bullets, or a combination of the two.

- ◆ Include all currently used and former versions of your company and product names, whether legal, formal, or casual.

- ◆ Include all versions of company and product names used in verbal or written communications by management, employees, sales personnel, vendors, and the press.

- ◆ Include all versions that appear on signage around your company.

- ◆ Include all former company names, including those appended, truncated, or changed in some manner.

- ◆ Include all frequent misspellings that may have appeared in the press.

- ◆ Include all abbreviations, letters, or nicknames.

- ◆ Include all company names that are similar but unrelated to your own.

- ◆ Include anything that a potential customer might use to locate your company on the Internet, whether you think it's even remotely possible or totally unappealing (you can eliminate the unappealing choices later, if you like).

What type of domain name would you like to create? (Check all that apply.)

❑ Company-specific (e.g., hp.com, ibm.com, microsoft.com, mcdonalds.com, fedex.com)

❑ Product-, brand-, or service-specific (e.g., laserjet.com, shoes.com, huntclub.com)

Figure 9.3   Brainstorming for domain names.

❑ Industry-specific (e.g., marketing.org, electronics.com, finance.com)

❑ Image-specific (e.g., targeting.com, ingenious.com, creative.com)

❑ Geography-specific (e.g., colorado.com, wintergreen.com, southcarolina. com)

❑ Other _____

Company-Specific Domain Names

What is the name of your company?

Your company's complete name:

_____

_____

Name variations

By your employees:

_____

_____

By your customers:

_____

_____

By members of the press:

_____

_____

By others:

_____

_____

Circle all of the names listed above that are trademarked by your company.

Figure 9.3 (*Continued*)

Image problems

Other companies whose names are similar to that of your company:

_____

_____

Any known translation problems in foreign languages:

_____

_____

Circle all of the names listed above that generate concern.

Product-, Brand-, or Service-Specific Domain Names

List your company's product names, brand names, or service marks.

_____   _____   _____   _____   _____

_____   _____   _____   _____   _____

_____   _____   _____   _____   _____

_____   _____   _____   _____   _____

Industry-Specific Domain Names

List keywords for your company.

_____   _____   _____   _____   _____

_____   _____   _____   _____   _____

_____   _____   _____   _____   _____

_____   _____   _____   _____   _____

Figure 9.3   (*Continued*)

Image-Specific Domain Names

List words, such as adjectives, that describe your company, products, or image.

_____ _____ _____ _____ _____

_____ _____ _____ _____ _____

_____ _____ _____ _____ _____

_____ _____ _____ _____ _____

Geography-Specific Domain Names

List streets, cities, states, regions, or other areas identifiable with your company.

_____ _____ _____ _____ _____

_____ _____ _____ _____ _____

_____ _____ _____ _____ _____

_____ _____ _____ _____ _____

Note: *Once you have selected a domain name, register it immediately with the appropriate issuing authority. Include the costs to register and renew it in your Internet marketing budget. If you're unsure who is responsible for domain name registration, start with InterNIC, http://rs.internic.com/, or contact your Internet service provider for assistance.*

Completed by: _____ Date: _____

Figure 9.3   (*Continued*)

Creating an Internet Style Manual

In the Internet addendum to your corporate style manual, or in your Internet style manual, you will specify two main items (Figure 9.4):

Instructions

- ◆ Review your traditional corporate identity manual, if you have one. If not, locate all art directions and type specifications for re-creating your company artwork.

- ◆ Adapt any applicable sections of your traditional identity guidelines for the Internet.

- ◆ If Internet substitutions are not available, for example, for corporate typefaces or colors, choose something close and make note of it.

- ◆ You may need to consult a book on Web design or HTML coding to cover all the possibilities. Check with your Web designer or interactive agency as well.

- ◆ For all cases, explain the guidelines and attach sample layouts, if applicable.

Placement of Internet Addresses on Off-Line Marketing Media

Business cards

_____

_____

_____

❑ Replace all inventory   ❑ Replace selected inventory

❑ Deplete inventory before ordering   ❑ Other: _____

❑ Do not include in program

Cost: _____

Company letterhead

_____

_____

_____

Figure 9.4   Drafting an Internet style manual.

❑ Replace all inventory   ❑ Replace selected inventory

❑ Deplete inventory before ordering   ❑ Other: _____

❑ Do not include in program

Cost: _____

Envelopes

_____

_____

_____

❑ Replace all inventory   ❑ Replace selected inventory

❑ Deplete inventory before ordering   ❑ Other: _____

❑ Do not include in program

Cost: _____

Fax cover sheets

_____

_____

_____

❑ Replace all inventory   ❑ Replace selected inventory

❑ Deplete inventory before ordering   ❑ Other: _____

❑ Do not include in program

Cost: _____

Mailing and shipping labels

_____

_____

_____

Figure 9.4   (*Continued*)

❑ Replace all inventory   ❑ Replace selected inventory

❑ Deplete inventory before ordering   ❑ Other: _____

❑ Do not include in program

Cost: _____

Interoffice memos

_____

_____

_____

❑ Replace all inventory   ❑ Replace selected inventory

❑ Deplete inventory before ordering   ❑ Other: _____

❑ Do not include in program

Cost: _____

News release letterhead

_____

_____

_____

❑ Replace all inventory   ❑ Replace selected inventory

❑ Deplete inventory before ordering   ❑ Other: _____

❑ Do not include in program

Cost: _____

Product literature (*Note:* You may have already addressed these costs in Chapter 8.)

_____

_____

_____

Figure 9.4   (*Continued*)

☐ Replace all inventory   ☐ Replace selected inventory

☐ Deplete inventory before ordering   ☐ Other: _____

☐ Do not include in program

Cost: _____

Employee name badges

_____

_____

_____

☐ Replace all inventory   ☐ Replace selected inventory

☐ Deplete inventory before ordering   ☐ Other: _____

☐ Do not include in program

Cost: _____

Visitor badges

_____

_____

_____

☐ Replace all inventory   ☐ Replace selected inventory

☐ Deplete inventory before ordering   ☐ Other: _____

☐ Do not include in program

Cost: _____

Signage

_____

_____

_____

Figure 9.4   (*Continued*)

❑ Replace all inventory ❑ Replace selected inventory
❑ Deplete inventory before ordering ❑ Other: _____
❑ Do not include in program

Cost: _____

Slide presentations

_____
_____
_____

❑ Replace all inventory ❑ Replace selected inventory
❑ Deplete inventory before ordering ❑ Other: _____
❑ Do not include in program

Cost: _____

Packaging

_____
_____
_____

❑ Replace all inventory ❑ Replace selected inventory
❑ Deplete inventory before ordering ❑ Other: _____
❑ Do not include in program

Cost: _____

Usage Guidelines for Corporate Identity Elements on the Internet

Logo application

_____
_____
_____

Figure 9.4 (*Continued*)

Graphic file dimensions

_____

_____

_____

Color restrictions

_____

_____

_____

Sizing

_____

_____

_____

Whitespace

_____

_____

_____

Address lines

_____

_____

_____

.signature blocks

_____

_____

_____

Figure 9.4　(*Continued*)

1. How your Internet presence will be publicized through your traditional corporate identity program
2. How your traditional corporate identity elements will be incorporated into and modified for the Internet

You may incur some costs for incorporating your Internet addresses into preexisting materials. You may choose to wait until your inventory of letterhead and business cards is depleted before reprinting. You may decide to use an interim solution. I wouldn't recommend using rubber stamps on your letterhead to signal your Internet marketing presence. Nothing ruins the professional image of a nicely designed set of company stationery more than a poorly inked, stamped impression of an e-mail address.

Establish formats for displaying your e-mail addresses on business cards, letterhead, interoffice memos, news releases, and so on. Your decision to include an identifying prefix, such as "e-mail," is up to you. Examples:

info@wolfBayne.com

e-mail info@wolfBayne.com

Contact info@wolfBayne.com

Establish formats for displaying your Web address as well. Your decision to include an identifying prefix, such as "Web" or "http://" is up to you. Examples:

www.wolfBayne.com

URL: www.wolfBayne.com

Web: http://www.wolfBayne.com

Remember, this format won't always work when you reproduce your Internet address on pens, mugs, T-shirts, or anything else. Try to be consistent but be flexible.

Contact Information

When you create pages for your Internet site, create a consistent format for inserting your contact information. The Web page placement and contents of your company copyright statement, company name, address, telephone number, and so forth should be included in your Internet style manual. Don't forget your traditional contact information for customers who want to change communication modes. For example, the Business Marketing Association uses this HTML format at the bottom of all of its Web pages:

<I>Copyright (c) 1995, Business Marketing Association, 150 N. Wacker Drive, Suite 1760, Chicago, IL 60606, Toll Free (800) 664-4BMA, Tel. (312) 409-4262, FAX (312) 409-4266. Email <A HREF="mailto:bma@marketing.org">bma@ marketing.org</A>.</I></P>

Signature Blocks

Internet signatures are those blocks of text found at the end of e-mail messages. You may wish to establish a consistent look for the messages that are distributed to the outside world through your company e-mail system. This allows you to take advantage of company communications throughout the Internet, yet maintain and reinforce a consistent look.

Create a boilerplate layout for your company, allowing individual employees to personalize it as needed. The following imaginary examples are brief, yet they manage to convey all the key information about the company and its sender, including the company name, traditional contact information, and the sender's claim to fame.

```
------------------------------------------------------

Tim Sturn                    http://www.tinkering.com

tsturn@tinkering.com              Tinker Weaving

Author: "World Wide Web Weaving"     580-555-4813

------------------------------------------------------
```

```
=================================================

Jan Danelle          http://www.danelle.com/

Author of "The Marvelous Online Cookbook"

"101 Briskets You Can Cook on the Internet"

501-555-1691             jan@danelle.com

=================================================
```

Your standard company signature block can be any combination of elements, as long as it is not too long and is easy to read. You might consider including an ASCII text version of your logo as well.

Logo

Your logo is that little design, picture, or "bug" that you keep using consistently on your company letterhead and stationery. If you don't have one already, have one professionally designed. A logo that is incorporated into your Web page design can help distinguish your site from many of the low-rent ones on the Web. If you *do* have a logo, you'll be concerned about its sizing.

Two ways to control the size of your logo on the Internet are (1) by resizing the graphics file that contains your logo before uploading it and (2) by using the image-width feature in your HTML code to specify how the image will display.

As you're deciding on the size for your logo, make sure you decide the maximum amount of graphics you'll tolerate on a page. You can specify this as the total number of bytes in graphics per page or as a percentage of graphics to pure text. Either way, you'll have a guideline that everyone can easily follow.

A good rule of thumb is to keep your logo relatively small. Small logos take less time to load, especially for those with slower modems, no patience, no bandwidth, or all of these. Small logos don't detract from what you are trying to do on the rest of the page. Don't make your logo *too* small. Remember, all monitors are not created equal. You want to create a *look* on the Web, not a speck of dirt.

Typeface

If you want to specify your corporate typeface as the one you'll use on the Web, make sure it exists online. If it does, go right ahead. But be forewarned. My browser is set to display all fonts as Times New Roman. I like it that way. You can try being consistent with this choice, if you wish, but don't lose any sleep over it.

Horizontal Rule

One of the features of HTML is the ability to include a horizontal rule or line. A rule helps break up large blocks of text and makes a page easier to read. Sometimes it's overused. Actually, many times it's overused. I overuse it myself on occasion. I just can't get over the fact that I can specify its look in so many ways simply by changing a few things in the coding.

The size, shading, alignment, or width of horizontal rules on your Web page might be one of those areas that needs definition. It's certainly easy to say that the standard for horizontal lines in your site is a size 1, no shading, and a width at 60 percent. It's easier to show it this way:

```
<hr SIZE=1 NOSHADE width=60%>
```

Navigational Links

Any element you use, such as icons or a special arrangement of text and lines, to help your user navigate your site should be repeated on subsequent pages. If more than one person is designing your site, it's a good idea to provide them with an example of how this should appear, too.

Colors

Nice logo. Funny how it looks green on my monitor. Did you intend for that to happen? Sorry, but my browser doesn't recognize it as gold. I also like the way you've specified the text color for your page links. Did I tell you that I've set my browser to something different and my choices always override yours?

If you're going to specify link colors, be realistic. Give it your best shot and then get over it. The best advice for specifying your corporate identity guidelines for links on your Web page is to quote the help provided under "colors" on the Netscape browser: "Ideally, text colors are in good contrast with the document background."

Signage

You have signage around your company (Figure 9.5) and signage in your trade show booth. You may even have signage on your company vehicles. Who says you can't publicize your Internet presence on all three? I can't think of a better way to let both employees and customers know that you're serious about marketing online.

Figure 9.5 Interse' Corporation shows its Internet pride by displaying its URL around a door frame in the company lobby. *Credit:* Interse' Corporation, 111 W. Evelyn Ave., Suite 213, Sunnyvale, CA 94086, www.interse.com.

Designing for a Specific Browser

Many companies will tell you if their site looks better with a certain browser. If you design your Web site to appeal to a select portion of the Internet audience, don't forget to mention it in your style manual. If you specify that your site will be designed for Netscape version 3.0 or higher, then you've dictated that certain sophisticated users are welcome, while others are not. This decision may or may not coincide with your market. Deciding to have a cutting-edge site can be tricky. Just make sure you also define the parameters for the alternate version of your pages.

Your Internet style manual should contain guidelines in several areas, and they should be applied as consistently as possible throughout your site. If your Web visitor tinkers with the color options on his or her browser, at least the colors won't change from page to page.

A list of Web design options could make up another book on HTML. There are several on the market that will help you in that area. This book isn't one of them. If you get a good designer, whether that person is in-house or at an agency, make sure you get documentation for all the specifications used to develop your Web site. Decide if any of these specs conflict in any way with your traditional corporate identity. Then decide what you can live with. Make changes if you prefer, but remember that the user has the final say in how your pages will appear. Take your specifications and integrate them into your written corporate identity manual. Make sure you make plenty of copies to distribute to anyone who has anything to do with your Internet presence.

Answers to the Riddle

You already know that SHOES.COM belongs to Alan's Shoes in Tucson, Arizona. If you haven't solved the others, here are the answers to the shoe domain name riddle posed earlier in this chapter:

◆ SHOE.COM belongs to Future Industries, Nashville, Tennessee

- SHOE.ORG belongs to InterNetWorx, Inc., New York, New York
- SHOES.ORG belongs to Footwear Retailers & Distributors Association, Washington, D.C.
- SHOEBOX.COM belongs to Shoebox Inc., Phoenix, Arizona
- SHOE-BOX.COM belongs to Shoe Boxes for Shoes, Inc., Glendale, Arizona

Betcha didn't know that selling shoes on the Internet could be so confusing!

chapter ten

Conducting Market Research

This chapter discusses how you can use the Internet to gather competitive and market research information for use in your marketing communications program. Keeping track of your company's image and competitors is an important part of managing your company's reputation. If you've already spent some time surfing the Internet, this chapter will be a review for you. If you're new to online searching, you'll enjoy the number of free resources now available online.

In Chapter 9, *Developing a Corporate Identity,* you drafted guidelines for including your Internet presence in your existing corporate identity program. In addition, you applied corporate identity principles to the Internet.

In Chapter 10, *Conducting Market Research,* you will continue to strengthen your marketing mix with the addition of market research. This chapter will contribute to the further development of Section Six of your Internet marketing plan.

Effective Supporting Materials for the Plan

Your Internet marketing plan is best supported by including data that reinforces your decision to market on the Internet. Section Six of your Internet marketing plan can be expanded by including any combination of the following:

- ◆ Plan of action for teaming portions of selected market research activities with Internet activities

- Recommendations for cost savings in traditional market research
- A summary of how incorporating the Internet into market research will improve your marketing communications program efficiency

Getting the Most out of This Chapter

This chapter consists of getting online and searching for information. If you don't have the time or the inclination to log in to the Internet right now, come back and read this chapter later. If you're ready, make sure you have decided what you're looking for before you get online. If you're paying for the connect time, this is important.

Market Research, the Internet, and Business Ethics

Finding information about your competitors today couldn't be any easier. You have only to sit down at your desk and get online. Never before has so much information been contained in one place. It's refreshing to be able to gather market data and not have to leave the office for the library anymore.

There is a lot of free information online. Sometimes there's *very good* information online. Sometimes the really good information costs money. This chapter will concentrate on how much you can find out without adding to your budget. If you want more than that, there are plenty of companies waiting to serve you. I already mentioned some of them in Chapter 3, *Analyzing Internet Market Statistics.*

I suppose I could warn you about invasions of privacy, competitive espionage, and the works. Where do you draw the line? These are decisions you'll have to make yourself. Just in case you were wondering, these are the guidelines I personally follow when researching on the Internet:

- Any factual information about a public entity, such as a business, found on the Internet is fair game to read and analyze for inclusion in internal market research reports. If a company puts its annual report at its Web site, it's safe to say that you can use that information for competitive analysis purposes.

◆ Be careful about including opinions instead of facts. Internet users post their convictions, philosophies, and wishful thinking to newsgroups and Web sites all the time. Don't take everything at face value.

◆ Do not repost derogatory information about another company found online, even if you quote its source. This guideline is even more important if you are sending e-mail from your company's server. You and your employer could be a party to a defamation lawsuit, even if you weren't the originator of the information. If you have to bring a source to your colleagues' attention, tell them where to look so they can read and interpret it themselves.

◆ Any personal information about individuals found on the Internet should *not* be included in market research reports, unless it already appears in a public document, such as a magazine or newspaper. Too many companies are putting their marketing databases online, allowing criminals and other busybodies to gather all kinds of detailed personal information for illegal and invasive purposes.

◆ E-mail messages to individuals are private. If someone e-mails information to you by mistake, don't use it unless you have the originator's permission. Obviously, your competitor is not going to give you permission. In that case, get rid of it. I've received enough misdirected and bounced e-mails to know that sometimes "technology happens." In that case, the only real decision is spelled "CONTROL D."

◆ Remember, however you gather and use market research or track your competitors, someone else on the Internet is doing it the same way. Don't publish anything you don't want used by someone else.

Searching Tips

Why would you want to conduct research on the Internet? You can easily accomplish competitive tracking activities by frequenting the ClariNet newsgroups. These newsgroups receive newswire feeds from such sources as Associated Press, Newsbytes and Reuters Online. You can use information you find on the Internet as an inexpensive substitute for an outside clipping service, provided you're not reselling this information and only applying it for internal use. This will be extremely useful for tracking your own company's editorial coverage as well. Databases from various government and business resources reside on the Internet. You can read information in electronic business and trade journals to keep up on the current news in your industry and around the world.

Figure 10.1 lists a few advantages and disadvantages of doing research on the Internet.

What Search Strategy? Oh, I'll Just Surf until I Find It!

Before you start searching, it's a good idea to decide off-line how and what you're going to retrieve. You do this by developing a good, solid search strategy. If you don't know where you're going, you won't know when you get there. Become familiar with the terminology in your industry so your search will be productive.

Take the time to become familiar with and use different Internet tools. You won't become versed in online market research until

Advantages	Disadvantages
Growth is much faster than in print publications.	Links to online resources are outdated quickly.
The amount of free information is unknown.	Free versus fee: The Internet has its share of inconsistent and inaccurate search tools.
You have access to many worldwide resources at once.	Service and access problems can overshadow convenience.

Figure 10.1   Advantages versus disadvantages to searching on the Internet.

you actually practice. If you need some encouragement, there are hundreds of free tutorials on the Internet. Start by searching in Yahoo!, http://www.yahoo.com, with the keywords "Internet search tutorial."

Searching effectively and surfing the Net are not identical concepts. Develop your own set of basic searching techniques. Develop personal methods for covering all the bases: Using a checklist and writing things down helps a lot. Search time can be pretty hectic. If you don't have a closed office situation or you work in a cubicle, try to convince someone to loan you a private office for an hour or two. Lock the door if you have to. Many times, I've been interrupted in the middle of an expensive search in a subscriber-restricted database. I've learned not to answer the telephone. Fortunately, you'll be doing your research on the Internet, so you don't have to worry about ringing up these types of access charges. Interruptions can still be distracting, because you'll lose track of where you are. That's where the bookmarks on your browser come in handy. Use them often.

Now about that search strategy worksheet. Figure 10.2 shows mine. Feel free to use it.

Resources

Mailbot Addresses

E-mail addresses such as info@wolfBayne.com are information e-mail addresses. These are not accounts for a specific individual. These are e-mail accounts set up to automatically manage inquiry traffic. E-mail autoresponders or mailbots are configured to send you boilerplate company data, such as services and pricing, in response to your e-mail request. They do not necessarily respond immediately. Internet and server traffic can slow response time. Some addresses look like autoresponders, but they are really used to weed out competitive inquiries. These responses are sent manually by a person at the company.

- ◆ Info@ E-mail Auto-Responder Directory, http://www .autoresponders.com/
  This is a good source of company information that's available for retrieval by e-mail.

Instructions

- ◆ Complete this form for each topic before you go online.
- ◆ Once you're on the Internet, make bookmarks for all the resources you find.
- ◆ Go back and search each one individually.
- ◆ If you find another hyperlinked resource, bookmark it and then come back to it.
- ◆ Save files and pages to disk in one separate, but new, directory.
- ◆ Print out information only if you need to and only after you've logged off.

What are you looking for? (State your concept in complete sentences.)

_____

_____

_____

_____

_____

Why are you looking for this information? (Check all that apply.)

❑ Competitive analysis   ❑ Educational purposes   ❑ Statistics

❑ Market research   ❑ Product and service opportunities

❑ Other (specify): _____

What factors will affect this search? (Check all that apply.)

❑ Some information has already been found. Specify: _____

❑ Avoid searches at competitor's sites that require registration.

❑ This data is needed by (specify date and time): _____

❑ Other (specify): _____

Figure 10.2   Search strategy worksheet.

What type of information do you want to find?

❏ Financial data   ❏ Case studies

❏ Technical bulletins   ❏ Product specifications

❏ Data sheets   ❏ News articles

❏ Company background   ❏ Data on similar companies

❏ Only information on the Internet (Note: Many Internet resources will point you to off-line resources.)

❏ Other (specify): _____

List keywords, companies, and phrases to *include* in this search.

_____ _____ _____ _____ _____

_____ _____ _____ _____ _____

_____ _____ _____ _____ _____

_____ _____ _____ _____ _____

List keywords, companies, and phrases to *exclude* from this search.

Note: Some Web search engines will allow you to eliminate concepts. This will save you time, especially if you receive too many responses to your search.

_____ _____ _____ _____ _____

_____ _____ _____ _____ _____

_____ _____ _____ _____ _____

_____ _____ _____ _____ _____

Completed by: _____ Date: _____

Figure 10.2   (*Continued*)

Newsgroups

The majority of newsgroups contain opinion and discussion. A few contain news releases. Many newsgroups contain messages with references to information elsewhere online. Newsgroups are accessible immediately, so you can dial right in and download whatever you see.

- InReference, Inc., http://www.reference.com
  Reference.COM lets you search for information in over
  16,000 Usenet newsgroups and hundreds of publicly
  accessible mailing lists.

- DejaNews, http://www.dejanews.com
  DejaNews helps you locate discussions in thousands of
  newsgroups by keyword, e-mail address, and newsgroup.

Mailing Lists

Mailing lists, or e-mail discussion groups, usually contain opinion
and discussion. A few contain news releases. Many lists contain
messages with references to information elsewhere online. There
is a delay in receiving messages from lists. Many list owners
archive back issues and digests of the list. Some list archives may
be searchable by keyword.

- Find It! @LISTSERV Mailing Lists and USENET Newsgroups, http://www.webcom.com/teddy/listserv.html

- Liszt: Searchable Directory of e-Mail Discussion Groups,
  http://www.liszt.com/
  If you're trying to locate a mailing list, this directory has
  cataloged over 66,000 of them.

- Interlinks at Nova Southeastern University, http://www
  .nova.edu/Inter-Links/cgi-bin/lists

- Kim Bayne's Marketing Lists on the Internet,
  http://www.bayne.com/wolfBayne/htmarcom/mktglist
  .html
  This directory lists 90-plus lists, newsgroups, and
  forums that discuss various marketing-related topics. If
  you are looking for other online marketers, you'll find
  where they network by checking this site.

- Publicly Accessible Mailing Lists, http://www.neosoft
  .com/internet/paml/
  This is a list of mailing lists available primarily through
  the Internet and the UUCP network.

- Tile.net/listserv, http://www.tile.net/tile/listserv/index.html
  This reference to Internet discussion groups catalogs them by name, description, subject, country, and organization.

FTP

FTP sites contain directories with files. Most of the files require that you download them before you read them. For help, look for a file labeled "readme.1st" or something similar.

- FTP search v3.3, http://ftpsearch.ntnu.no/ftpsearch

The Web

The World Wide Web currently has the easiest-to-locate information. There are hundreds of searching sources on the Web. If that isn't enough, some sites even search the search engines.

Consolidated search sites.   *Note:* These sites search other search engines, reference resources on the Internet, and a host of business indexes.

- IBM Infomarket, http://www.infomkt.ibm.com/
- StartHere, http://www.starthere.com
- Search Engines Forms by Beaucoup!, http://www.beaucoup.com/formengs.html
- The Information Superlibrary, http://www.mcp.com/superseek
- The LLNL List of Lists, A List of Internet Searching Resources, http://www.llnl.gov/llnl/lists/listsl.html
- Nlightn (pronounced "enlighten"), http://www.nlightn.com/
- Northwestern College—SearchIt, http://www.netins.net/showcase/nwc-iowa/
- SavvySearch, http://www.cs.colostate.edu/~dreiling/smartform.html
- All-in-One Search Page, http://www.albany.net/allinone/

Business directories

- AT&T Toll-Free Internet Directory, http://www
  .tollfree.att.net/dir800/
- The Better Business Bureau, http://www.bbb.org/
  council/main/index.html
- The Internet Business Directory's Catalogue of Businesses, http://www.tibd.com

News

- Electronic Newsstand, http://www.image.dk/~knud-sor/en/
- CNN/CNNfn/AllPolitics Searcher, http://cnn.com/
  SEARCH/index.html
- USA Today News Search, http://167.8.29.8/plweb-cgi/ixacct.pl

Market research

- ANYwhere Online Market Research Center,
  http://www.anywhereonline.com/
- Market Research Organization Web Sites,
  http://www.asiresearch.com/links/mrlinks.htm
- FIND/SVP's Best Finds for Research Resources,
  http://www.findsvp.com/findsvp/bestfnds.html/tigcc8d

Financial information

- IPOnet, http://www.zanax.com/iponet/
- The Internet IPO Monitor, http://www.netipomonitor
  .com

Federal resources

- GPO Access Databases, http://www.access.gpo.gov/
  su_docs/aces/aaces002.html

Legal research

- Meta-Index for U.S. Legal Research, http://gsulaw .gsu.edu/metaindex/

Conducting Market Research via E-mail

If you wish to gather your own market research by using internal customer surveys, you may have thought about using e-mail for this purpose. Many Internet market researchers use e-mail to bulk-distribute surveys. Problems with this approach include the following:

- It used to be that e-mail would get someone's attention quickly, but now e-mail is actually easier to ignore. Recipients are using filters in their e-mail programs to sort incoming mail by the various header fields and message text. Finally, if the recipient is not interested, there is no paper sitting around after the message has been deleted.

- You can't include a monetary incentive to reply in e-mail. Some surveys include dollar bills or an inexpensive gift as a pre–thank you to participating. For example, I recently received an opinion survey from a manufacturer that contained a dollar bill as a "small token of our appreciation." Companies who include money with a survey feel that the recipient will be more inclined to answer questions if they've already been "paid" to do so. Marketers rely on a recipient's guilt or sense of obligation for this strategy to work. A market researcher can always include an offer of a special report in an e-mail survey, but it's still not as good as having something in your hand.

- E-mail surveys exclude everyone who is not online or doesn't want to respond via e-mail. This can eliminate responses by a good portion of your audience. If you are trying to survey only individuals who actually use the

Internet, you avoid having a control group with which to compare answers.

◆ Results from e-mail surveys may be skewed by false, forged, and anonymous responses. However, this problem is not restricted to just Internet surveys. Some surveyors feel that anonymous responses yield more honest results. Others feel that anonymous responses can yield more false results, since anonymous responders have nothing to lose by lying.

◆ Often, e-mail surveyors use addresses gathered from special-interest lists or newsgroups. The addresses are compiled using software packages that allow keyword searches. There are more youngsters on the Internet than ever before, and it is often impossible to determine if an e-mail address belongs to a working professional or a young high school student. E-mail surveyors often forget that students are less likely to subscribe to professional print journals, which produce a more accurate demographic mix.

◆ E-mail responses are not necessarily completed in a timely manner. For some reason, people allow e-mail surveys to accumulate and then send in the response whenever they have time. Surveyors often forget to include a deadline on these e-mail surveys, thinking that everyone will respond immediately since it's on the Internet. It just isn't so.

◆ There are many marketing novices who think that e-mail surveys will answer all their questions. When you interview someone on the telephone, you have an opportunity to ask that person to qualify their statements, which can give you additional information for this and future surveys.

◆ Surveyors may believe that the results from e-mail surveys are easier to compile. E-mail surveys, like other types of surveys, have their percentage of incomplete answers. This forces the surveyor to either ignore the response, compile inaccurate results based on half answers, or recontact the respondent for complete data. Surveyors should state that incomplete surveys will not be accepted. However, without the aid of a software program to read and sort incoming surveys and calculate results, each e-mail message must be manually handled.

For those marketers who still wish to conduct surveys via e-mail, there are software packages, such as one by Decisive Surveys at http://www.decisive.com, that will make the job easier.

Web sites, with survey forms that have required fields, have a better chance for accuracy than e-mail surveys. Surveyors will receive complete information from a motivated individual. If someone has chosen to visit a site, complete a form, and register an opinion, he or she is motivated. Also, once the deadline for the survey has passed, late responses are eliminated from the mix by removing the form from the Web site.

chapter eleven

Executing Public Relations and Promotional Programs

This chapter discusses how you can use the Internet to enhance your public relations activities. If you are responsible for media relations in your company, you may already be using the Internet for this purpose. You have developed a proprietary list of editorial contacts used to disseminate company and product information on a regular basis. You contact reporters and editors via telephone, facsimile transmission, regular mail, and at trade shows. Now you're using the Internet as well.

In Chapter 10, *Conducting Market Research,* you learned to develop your own search strategy off-line. You also learned about some excellent Internet resources for gathering competitive intelligence.

In Chapter 11, *Executing Public Relations and Promotional Programs,* you will continue to strengthen your marketing mix with the addition of public relations. This chapter will contribute to the further development of Section Six of your Internet marketing plan.

Effective Supporting Materials for the Plan

Your Internet marketing plan is best supported by including data that reinforces your decision to market on the Internet. Section Six of your Internet marketing plan can be expanded by including any combination of the following:

- Plan of action for teaming portions of selected public relations activities with the Internet
- Recommendations for cost savings in traditional public relations
- A summary of how incorporating the Internet into public relations will improve your marketing communications program efficiency

Getting the Most out of This Chapter

This chapter discusses using online resources to distribute news and information about your company to the public. This can be accomplished through a number of ways. However, it is best to use the Internet selectively in this capacity. Editors' addresses are published everywhere online. This does not mean that a particular editor prefers to be contacted in this manner. Use the Internet as you would use any other form of contact, with informed discretion.

Internet Communications and the Changing Face of PR

In January 1995, *Business Marketing* magazine's front page carried the headline: "Intel Wipes Out Surfing the 'Net: Few Master Online PR Wave." The story was but one of several on Intel and its Pentium problems. The *Business Marketing* article pointed out that Intel also had problems with its Internet public relations. Intel received a tremendous amount of coverage, but it was not alone. An *Electronic Engineering Times* story around the same time reported that an engineer from LSI Logic of Canada posted his condemning opinion about Viewlogic's ASIC design tools to a newsgroup. His company responded on the Internet with an apology and the promise that this type of post would never happen again. On CompuServe, a user was posting bad reviews of a certain company's products in a variety of forums. Reportedly, the user was the employee of a competitor.

Risk and Opportunities

Companies still continue to evaluate whether they should take advantage of the Internet as part of their public relations program. The Internet can be a very dangerous place when it comes to marketing. But it doesn't have to be. Intel failed because they were blind to what was happening; they didn't recognize that the Internet had taken on so much clout; and they wasted time by not dealing with the problem as it occurred. By failing to act appropriately, they secured their place in Internet history. Your company doesn't have to make the same mistakes.

Marketing communications and public relations staff must monitor and respond to online communications and not stick their heads in the sand. I'm always amazed when I meet communications specialists who aren't online or who are online once a month or less. Yes, scheduling regular time to observe Internet discussions and news requires dedication. Sometimes it can even be boring. Think about how bored you'd be if you were out of work because your company went under . . . all because of bad press on the Internet.

Like everything else, Internet PR has its advantages and disadvantages. By using the Internet to disseminate information directly to the public you eliminate the middleman, those publishers and editors who sift through the news and decide what their audience should read and see. The news is distributed exactly in the manner you meant for it to be. In this way, there's less chance that a publication will misinterpret what you have to say or even insert its own editorial interpretation.

The risk you take by relying entirely on the Internet for news dissemination is that you now lose the third-party endorsement of the press. The public knows there's no filtering process in place, which means that your message may have less credibility than traditional editorial coverage. Furthermore, anything that you do online, you do for keeps. Take the Intel incident. All you have to do is visit Dejanews, http://www.dejanews.com, and search old newsgroup discussions for the keywords "Pentium" and "Intel." You'll be treated to a menu of endless Pentium jokes and tirades. Working with the press and the public online can be a humbling experience.

Working Tips for Internet PR

Many Internet marketers feel that the Internet will replace traditional public relations. Everything will be done electronically, without the need to build relationships. Yet it's even more important that Internet marketers build relationships now because of the volume of Internet marketers operating under that same misconception. If you thought your finely crafted news release was good enough to get that reporter's attention a year ago, remember this. That reporter now has 500 other finely crafted electronic news releases to sift thorough each day.

The rules for building relationships with the press are the same whether you use the Internet, the telephone, a facsimile machine, or a traditionally mailed press kit. Take your time to become familiar with the publication *and* the editor who covers your industry and products. Whichever method you use to contact the press, be as helpful as possible to help them do their job. Provide as much background material as possible and bring your editorial contact up to date. Contact the editor on a regular basis to share news and get news. Nothing substitutes for relationships, not even the Internet. If you can't do this personally, find someone who can.

Use the Internet to Enhance External Communications

Continue using the same modes of communication you have used before, using the Internet as an adjunct or complement to these other activities. Limit your distribution of news via e-mail to editors who prefer e-mail, *and* post news at your Web site for those who don't (Figures 11.1 and 11.3).

While we're on the subject, news releases on the Web are not just for editors. You want your customers to read this information as well. Provide unrestricted access to news at your Web site. Allow customers to see the news and don't require registration. You can always provide additional information to the press that the public can't reach, if you prefer. The main news should be available to anyone who asks.

To simplify the use of your online news library, consider installing a search engine at your site. This will allow reporters who are researching a background piece to immediately find what they are looking for without having to track you down and wait for a response.

Web Embargos

Some public relations professionals will warn you not to use the Web at all to disseminate news. They say that editors who find that your news is on the Web will avoid covering you, since most publications don't want to reprint "old" information. You can't please everyone, but you can try. Contact those editors with whom you've built a relationship (Figure 11.2). Ask each how your Web posting will affect coverage of your news in its print publication. If you've determined that the majority of editors you're trying to reach don't like the idea, then you'll have to negotiate.

Agree to avoid posting your news *immediately* on the Web. Select a time after the release date for posting the news at your site. Tell editors that they can receive the news immediately in the form they prefer, but that you will still post the news at your Web site after they've been given a chance to use it. You may wish to include a note to that effect in your release. By allowing editors to interpret your news and publish it first, you'll avoid diluting its value to them. One more tip: Show your appreciation to publications who cover your company. Include a detailed bibliography of editorial coverage at your site with links to their online publications.

How Much Are You Going to Put OnLine?

Before converting your news releases to online use, make a master document list (Figure 11.4). You'll need these details so you can get accurate bids from outside services. If you don't use an outside firm, you'll still want to know how much work you're considering. Keep track of where the files reside, in both off-line and online form, even after you upload them to the Internet. Include the various options for distributing your news release, in both online and off-line forms.

Press Release

FOR IMMEDIATE RELEASE

SEE US AT DAC BOOTH #1050

Contact: Sonia Harrison
Public Relations
KVO, Inc.
(503) 221-2369
sonia_harrison@kvo.com

Diana Wickizer
Marketing Communications
Antares Corporation
(503) 641-3962
diana_wickizer@antaresco.com

ANTARES DETAILS DISTRIBUTION CHANNEL STRATEGY

Adds Independent Sales Affiliates; Expands Inside Sales and Electronic Connectivity to Customers

DESIGN AUTOMATION CONFERENCE, LAS VEGAS -- June 3, 1996 -- Antares Corporation, the recently launched corporate combination of industry-leading electronic design automation (EDA) providers, Model Technology and Exemplar Logic, today unfolded details of its novel distribution strategy. Executing its announced multi-tiered strategy, Antares has recruited four new independent sales representatives to increase direct regional sales coverage. The company has also expanded its inside sales team and increased its World Wide Web presence to provide customers with a cyber-sales resource. These actions supplement Antares' announced worldwide distribution channel strategy consisting of inside sales, direct field personnel, distributors, and original equipment manufacturers (OEMs).

"A strategic component of our business model when we announced Antares was a cost-effective, multi-tiered distribution channel that would meet the unique requirements of our customers," said Pepe Piedra, Antares president and CEO. "We've moved forward in implementing this strategy by expanding both external and internal sales groups as well as expanding our Web-based connectivity to better communicate with our worldwide customer base. Our continued goal is to develop the most efficient means of providing easy-to-understand, easy-to-buy, easy-to-use EDA products. At the same time, our customers benefit by understanding that an Antares product purchase funds ongoing product development rather than supporting a costly field sales infrastructure."

- more -

Antares

8905 SW Nimbus Ave., Suite 155, Beaverton, OR 97008
Phone: 503-526-2025, Fax: 503-526-8742

Figure 11.1   Antares Corporation reminds its editorial contacts of its Internet presence by including its URL and e-mail addresses in all company news releases. *Source:* Antares Corporation, 8905 SW Nimbus Avenue, Suite 155, Beaverton, OR 97008. www.antaresco.com.

Antares' new independent sales representatives, called "affiliates," provide technology experience and dedicated attention to regional customers. The affiliates are focused on Antares' products, including Model Technology simulation and Exemplar Logic synthesis environments.

In addition to its affiliate program, Antares has expanded its inside sales presence to drive regional sales activities throughout North America from its headquarters in Oregon. "Our inside sales team has already distinguished themselves as a self-sufficient channel," noted Kelly Rupp, Antares vice-president of sales. "The inside team is co-incented with our field and affiliate sales to leverage each other as well as independently secure business and provide more direct contact with customers."

New affiliates include Jeff Forristall, supporting the Mountain states, Gene Wesolaski in New England, Nicholas Dean in Southern California, and Debra Klein in the Southeast. In addition, the complete Antares product family is now available from Ernie Liu in the Mid-Atlantic states and distributors J-Squared Technologies in Canada and I&C Microsystems in Korea.

Beyond its human component, Antares relies upon the World Wide Web to promote its products, feature on-line demonstrations and qualify customers for product evaluations. Antares' goal with its Web capabilities aims to provide customers a complete cyber-salesperson, not merely to promote its products but to allow interested prospects to study the products' capabilities and evaluate their application. To maximize sales efficiency, and ensure an educated, well-informed sales team, the Web is also being used as an internal tool to arm the Antares sales team with presentations, product information and current industry news and analysis.

Antares' sales representatives may be reached at 503-643-5800, and its Web site address is www.antaresco.com.

Antares is the leading provider of industry-best language-based simulation and synthesis environments for field programmable gate array (FPGA), application-specific integrated circuit (ASIC), and printed circuit board (PCB) designs. The company's headquarters are located at 8905 S.W. Nimbus Avenue, Suite 155, Beaverton, Oregon 97008. Phone: 503-526-2025. Fax: 503-526-8742. WWW site: http://www.antaresco.com.

###

Figure 11.1 (*Continued*)

Instructions

- If you have an external PR agency, use this form to update them on editors who contact your company directly.
- If you do not employ a PR agency, subscribe to a press-list service. Many include editors' e-mail addresses and preferences for communication.
- Use this form to build, update, and/or enhance your in-house list.
- This form can be e-mailed, mailed, and faxed.
- You can convert this form to HTML and post it at your Web site in the press area.
- You can use this form to interview editors while you already have them on the phone.
- Follow up personally with individuals who do not respond.

Editor's name: _____

Job title: _____

Publication: _____

Publishing company: _____

Address: _____

_____

City: _____ State: _____ Zip: _____

Telephone: ( ) _____ Extension: _____

Fax: ( ) _____

E-mail: _____ @ _____

Figure 11.2   Editorial contact database update.

Publication's URL: http:// _____

Other: _____

Which topics do you cover for this publication?

❑ _____ ❑ _____ ❑ _____
❑ _____ ❑ _____ ❑ _____
❑ _____ ❑ _____ ❑ _____
❑ _____ ❑ _____ ❑ _____
❑ _____ ❑ _____ ❑ _____
❑ _____ ❑ _____ ❑ _____

Name two other editorial contacts at this publication who cover these topics.

Editor's name: _____

Job title: _____

Telephone: (____) _____ Extension: _____

Editor's name: _____

Job title: _____

Telephone: (____) _____ Extension: _____

What is your contact preference? (Number in order of preference for standard news releases.)

_____ Mail

_____ Telephone

_____ Facsimile

_____ Electronic mail

_____ Newswire

Figure 11.2 (*Continued*)

_____ ASCII text on disk

_____ FTP site   ❑ Password-protected   ❑ Open access

_____ E-mail autosponder

_____ Internet mailing list

_____ Web site   ❑ Password-protected   ❑ Open access

_____ Other (specify): _____

Circle the method you most prefer for breaking news.

Our company would like to include news releases at its Web site. If our news appears at our Web site, how likely is it that you will still consider it for publication?

Highly unlikely   **1   2   3   4   5   6   7   8   9   10**   Highly likely

Comments: _____

_____

_____

_____

If you preferred an embargo period prior to posting news on the Web, what would that be?

❑ Do not post on the Web   ❑ One month   ❑ Three weeks

❑ Two weeks   ❑ One week   ❑ 48-hours   ❑ One day

❑ Other _____

Please return this form to: _____

E-mail: _____   Address: _____

Fax: _____   Other: _____

Figure 11.2   (*Continued*)

Instructions
- ◆ Use this list as a reminder of the different ways to distribute your news.
- ◆ Check off all activities as you complete them.

❑ Distribute your news by regular mail.

❑ Distribute your news by fax to editors who prefer it.

❑ Distribute your news through the newswire services for thorough coverage in print and online.

❑ Distribute your news by e-mail to editors who prefer it.

❑ Post rewritten and brief excerpts of your announcement to *appropriate* newsgroups.

❑ Distribute your news to individuals who have *voluntarily* signed up for a company-managed Internet mailing list. Cost to manage mailing list:

Setup fee _____ Monthly maintenance _____

Contact your local Internet service provider or your computing services department for costs to add to your budget.

❑ Upload your news in HTML to your Web site.

❑ Upload your news in ASCII text to an FTP directory.

❑ Upload your news in ASCII text for use by mailbots.

❑ Provide your news in ASCII text on diskettes.

❑ Include all Internet addresses in your news releases, either preprinted on letterhead or included in the body of the release.

❑ Include all traditional contact information, such as telephone, address, and fax, in all news releases regardless of their format.

❑ Participate frequently in online discussion groups by providing answers from your news that directly addresses users' concerns.

❑ Refresh your online files by removing old news or archiving it.

❑ Distribute news via other traditional methods to reach those editors who prefer it.

Figure 11.3 Internet news dissemination PR checklist.

❑ Follow up with editors by telephone or in person to provide them with additional or new information.

❑ Other: _____

❑ Other: _____

❑ Other: _____

❑ Other: _____

Figure 11.3   (*Continued*)

Resources

Most of these companies charge for their services and products. Include this information in your Internet marketing budget.

Media Directories, Mailing and Clipping Services

◆ American College Media Directory, http://www.webcom .com/shambhu/acmd/home.html
Includes contact information on 3,000 college newspapers, radio stations, and television stations that deliver news and information to millions of students in campuses across the nation.

◆ Bacon's Media Directories, http://www.baconsinfo.com
Directories include newspapers, magazines, radio, TV, and cable contacts in all industries. Bacon's Information, Inc., 332 S. Michigan Ave., Chicago, IL 60604. Toll free (800) 621-0561, in Illinois (312) 922-2400, fax 312-922-3127. Directories: directories@baconsifo.com. Clipping service: clipping@baconsinfo.com. Mailings: mailings@baconsinfo.com.

◆ Burrelle's Media Directories, http://www.burrelles.com
Media directories are available in print, on disk, on CD-ROM, and on the Internet. Burrelle's Information Services, 75 E. Northfield Road, Livingston, NJ 07039. Toll

Press Release	Release Date(s)	Internet Distribution
wolfBayne announces CyberSleuth 2000 Internet PR Tracking Software	Press—January 1, 1999; Web site— January 14, 1999	E-mail, HTML—Web; ASCII text—FTP and mailbot; HTMARCOM list
Other Distribution	**Total Text**	**Graphics No., Types, Sizes**
ASCII diskette in product announcement kit, mail, fax, newswire	Pages = 2; word count = 652	One screen capture opening screen, *.GIF format for Web
Conversion Costs	**Archive Location**	**Online Location**
To HTML and ASCII— none, complete in-house	c:\wb\sleuth.htm plus disk #24	../nash/music.htm
Uploaded	**Updated**	**Initials**
7/25/96	8/25/96	

Figure 11.4 Master PR document list.

free (800) 631-1160, toll free fax 800-898-6677. Directories: directory@burrelles.com.

- ◆ Luce Press Clippings Inc., http://www.lucepress.com/ 42 S. Center, Mesa, AZ 85210. Toll free (800) 528-8226.

- ◆ MediaMap, http://www.mediamap.com/ Subscriptions include the computer industry editorial calendars online, PR report service, software and data service, trade show report, and the electronics trade press service. MediaMap, 215 First Street, Cambridge, MA 02142. Tel. (617) 374-9300, fax 617-374-9345. E-mail: info@mediamap.com.

- ◆ Press Access, http://www.pressaccess.com Editor's directory and databases in the high-tech arena, North American computer trade and business press. Press Access, 120 Boylston St., Boston, MA 02116. Tel. (617) 542-6670, fax 617-542-6671. E-mail: info@PressAccess.com.

- ◆ SRDS, http://www.srds.com SRDS, 1700 Higging Road, Des Plaines, IL 60017. Toll free (800) 851-7737. Tel. (847) 375-5000, fax 847-375-5003.

News Distribution and Wire Services

Some news distribution services can also be found on America Online, CompuServe, and Prodigy.

- ◆ Business Wire, http://www.businesswire.com/
- ◆ ClariNet, http://www.clarinet.com/
- ◆ global internet news agency, http://www.gina.com/
- ◆ Newsbytes News Network, http://www.nbnn.com/
- ◆ North American Precis Syndicate, http://www.napsnet .com/
- ◆ PR Newswire, http://www.prnewswire.com/

Miscellaneous PR Resources

- Editor and Publisher, http://www.mediainfo.com/
- Media Online Yellow Pages, http://www.webcom.com/~nlnnet/yellowp.html
- National Press Club, http://npc.press.org/
- PiMS, http://www.pimsinc.com/

chapter twelve

Incorporating Sales Support Functions

This chapter discusses how you can use the Internet to enhance your sales support activities. Sales support is a mixed bag of activities at any given company. These activities may simply include customer service, such as assigning individuals to handle incoming inquiries from various sources, including the Internet. If you have sales support responsibilities for your company, your duties could include anything from developing distributor and reseller programs to handling sales meetings. As diverse as this field appears to be, there are a few activities without which your Internet marketing presence would not be complete: order processing and leads management. This chapter will focus on those two.

In Chapter 11, *Executing Public Relations and Promotional Programs,* you continued to strengthen your marketing mix with the addition of public relations. You reviewed examples of how you could use the Internet for media relations and promotion. You located Internet resources for press directories, clipping services, and news distribution.

In Chapter 12, *Incorporating Sales Support Functions,* you will continue to strengthen your Internet marketing mix with the addition of sales support. This chapter will contribute to the further development of Section Six of your Internet marketing plan.

Effective Supporting Materials for the Plan

Your Internet marketing plan is best supported by including data that reinforces your decision to market on the Internet. Section

Six of your Internet marketing plan can be augmented by including any combination of the following:

- Plan of action for teaming portions of selected sales support activities with the Internet
- Recommendations for cost savings in traditional sales support
- Evaluations of outside services for leads management activities
- A summary of how incorporating the Internet into sales support will improve your marketing communications program efficiency

Applying the Internet to Sales Support

As in all other activities associated with your company's marketing communications, use your Internet addresses in all the materials you distribute or display for your sales support activities. This simple inclusion is essential to publicizing your Internet marketing presence in a cost-effective manner (Figure 12.1). Internet marketers are teaming the technology of the Internet with other technologies as well. Provide your Internet address on product demonstration diskettes, telephone cards (Figure 12.2), and browsers configured to open to your Web page. Reinforce both your traditional and Internet marketing message in multiple ways.

Include technical support literature, such as product specifications, in your Internet promotional campaign. By duplicating this content on the Web, you may more than double the reach of your traditional literature-fulfillment activities (Figure 12.3).

Autoresponders, Mailbots, and Other Devices

The term *autoresponder* refers to an e-mail account, such as info@interse.com, or the software or script used to filter that account. The account is configured for the purpose of responding automatically to e-mail requests for company and/or product

SCUDDER

Scudder Canada Investor Services Ltd.
BCE Place
161 Bay Street
P.O. Box 712
Toronto, Ontario M5J 2S1
416 943 8665
Fax 416 350 2018
www.scudder.ca

With Compliments

Shabina Bahl
Marketing Assistant

Figure 12.1 Scudder Funds of Canada takes full advantage of opportunities to include its URL on sales materials, including this "with compliments" package insert. *Source:* Scudder Canada Investor Services Ltd., BCE Place, 161 Bay Street, PO Box 712, Toronto, Ontario M5J 2S1, www.scudder.ca.

Figure 12.2 Customers of Prairie Systems enjoy the convenience of using a collectable TeleCard displaying a Web address and toll-free telephone number. *Source:* Prairie Systems, 7200 World Communications Dr., Omaha, NE 68122, toll free (800) 964-3032, www.prairiesys.com.

𝓖𝓪𝓽𝓮𝓼 News Release

The Gates Rubber Company
P.O. Box 5887 • Denver, Colo. 80217
(303) – 744-1911

Release: IMMEDIATELY

Contact: Jerry Donovan
             Publicity Manager
             303-744-5520; jdonovan@gates.com

October 24, 1995

**Hose, Belt Technical Tips
On Gates Internet Page**

An Internet home page, containing technical tips on coolant hoses and serpentine belts, has been created by The Gates Rubber Company.

The World Wide Web site is accessible from any computer connected to an Internet service provider or gateway such as Compuserve, America Online or Prodigy. A Web browser (Netscape or Mosaic) is required.

Gates Internet WWW site has information on selecting, installing and maintaining engine hoses, and recommendations for reducing noise from belt drives. Headlines are "Give a good squeeze to detect a bad hose," "Troubleshooting cooling system hoses," "Hot news about coolant hose failure," "Replacing small molded coolant hoses," and " Troubleshooting V-ribbed belt noise." Each of the five tips has several illustrations.

The home page also includes various news items under the headings of "What's new at Gates" and "Special Offers." The items have an email address for obtaining product literature that will be mailed to the inquirer within 24 hours. Gates also has set up several links for reaching other automotive aftermarket WWW sites.

Gates Internet page can be found at http://www.gates.com/gates/

# # #

intnetpr

Figure 12.3   Gates Rubber Company points its customers to the technical support literature now available on Gates' Web site. *Source:* Gates Rubber Company, PO Box 5887, Denver, CO 80217, www.gates.com/gates/.

information. Autoresponders "automatically respond," hence the name. *Mailbot* is another term commonly used to refer to essentially the same activity. Mailbot is an abbreviation of "mail robot" and the implication is that your mail is being handled by an automaton of sorts. In either case, the purpose for using an autoresponder is to automate the distribution of news, facts, and other information via electronic mail without human intervention.

Of course, humans *are* still involved. They have to put the autoresponder in place to begin with. They also have to decide on file content. Finally, the human, or Internet marketer, must remember to update this file regularly. Autoresponders are a nice feature that can save you hours of repetitive customer service, especially if you send the same materials via e-mail repeatedly.

Installing and using autoresponders can be a boon to customer-service staff. The content included in the files these mailbots deliver should include direct e-mail addresses of key personnel along with all traditional contact information, just in case your form letter or automated answer generates more interest. Publicize your e-mail autoresponder address on your product literature and take advantage of it as much as possible. You can use autoresponders for as many applications as you need and/or you wish to track.

A Quick List of Autoresponder Applications

- *Advertising.* Use mailbots for each ad that runs in a different publication in order to track where your Internet sales leads are coming from (i.e., mt@wolfBayne.com, busmar@wolfBayne.com, mc@wolfBayne.com).
- *Collateral materials.* Use mailbots for each brochure to provide product-specific price lists and updated information (i.e., book@wolfBayne.com).
- *Market research.* Use mailbots for incoming e-mail responses to an online survey (i.e., survey-wiley@wolfBayne.com).

- *Public relations.* Use mailbots for requests by journalists and editors to provide news releases in text format (i.e., news@wolfBayne.com).
- *Sales support.* Use mailbots to e-mail updated lists of distributors or resellers of your products (i.e., sales@ wolfBayne.com).
- *Trade shows.* Use mailbots to e-mail updates of where your company exhibits next (i.e., tradeshows@ wolfBayne.com).

You can create an autoresponder of your own if you are ambitious and/or have some programming skills. At the system level, sometimes it's a matter of defining a script, filter rules, and files. You can include lines of instructions to accompany your online files. For example, a line in a filter-rules file might look like this:

```
if (to = "info@wolfBayne.com" ) then exec "send.script INFO %r"
```

While the corresponding lines in the script file might look like this:

```
INFO ) filename="company-info.txt"

nicename="wolfBayne Communications Information"
```

A customer sends e-mail to info@wolfBayne.com. Upon receipt, the UNIX system (where my Internet e-mail account resides) sifts through or filters the messages, looking for matches in my filter rules. If it finds a match, it sends a command to my script file, which then determines what to send back to the person at the other end. That person is designated by the %r seen above and the system replies to the e-mail address found in the header of that message.

By the way, I didn't design this particular mailbot. I just modified it. Dave Taylor of Intuitive Systems created and distributed the code for this particular mailbot on the Internet a few years ago. It works quite nicely. Dave has released several versions of the Embot since then. If you'd like a copy of Dave's Embot for your own use, go to http://www.intuitive.com/taylor/embot.html to read all about it.

Taking Orders on the Internet

The Internet allows you to automate the sales order process in a very dramatic way. Companies that offer order entry, order tracking, and additional product information in one location on the Web do it best. One of the reasons Internet commerce stalled for so long was because there wasn't a secure way to handle transactions online. Sometimes your browser can tell you if you are accessing a secure server on the Internet. Sometimes the customer still prefers to pick up the phone and call someone, rather than risk putting his or her credit card number online. Still, many companies continue to host their Web pages on unsecure servers, mainly because they haven't yet decided to incorporate direct sales into their site design.

If you decide to incorporate order processing at your site, discuss this with your computing services department and/or your Internet service provider. Some service providers design different, more secure, Internet servers for their business customer. For in-house Web servers, upgrading your server may impact your budget. They may have a cost-effective solution for you already in place.

Sales Leads Management

Market studies show that sales personnel contact only a small percentage of total sales leads generated by a company's marketing programs. On the Internet, the problem is even more rampant, due to the sheer volume in e-mail transmitted daily. During an on-site visit at a high-tech company, I watched while the vice president of sales inadvertently deleted the directory that contained his Internet e-mail inquiries. Rather than recover the file, he responded with indifference. "They're only e-mail leads," he chuckled. "If they were serious leads, they would have called us."

E-mail inquiries have fast become the "bingo" lead of the 1990s. *Bingos,* or reader service cards, are those postcards that trade publication subscribers use to request additional information. Readers fill out their interests by circling numbers on the card and mailing it to the publishing company. The publishing company processes the leads and generates a report for the advertiser. Many companies mail out literature packets to these leads, using the prepasted labels provided by the magazine, but that's about it. Marketing and sales managers alike apparently feel that these leads are hardly worth the trouble. Many companies don't even bother to follow up on these leads at all. They treat them as "tire kickers" or trade show "trick or treaters."

Companies are spending thousands of dollars to generate leads on the Internet. Most of these companies process leads either poorly or not at all. Remember, your presence on the Internet may be the first time a prospect has heard about your company. If you disregard an Internet user's interest, how do you know that user won't go to your competitors? You've lost a sale, all because you discounted the seriousness or credentials of the inquirer at the other end of the Internet connection.

If you're discounting Internet leads, revamp your leads-management system, as well as your attitude. If you're trying to demonstrate that your Internet marketing presence is worthwhile, you'll need to take advantage of every lead the Internet generates for you. If you are short-staffed or unable to develop an effective in-house leads-management system, evaluate outside firms (Figure 12.5). Outside leads-management firms, such as Saligent, Inc., http://www.saligent.com (Figure 12.4), offer services in just about every aspect of sales leads and inquiry management. Many of these outside firms will generate detailed analysis reports to support your Internet marketing program.

Fun with Java and Frames

One of the biggest complaints about directing customers to place orders online has been the navigational problems associated with Web sites. The bare minimum Web approach to sales includes

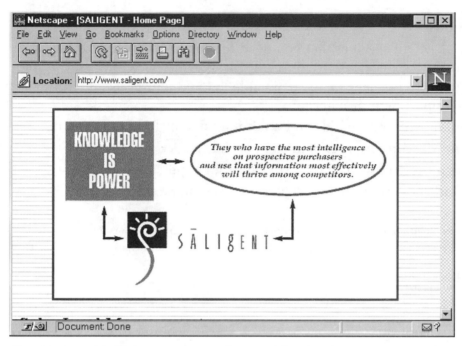

Figure 12.4   Saligent taps into the wealth of information found in a variety of leads generated by both traditional and online sources.

making sure that every page contains a menu bar and every menu bar contains a link to the online order form. Repetitive menu bars at the tops and bottoms of Web pages still require the user to scroll up or down to find them. If your document is long, this can be one more barrier to getting that online sale.

Webmasters have started to solve this problem by using Web features designed to keep the "order button" visible at all times: frames and remotes. Frames divide up one Web page into two or more adjacent "windowpanes" within the browser window. Frames allow you to keep a selected portion of your Web page, such as an order button, visible at all times. Web sites that use frames allow users to browse freely yet maintain the ability to jump to any page at any time (Figure 12.6). For more information on frames, search the Web with the keywords "frames," "Web page layout," or "Web design."

Instructions

- ◆ Check off all services that you need for your Internet marketing program.
- ◆ Note those services that you are able to handle in-house by filling in that department or manager.
- ◆ Obtain competitive bids on remaining services from outside vendors.
- ◆ Insert the top three companies in each category and the costs.
- ◆ Weigh these costs against hiring additional personnel in-house.
- ◆ Include cost information in your Internet marketing budget.

Services Needed/ Description	In-House/ Assigned To	Outside Service Bureau	Cost
❑ Consulting services		1. _____	_____
		2. _____	_____
		3. _____	_____
❑ Data entry		1. _____	_____
		2. _____	_____
		3. _____	_____
❑ Database development		1. _____	_____
		2. _____	_____
		3. _____	_____
❑ Inquiry tracking		1. _____	_____
		2. _____	_____
		3. _____	_____
❑ Inbound telequalification		1. _____	_____
		2. _____	_____
		3. _____	_____
❑ Lead generation		1. _____	_____
		2. _____	_____
		3. _____	_____

Figure 12.5   Checklist for sales leads management services.

❑ Literature fulfillment

    1. _____   _____

    2. _____   _____

    3. _____   _____

❑ Outbound telemarketing

    1. _____   _____

    2. _____   _____

    3. _____   _____

❑ Product shipping

    1. _____   _____

    2. _____   _____

    3. _____   _____

❑ Sales lead distribution

    1. _____   _____

    2. _____   _____

    3. _____   _____

❑ Staff training

    1. _____   _____

    2. _____   _____

    3. _____   _____

❑ Other: _____

    1. _____   _____

    2. _____   _____

    3. _____   _____

❑ Other: _____

    1. _____   _____

    2. _____   _____

    3. _____   _____

❑ Other: _____

    1. _____   _____

    2. _____   _____

    3. _____   _____

❑ Other: _____

    1. _____   _____

    2. _____   _____

    3. _____   _____

❑ Other: _____

    1. _____   _____

    2. _____   _____

    3. _____   _____

Figure 12.5 (*Continued*)

Remotes are pop-up windows used to navigate a Web site. These windows are created using the Java programming code. A good example of a remote in action is located at the Yahoo! site, http://www.yahoo.com (Figure 12.6). If you're in the pre-liminary stages of Web design, now's the time to direct your Web-master to include some of these sales-enabling features in your site.

Resources

Secure Payments

♦ CheckFree Corporation, http://www.checkfree.com/
Provider of electronic commerce services, software, and

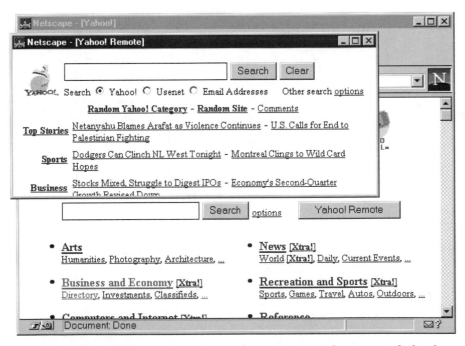

Figure 12.6   Yahoo's pop-up window stays with users while they browse the site, allowing them to search the index at any time.

related products. CheckFree designs, develops, and markets services that enable its customers to make electronic payments and conduct secure transactions.

- CyberCash, http://www.cybercash.com/
  Provides secure financial transactions services over the Internet, including secure credit card transactions, electronic checks, and microtransactions.

- DigiCash, http://www.digicash.com/
  Developer of electronic payment mechanisms for open, closed, and network systems that provide security and privacy.

- First Virtual, http://www.fv.com/
  Its Internet Payment System (IPS) uses VirtualPINs for online transactions. Credit card numbers are preregistered over secure telephone links with confirmation sent by e-mail.

- NetCash, http://www.netbank.com/~netcash/
  An electronic payment system for merchants, based on trading payment coupons through e-mail.

chapter thirteen

Planning Trade Shows

This chapter will discuss the different elements of trade shows, conventions, and event planning as they are related to Internet marketing. This chapter will help you better understand how the execution of your exhibit and meeting duties will be made easier by utilizing the many resources the Internet has to offer.

Many of the activities in this chapter will involve no additional expenditures at all from your marketing budget. Using the Internet in your trade show programs may involve little more than adding an action item or two to the list of activities. You will simply change your mode of communication when contacting the various vendors, trade show producers, and sales personnel. A few activities will involve an investment in order to update your trade show image. If you choose to implement these activities, you will need to obtain bids so you can include this information in your trade show booth.

In Chapter 12, *Incorporating Sales Support Functions,* you reviewed and enhanced traditional sales support operations, such as customer service, reseller programs, field sales activities, and technical support, with the addition of the Internet into the marketing mix.

In Chapter 13, *Planning Trade Shows,* you will continue to strengthen your marketing mix with the addition of Internet elements into your trade show and event-related functions. This chapter will contribute to the further development of Section Six of your Internet marketing plan.

Effective Supporting Materials for the Plan

Your Internet marketing plan is best supported by including data that reinforces your decision to market on the Internet. Section Six of your Internet marketing plan can be expanded by including any combination of the following:

- ◆ Plan of action for converting selected trade show activities to the Internet
- ◆ Plan of action for teaming portions of selected trade show activities with Internet activities
- ◆ Suggestions for incorporating Internet addresses and your Web presence into displays
- ◆ Recommendations for outside service firms that conduct business on the Internet
- ◆ Recommendations for participating in virtual trade shows
- ◆ A summary of how incorporating the Internet into the trade show function will improve the marketing communications program efficiency

Getting the Most out of This Chapter

The activities in this chapter include reviewing and comparing one or more options for enhancing your trade show activities. Throughout this chapter, I use the words *trade shows, conferences, expositions, seminars,* and *meetings* interchangeably. That does not mean that I am specifically referring to only those types of events when discussing any of the referenced Internet resources. During your reading, feel free to assume that I mean any type of special event that involves advance planning. Should you find a resource or approach that meets your needs, take advantage of it. For example, if you are interested in booking your company executives at industry conferences as part of your public relations campaign, use the Internet trade show directories to request information on applicable shows by e-mail.

The suggestions in this chapter are not all-inclusive. You will begin to discover many other uses for the Internet that are not covered here. I recommend that you keep a checklist of trade show functions and start jotting down how each can be improved by incorporating the Internet. Ask your colleagues how they are using the Internet to enhance their trade show functions. Visit trade shows and stop by booths to observe how prominent industry players and competitors are taking advantage of all that the Internet has to offer. As you select specific cost-related Internet activities for inclusion in your Internet marketing plan, obtain bids from outside vendors to include in the Internet marketing budget. The Internet is perfect for requesting bids via e-mail as well.

Applying the Internet to the Trade Show Function

Considering the important role that the Internet is playing in marketing communications, its impact on the trade show industry has been nothing short of phenomenal. Trade shows have taken on a new life online, and marketers are flocking to take advantage of it. If one of your responsibilities as a marketing communicator involves scheduling, planning, and following up on your company's trade shows, conferences, and seminars, you will be pleased at the variety of planning functions that can now be completed by using the Internet. In addition, as part of your marketing promotional activities, you can now include the Internet as one more tool to help draw visitors to your booth.

Dressing for Success

You know your company is exhibiting at an upcoming trade show. You've just launched your Web site and you need a unique way to get the word out about your Internet presence. You have several weeks to go before the show and you think about ordering something special. How about establishing a new dress code for your booth staff? Nothing gets an attendee's attention faster than trade show staff dressed in matching garb. Print your Web address on the back of brightly colored T-shirts or golf shirts so that visitors to your booth will have a constant reminder of your online presence (Figure 13.1).

Figure 13.1 Synergex employees sport casual wear emblazoned with the company's Web page URL. Photo courtesy of Synergex, 2330 Gold Meadow Way, Gold River, CA 95670.

If your Web page address is long and difficult to remember, you may wish to provide the booth visitor with your URL in print. Along with the product literature that you distribute in the booth, hand out a reminder (Figure 13.2), such as an advertising reprint or small business card. If the attendee requests that you mail the literature after the show, don't forget to send the Web page data along with it.

There are several other ways to bring attention to your Internet presence while you are exhibiting. Neon signs shaped like the letters that make up your company domain name are effective, as are scrolling message boards that state, "Visit our Web page at www

Why Ordering A Molded Heater Hose Isn't The Run Around It Used To Be.

Before, when you needed a molded heater hose, you went to a new car dealer. Now it's as close as your nearest jobber, which means you'll get higher quality at a competitive price. And with our Hose Locator Guide, finding the location and routing of a hose will be easier than ever before. For details, talk to your Gates jobber or call 1-800-788-2358.

THE WORLD'S MOST TRUSTED NAME IN BELTS AND HOSE.

The Gates Rubber Company, Denver CO 80217   Gates internet home page: http:// www.gates.com/gates/

Ad code: 313
Job #: GAU-41801
Ad size: 1/2 PG 4C Hort.
Description: Molded Coolant Hose
Date prepared: 5/95
Prepared by: Bozell/Omaha

With their abrasive rocks, the mines of central Wyoming used to chew up a good hose in about a month -- until the Terminator™ hose arrived. With its rugged synthetic rubber cover and resilient polyester reinforcement, the Terminator hose will outperform any multi-purpose hose on the market today. If you work in a tough environment, the Terminator hose makes sense. It can handle intense heat, and covers hundreds of applications, including oil, water, air, chemicals, grease sprays, paraffin wax and salt solutions, so practically anyone can use it. The Terminator hose will take more punishment and cause less downtime than any other leading hose. So call your Gates distributor and place your order today. Because while the Terminator hose may be tough, the decision to buy one shouldn't be.

THE WORLD'S MOST TRUSTED NAME IN BELTS, HOSE AND HYDRAULICS.

The Gates Rubber Company, Denver CO 80217 (800) 788-2358 FAX (303) 744-5771 Gates internet home page: http://www.gates.com/gates/

Figure 13.2 Ad reprints can be distributed at trade shows and included in literature packets as a reminder that a company is online. *Source:* Gates Rubber Company, PO Box 5887, Denver, CO 80217, www.gates.com/gates/.

.company.com." Include your URL on portable signage that can be taken from trade show to trade show, regardless of your booth configuration. Small and inexpensive desktop signs are useful in this regard.

If you stage presentations in your booth, you may have to order seats to accommodate the weary trade show visitor. This provides you with yet another opportunity to show your Internet pride. Re-create your Web address on the backs of chairs. Imagine the reinforced message you'll be sending your guests if, during the course of a 10-minute presentation, they glance at the seat backs a few times.

If you are accustomed to renting carpet for installation in your booth, think about the convenience of purchasing your own. By purchasing, you guarantee that the color will match your booth decor and will not change from show to show. This would allow you the option of ordering carpeting with your domain name dyed or woven into the threads. Of course, if the cost of ordering your Internet address woven into specialty carpeting is cost-prohibitive, you might try another, equally as effective solution to decorating your booth. Try ordering a small area rug that can be placed at the front of the booth or in front of the registration desk. Small rugs and counter placemats can be ordered with a color picture of your Web site's home page, for placement in strategic locations throughout the booth.

That's It? I Just Reproduce My Web URL on Everything?

Well, not exactly. Those examples were the easiest to implement. If you're looking for something less passive and more impressive, think about getting the booth visitor involved with your site. After all, the Internet is supposed to be interactive, isn't it? It would be a shame not to take advantage of it. If you have computers in your trade show booth, or if you can rent them, it is always a good idea to let booth visitors test-drive your Web site on the spot. You're right there to answer any questions they may have, and you can point them precisely to the best material. Demonstrating your Web site on the show floor can reinforce your product information as well.

Show Selection

Let's think back a moment. Weeks, months, or even a year before this date, you selected this show for your company. How did you do it? Did an exhibit-space sales representative call you on the telephone and discuss the show's opportunities? Did you see a competitor at this show last year and decide you needed to be there? Just how did you get enough information to make your decision to exhibit?

Prior to the use of the Internet for marketing purposes, company trade show coordinators, administrators, and exhibit managers had to compile show information manually. They would read trade and business publications and gather conference brochures from various sources. The conference ads found in industry publications would remind marketing professionals of an upcoming event and they would call for additional information. If they needed information on several shows, they would, in turn, make several time-consuming telephone calls. In response, the conference brochures would be either faxed to the office or would arrive in the mail. Many times, brochures would arrive on their own, only to be stacked in the office corner or tucked away in a file cabinet.

Eventually, the marketer required another, more consolidated resource for keeping track of all the possible exhibit opportunities. The printed trade show directory, a compilation of show listings by industry and geography, was the perfect solution. As a reference tool, it was a handy yet bulky reminder of the overabundant choices available to the exhibitor. The trade show companion would quickly become out of date. Quarterly updates were received, but they just weren't timely enough. Each year the trade show manager would subscribe to this paperbound resource and each year he or she would reevaluate whether the expenditure was actually worth it.

Today, there is an alternative which takes up no shelf space and is easily accessible from anywhere in the world, including the computer in your office. On the World Wide Web, there reside several dozen free and easily searchable directories of conferences and expositions that a marketer can use to assist in the planning process. For example, Trade Show Central, http://www.tscentral.com/html/tsc-search.html (Figure 13.3), was created to help marketers quickly find information on over 10,000 different trade shows in a frequently updated online database. An exhibit services directory, trade show profiles, and information for trade show organizers can be found here as well. Another Internet trade show resource, EXPOguide, http://www.expoguide.com/, is a directory of trade shows, conferences, exhibition halls, show services, and show-related classifieds (Figure 13.4). EXPOguide also allows you to search by location, date, or general keywords. Once you locate an appropriate show, you can request additional information through an e-mail form at the Web site (Figure 13.5). Now the process of locating contact and show management information, reviewing show locations and dates, surveying exhibitor profiles, and contacting show management has been simplified. Yet the trade show manager still has work to do.

Figure 13.3 Trade Show Central offers trade show managers a variety of information in its extensive online database.

Figure 13.4 EXPOguide offers searching capabilities to speed the process of locating targeted shows.

Once the trade show manager has reviewed the choices, made the selections, and compiled the annual show schedule, the process of arranging services for these shows begins. If you are this manager and your company participates in 20 or more shows per year, you are well aware of the amount of paperwork, including service orders and invoices, that is involved. You could choose to have an exhibitor management firm handle these details, hire or assign someone in-house to fill out all the paperwork for you, or complete these activities through the Internet.

Exhibitor Services Firms

If you're in charge of exhibit design and logistics, your job has been made easier by exhibitor services companies on the Internet.

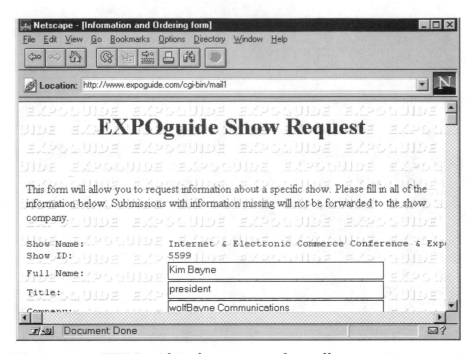

Figure 13.5 EXPOguide's show request form allows users to request information from a variety of events.

Turnkey exhibitor service firms, such as Condit Exhibits at http://www.condit.com/CoolJobs.html, will handle every aspect of your display.

Displays for Rent

If you haven't yet ordered that pop-up exhibit for that 10 by 10 booth next month, there is still time to locate an exhibit design house. The Internet has its share of companies who manufacture pop-up displays, tabletop displays, and modular units. Some vendors will also allow you to reserve a rental exhibit at their site if you're not yet in the market to buy one. Don't forget to order those custom booth graphics online, too.

Accommodations and Travel

Nothing is worse than waiting until the last minute to book hotel reservations. Sometimes, your frantic request to a busy travel agent is nothing more than another checkmark on his or her list of last-minute requests. Since you have to find a place to stay while you're in that out-of-town location, why not book it through one of the various travel-reservation sites online?

Many Internet travel Web sites serve as a turnkey solution for your convention planning needs, but you may still not have the time to book travel yourself. If you already have an established relationship with a responsive travel agent, you might even ask if the company has an e-mail address to which you can send in travel requests. Think about how much easier it will be to receive an e-mail response from a show producer and make your reservations for the same show through e-mail, by simply cutting and pasting the show dates into place.

On the Internet, you'll find traditional, independent travel agents with years of experience who have recently developed an Internet presence. You will also find those who service only online customers. Some Internet travel agents provide an incentive to those who take advantage of their online services. Travelocity, http://www.travelocity.com/ (Figure 13.6), offers individuals airline bonus miles when they purchase a ticket through the company's site. Last-minute business travelers can save on airline expenses by taking advantage of low prices on last-minute deals as well.

If you're someone who prefers to book directly with the airlines, commercial airlines sites such as America West's, http://www.americawest.com/, allow you to enter departure city, destination city, travel dates, and preferred time of day. You'll receive a listing of flights from which to choose and you can buy your tickets directly online.

National Reservation Bureau, Inc., http://www.vacationweb.com/alv_nrb/, which offers discount rooms at hotels, resorts, and casinos, handles lodging requests for such shows as Comdex and Interop and other conventions (Figure 13.7). Individual major

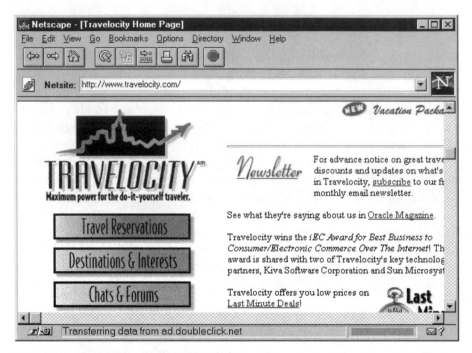

Figure 13.6 Travelocity is making waves in the travel industry with its discount Web shop.

hotel chains have a visible Internet presence worth investigating. Hilton Hotels has its Internet Travel Center, http://www.hilton .com (Figure 13.8). On HiltonNet, event planners can make reservations and find out about gaming and entertainment features at various properties. HiltonNet allows visitors to make reservations at international destinations and provides extra services online to members of the Hilton HHonors frequent-guest program. Its site is easily searchable by keyword or phrase.

Most Internet travel sites offer extensive hotel information, including the following:

- Addresses
- Telephone numbers
- Facsimile numbers

- Number of rooms
- Available meeting space
- Nearby airports
- Courtesy car
- Room rates

These detailed listings can save the company much more in the long run than trade show planning. Finding a hotel's facsimile number at its Web site can be a big help when you need to send that time-sensitive document to the company president. Reminding your sales force of the hotel's courtesy car can cut down on the number of multiple-taxi fares from the airport to the hotel.

Occasionally, hotels will offer packages and promotions to Internet users who book reservations through their Web sites.

Netscape - [Las Vegas: Hotels - Casinos - Resorts]

File Edit View Go Bookmarks Options Directory Window Help

Location: http://www.vacationweb.com/alv_nrb/

Luxury Hotels & Casinos

Hotel/Casino	Location	Special Internet Rates
Ballys Hotel & Casino	On the Strip	from ... $78
Caesars Hotel & Casino	On the Strip	from . $130
Flamingo Hotel & Casino	On the Strip	from ... $85
L.V. Hilton Hotel & Casino	Off the Strip	from ... $89
Luxor Hotel & Casino	On the Strip	from ... $65
New York New York	On the Strip	from ... $89
Rio Suites Hotel & Casino	Off the Strip	from ... $69
Tropicana Hotel & Casino	On the Strip	from ... $69

Plus tax. Weekends rates slightly Higher. Rates can vary daily. Holidays & Conventions

Document: Done

Figure 13.7 National Reservation Bureau's Vacationweb offers low rates for Las Vegas conventioneers.

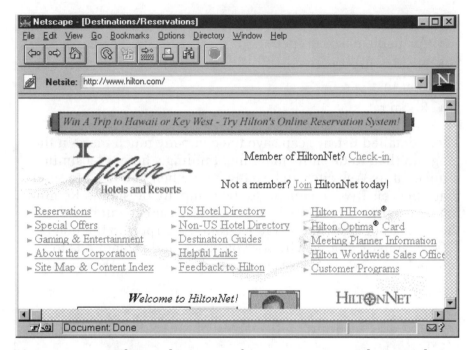

Figure 13.8   Hilton takes care of its customers with special programs and an online concierge.

Hyatt Hotels supplements its traditional advertising and promotional programs by including descriptions of special packages. While current members of frequent-guest clubs may already be aware of these specials, your visit to the Web site has just saved your company travel budget. Hyatt, being fully aware of the dangers of relying solely on the Internet for customer feedback, prominently displays their toll-free reservation number at its site.

International Exhibits

If you plan to exhibit internationally, Hotels on the Net at http://www.asiahotels.com/ (Figure 13.9) catalogs hotels in the Asia-Pacific region, in such locations as Australia, China, Hong Kong, Guam, India, Indonesia, Japan, Korea, Malaysia, Philippines, Singapore, Taiwan, and Vietnam. This site includes detailed information on conference facilities, health clubs, and restaurants.

Convention Facilities and Amenities

Georgia World Congress Center and the Georgia Dome home page, http://www.gwcc.com/ (Figure 13.10), includes information on the city of Atlanta and how to get around. GWCC provides directions to its facility with an easy-to-read street map (Figure 13.11). GWCC offers exhibiting companies a direct connection to the Internet from the trade show floor. Aside from telling your booth visitor that your company exhibits on the Internet, this service allows you to show them your pages. While just about any conference facility will run a telephone line to your booth, the quality of the connections leaves something to be desired. GWCC, in cooperation with BellSouth Communication Systems, has made a special effort to offer T-1 line connections and computer and software rental. If you're not exhibiting in Georgia any time soon, you might want to bring along a laptop loaded with your Web pages and an Internet software suite. Should the line in your booth

Figure 13.9 Hotels on the Net's Asia-Pacific hotel directory.

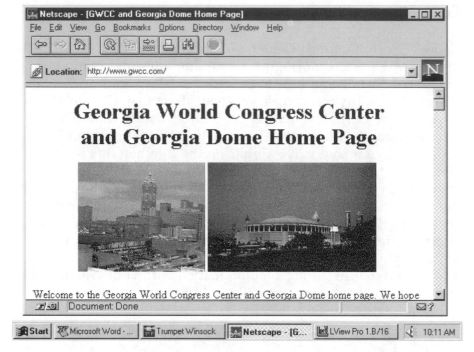

Figure 13.10 The Georgia World Congress Center has made special arrangements to offer T-1 lines to an exhibitor's booth.

experience problems, you will still have the option of showing your Web pages directly from the laptop's hard drive.

Graphics Creation

PosterWorks for Windows is a useful PC software tool for creating very large trade show display images. More information is available at http://www.posterworks.com/. Use it to create a booth-size version of your Web site that users can walk through.

Booking Entertainment

Speakers, Consultants & Entertainment Online Directory, http://www.a2zpros.com/, is a one-stop index for meeting and program

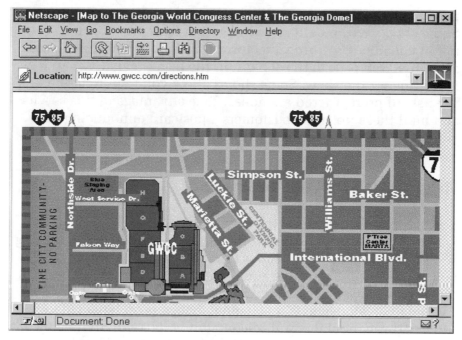

Figure 13.11 GWCC's street map can get you to your show destination.

planners. It provides resources for locating presenters, consultants, entertainers, and related entertainment services for your next show.

Keep Current on Trade Show Developments

Check out *Exhibitor* magazine's site, The Exhibitor Network, http://www.exhibitornet.com/, for the latest issue, tips on exhibiting, new show information, and a resource center of trade show suppliers. Another good source of exhibiting information is the Trade Show Exhibitors Association, located at http://www.ieabbs.org.

Getting the Word Out about Your Event

Adding your trade show schedule to your Web site will inform users of your presence at a show they plan to attend. Trade show producers on the Internet will also list exhibiting companies. Some shows will provide free links from their site to yours. You might consider providing a reciprocal link from your trade show schedule Web page to the show's profile page so visitors can register online for the show. Some shows allow you to purchase mailing lists of preregistered attendees. Take advantage of this service and mail these potential customers a postcard announcing both your Web site and your booth.

Virtual Trade Shows and Other Ideas

You can take advantage of the way in which trade shows have materialized in other forms online. Producers of the long-running computer and electronics show, Comdex Fall, now employ full-motion video and real-time audio telecasts on the Internet as part of their show. Comdex TV Online is the counterpart to Comdex TV, the dedicated television channel that runs on large video screens throughout the multiple exhibit halls. Comdex TV covers show news, reviews, and interviews on exhibitors. If you are exhibiting at this type of technology exposition, you can get your message out on the Internet at the same time. Visitors to the Comdex TV site must download Xing Technology's viewer software before they can see the show (Figure 13.12).

Finally, this brings us to the idea of virtual trade shows. *Virtual trade show* is a concept that has many definitions. A virtual trade show is "almost" a trade show, which means that the Internet is used to simulate the activities that would normally take place on the trade show floor. Virtual trade shows, like InterAct'96, consist of interactive product demonstrations and three-dimensional "booths" (Figure 13.13). Like their traditional counterparts, virtual trade show producers target an industry, technology, or theme for the event, and invite various companies to exhibit online.

In a virtual trade show, exhibitors and attendees meet on the Internet to exchange product and company information. Product literature can be placed online, just at it appears at the exhibitor's own Web site. A few of these shows coincided with the actual off-line event of the same name that was held simultaneously.

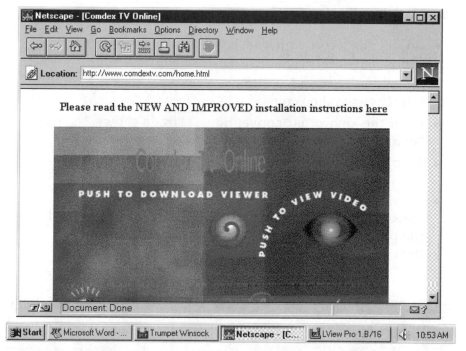

Figure 13.12   Comdex, producer of technology expos, takes charge on the Internet, with its implementation of a growing activity.

The virtual trade show concept was born out of necessity. With costs for show participation climbing, small companies lacked the resources to exhibit at multiple shows. Even in those few shows at which they exhibited, the smaller firms were often dwarfed by the bigger ones, with a proportional number of visitors stopping by. The advantage to the exhibitor in participating in one of these virtual events is that there are no booth-setup costs, no travel to outlying convention halls, no out-of-town booth staff to coordinate, and certainly far less in the way of expenses. If virtual trade shows are used in conjunction with the actual physical event, the advantage is that you are reaching customers who would otherwise be unable to see your product demos in person. Initially stalled by exhibitor resistance and technological limitations, the concept of virtual trade shows is slowly gaining acceptance (Figure 13.14).

Some Activities You Can Do Now

- ◆ Go to your favorite Internet search index or directory site.
- ◆ If you don't have a favorite search engine, start at Yahoo!, http://www.yahoo.com.
- ◆ Enter the keywords "conventions," "trade shows," "exhibits," "virtual trade show," "conferences."
- ◆ Take notes on the various Internet trade show options and examples.
- ◆ If you don't get enough results from your search here, click on the other directory links found at the bottom of the page. Yahoo! will send your search with you to the next location.

Figure 13.13 InterAct'96, held April 23–25, 1996, was the Web's first successful and true virtual trade show, registering 50,000 visitors.

Traditional	Virtual
Exhibit costs run in the tens of thousands of dollars.	Exhibit costs are insignificant by comparison.
Show planning can take months to complete.	Show planning time is much shorter.
Prime booth locations are usually sold out early.	Prime booth locations are nonexistent; however, logo of big budget exhibitors may appear on the Web's home page.
Booth setup involves shipping crates, hiring labor, and spending hours getting all the details right.	Booth setup involves uploading a few files and some demo versions of software and letting the show producer do the rest.
Attendees stop by for an in-person product demo.	Attendees get online for a 3D product demo.
Product demonstrations occur in real time.	Product demonstrations are hampered by bandwidth.
Visitors to the booth are treated to giveaways.	Visitors to the booth are treated to software.
Company executives meet in a conference or hotel room to discuss pricing and negotiate contracts.	Company executives meet on the Internet through chat tools and videoconferencing.
Booth entertainment consists of live performers, who present, sing, dance, and juggle to draw people in.	Booth entertainment is simulated with video and audio clips placed online for downloading.
Attendees walk for hours and get sore feet.	Attendees browse for hours and get carpal tunnel syndrome.

Figure 13.14   Traditional versus virtual trade shows.

◆ Read the services offered by companies at the various
Web sites.

Bookmark any site that may be useful to you in writing your Internet marketing plan.

Cross-Pollinate

Here are some simple ways you can quickly marry your trade show programs with your Internet marketing programs (Figure 13.15)

❑ Update all print ads, including those that run in show dailies, to reflect both exhibit locations: "See us at Comdex Fall, Booth 1234" and "Visit us on the Web at http://www.comdex.com/."

❑ Hand out T-shirts with a silk-screened copy of your Web page to qualified booth visitors.

❑ Ask booth visitors if they would like to receive product information via e-mail. Include an extra line for Internet addresses on your show leads' qualification forms or in your leads database.

❑ Offer a free gift to booth visitors who register online before the show.

❑ Offer a free gift to booth visitors who download a designated page from your site and bring it to the show.

❑ Create a password-protected Web page with a clickable schedule where editors can register for a show-site meeting with company executives based on currently available time slots.

❑ Investigate virtual trade shows as a way to complement your physical trade show exhibits (Figure 13.17).

❑ Use the Internet to send booth staff updated schedules for booth-duty assignments.

❑ Use the Internet to order food and beverages for your show's hospitality suite.

❑ Set up a touch-screen kiosk in your booth containing your complete Web site.

Figure 13.15   Brainstorming ideas for fitting the Internet into your trade show mix.

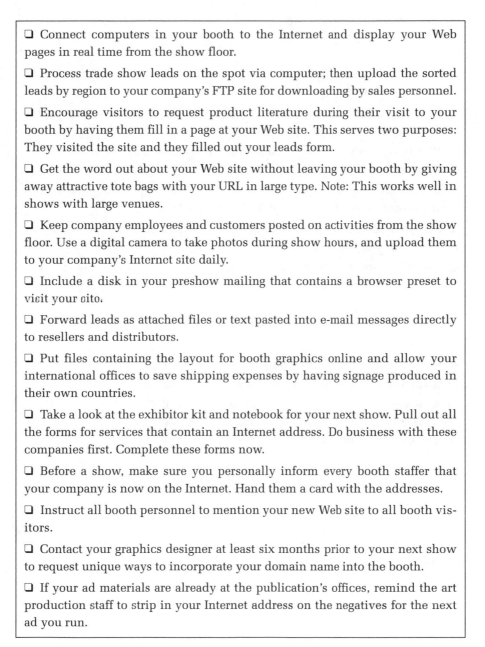

❑ Connect computers in your booth to the Internet and display your Web pages in real time from the show floor.

❑ Process trade show leads on the spot via computer; then upload the sorted leads by region to your company's FTP site for downloading by sales personnel.

❑ Encourage visitors to request product literature during their visit to your booth by having them fill in a page at your Web site. This serves two purposes: They visited the site and they filled out your leads form.

❑ Get the word out about your Web site without leaving your booth by giving away attractive tote bags with your URL in large type. Note: This works well in shows with large venues.

❑ Keep company employees and customers posted on activities from the show floor. Use a digital camera to take photos during show hours, and upload them to your company's Internet site daily.

❑ Include a disk in your preshow mailing that contains a browser preset to visit your site.

❑ Forward leads as attached files or text pasted into e-mail messages directly to resellers and distributors.

❑ Put files containing the layout for booth graphics online and allow your international offices to save shipping expenses by having signage produced in their own countries.

❑ Take a look at the exhibitor kit and notebook for your next show. Pull out all the forms for services that contain an Internet address. Do business with these companies first. Complete these forms now.

❑ Before a show, make sure you personally inform every booth staffer that your company is now on the Internet. Hand them a card with the addresses.

❑ Instruct all booth personnel to mention your new Web site to all booth visitors.

❑ Contact your graphics designer at least six months prior to your next show to request unique ways to incorporate your domain name into the booth.

❑ If your ad materials are already at the publication's offices, remind the art production staff to strip in your Internet address on the negatives for the next ad you run.

Figure 13.15 (*Continued*)

❑ Make sure all trade show press releases contain a reference to your Internet presence.

❑ Create a sticker for the front of the press-kit folders that you plan to put in the show press-kit room.

❑ Include a color printout of your home page, along with bullets listing your site's features, in your show press kit.

❑ Wait to reprint your sales literature until just before the next trade show so you can add your URL.

❑ Use online freight and overnight courier Web sites to track the arrival of your packages and exhibits to and from the show floor.

❑ Sell your old trade show booth online by putting pictures, specifications, and price at your Web site.

❑ Upload conference presentations made by your executives on the Web immediately afterward for downloading by customers who could not attend the show.

❑ Order custom lanyards with your Internet addresses to wear with your trade show badges.

❑ Conduct preshow staff training during Internet chat sessions.

❑ Invite special customers to a hospitality suite debut of your Web site.

❑ Subscribe to the TRADESHOW mailing list (e-mail discussion group). Send a message to listproc@nevada.edu. In the body of the message type: *subscribe tradeshow your_full_name.*

❑ _____

❑ _____

❑ _____

❑ _____

Figure 13.15   (*Continued*)

Instructions
- ◆ Check off any of the following trade show activities you wish to implement for your trade show program.
- ◆ Search the Internet for trade show service firms that conduct business online.
- ◆ Bookmark their Web sites for future reference.
- ◆ Make notes on this form next to the trade show activity that needs enhancement.
- ◆ Begin gathering costs for incorporating the Internet into your trade show program.
- ◆ Use this data to create the next portion of your Internet marketing budget.

Exhibit Design

❑ Display ❑ Signage ❑ Carpeting ❑ Furniture
❑ Exhibit crates ❑ Photography ❑ Other: _____

_____
_____
_____
_____

Show Activities

❑ Live talent ❑ Presentation scripts ❑ Booth giveaways
❑ Staff training ❑ Leads forms ❑ Telephone lines
❑ Equipment ❑ Hospitality suites

_____
_____
_____
_____

Completed by: _____ Date: _____

Figure 13.16   Trade show functions checklist.

Show title: _____

Dates: _____ Contact person: _____

Web URL: _____ E-mail address: _____

Sponsor or show management: _____

Show description: _____

_____

_____

_____

_____

Check one:

❑ This is a new show.   ❑ This show was last held on (date): _____

❑ Last show: Total exhibitors: _____   Total attendees: _____

❑ Next show: Anticipated exhibitors: _____

Anticipated attendees: _____

How will the number of visitors be tallied?

❑ Hits   ❑ Registered visitors   ❑ Other: _____

If other, please explain: _____

_____

_____

_____

_____

Figure 13.17   Virtual trade show evaluation form.

How is the show being promoted? ❑ Internet ❑ Advertising ❑ Direct mail

❑ Other: _____

_____

_____

_____

_____

Notable companies exhibiting at this show: _____

_____

_____

_____

_____

List the technologies, such as software and programs, available for visitors during the show: _____

_____

_____

_____

_____

Costs to participate: _____

Payment terms: _____

Is this a true virtual trade show or just a Web site designed to look like a convention center? In other words, will this event be an interactive experience for attendees?

❑ Yes   ❑ No   ❑ Unsure

Completed by: _____ Date: _____

Figure 13.17   (*Continued*)

chapter fourteen

Launching Your Internet Marketing Program

This chapter will cover the steps needed to launch your Internet marketing program. This is one of the most fulfilling aspects of marketing communications—the launch. It's present in just about every activity. In advertising, the launch is the placement of ads in business and trade publications. It's the culmination of meetings with agency creatives, photographers, and copywriters. In trade shows, it's opening day, when that bell rings in the exhibit hall to let the attendees enter. The doors open, and you're exhausted after days of installing the booth and furnishings, but you're too excited to care. For public relations professionals, it's the climax of weeks spent interviewing company executives and product managers, days spent drafting releases for routing approval, and hours spent with a telephone receiver glued to your ear. The publications hit the stands and your company receives its due. A campaign launch is to marketers what opening night is to Broadway actors. Now get ready to begin scheduling and implementing activities in anticipation of a new launch—your Internet marketing program.

In Chapter 13, *Planning Trade Shows,* you learned about the different Internet resources now available to aid in your trade show planning. You were introduced to virtual trade shows and compared them to the traditional kind. You found out about online resources designed to keep you current on conferences and events for your exhibit schedule planning.

In Chapter 14, *Launching Your Internet Marketing Program,* you will continue to strengthen your marketing communications program by finalizing plans for your Internet marketing program launch. This chapter will contribute to the further development of Section Six of your Internet marketing plan.

Effective Supporting Materials for the Plan

Your Internet marketing plan is best supported by including data that reinforces your decision to market on the Internet. Section Six of your Internet marketing plan can be expanded by including any combination of the following:

- Timeline charts showing Internet marketing activities alongside your traditional marketing activities
- Brief overview of each element in your online promotional plan
- A summary of your entire marketing communications program, including how traditional and Internet activities supplement each other

Getting the Most out of This Chapter

The activities in this chapter include summarizing your marketing communications program in its entirety and scheduling all activities in relationship to each other.

Plan of Action: The Schedule

Now that you've decided what kinds of activities you'll include in your Internet marketing plan, start to schedule them. Presumably, you'll want to synchronize the announcement of your Web site with another noteworthy event on your marketing calendar. This allows you to use the editorial coverage from one event to attract interest in your Internet marketing activities.

Merely launching your Web site will probably not invite much press interest, unless your site is substantially different from the majority of sites already in existence. You will need to make that assessment with brutal honesty. Editors are inundated with Web site announcements on a daily basis, and they rarely cover one as an event by itself.

Let's assume you're planning to exhibit at a major industry trade show six months into the future. During that show you also plan to announce a major extension of your product line. Announcing your Web site at the same time will allow you to use the Web to further enhance your public relations activities. In this case, your timing is scheduled strategically to take advantage of efforts that are already under way. Taking that six-month time frame into account, let's look at a sample schedule showing only the Internet marketing portion of the plan (Figure 14.1).

Six Months Before

  Compile first draft of Internet marketing program budget.

  Form Internet marketing task force.

  Establish Internet service account, upgrade access, or install Web server.

  Register domain name.

  Begin competitive research.

Five Months Before

  Flowchart or outline Web site content and navigational aspects of your Web site.

  Obtain bids from outside suppliers and vendors.

  Test Web site access.

  Purchase press directory, enhance in-house directory, or consult with PR firm.

Four Months Before

  Create Internet style manual.

  Hire interactive agency or Web design firm.

Figure 14.1   Sample Internet marketing program schedule.

Begin document conversion to HTML.

Begin developing new documents in HTML.

Alias domain name.

Test aliased Web site access.

Consult with outside inquiry management firm.

Consult with outside Internet measurement firm.

Three Months Before

Inventory stock of print marketing literature.

Plan for reprints to include e-mail and Web addresses.

Add URL and e-mail to all trade show ads.

Compile list of Web sites as targets for exchanging reciprocal links.

Update sales lead database with fields to accommodate customer e-mail address.

Two Months Before

Install and test Web site search engine.

Research and join appropriate industry- and technology-specific mailing lists.

One Month Before

Design HTML–to–e-mail forms.

Install Web tracking or measurement software.

Design standard company signature block for all outgoing e-mail.

Begin to register Web site in multiple search engines and directories.

Prepare traditional news release or press advisory outlining key features of Web site.

Install mailbot.

Upload completed Web pages and test download times and other problems.

Figure 14.1   (*Continued*)

Launch Week

Distribute news release or press advisory through traditional and electronic media.

Check Web statistical log.

Check autoresponder filter log.

Respond to Internet sales leads.

One Month After

Revisit search engines and directories to verify listings.

View editorial coverage in key publications.

Check Web statistical log.

Check autoresponder filter log.

Respond to Internet sales leads.

Update online documents.

Two Months After

Plan for site evaluation.

Begin planning next site revision landmark.

Continue market and competitive research.

Check Web statistical log.

Check autoresponder filter log.

Respond to Internet sales leads.

Update online documents.

Three Months After

Check Web statistical log.

Check autoresponder filter log.

Respond to Internet sales leads.

Plan for site relaunch.

Update online documents.

Figure 14.1   (*Continued*)

This sample Internet marketing plan format (Figure 14.1) is not going to work for everyone. You will have different elements in your Internet marketing program. You may already have a company domain name, but not a Web site. Registering a domain name and waiting for its approval won't be in your plans.

You'll notice four repetitive activities in the sample schedule, beginning with the week of the launch. They are as follows:

- Check Web statistical log.
- Check autoresponder filter log.
- Respond to Internet sales leads.
- Update online documents.

Once your program is under way, you must check on your progress. Aside from paying attention to incoming e-mail inquiries, checking your logs is the only way to verify that activity is actually occurring at your site. The third activity, responding to sales leads, should be done within 24 hours of receiving a message. The Internet is a fast-moving world. If you're fast to implement the technology, but slow at maintaining customer-service standards, your Internet reputation will suffer. Finally, the Internet requires a regular commitment to updating online documents. If you don't, and your site becomes static, you may find your company honored with one of the Internet's dubious distinctions, such as Ghost Sites of the Web, http://www.pathfinder.com/technology/ghostsites/ghost1.html, a graveyard of obsolete and abandoned Web sites.

How will your final schedule look after you combine it with your traditional program? That choice is up to you. You may wish to include only the Internet portion in your marketing plan. Conversely, you may decide to highlight only those activities directly affected by the Internet. Perhaps you'll show your entire marketing communications program, with the Internet marketing elements highlighted, to give management a better overall concept of how all the pieces fit together. Figure 14.2 shows another schedule variation.

	January	February	March	April	May	June
Adv. and direct mail		Create and update advertising materials, insertion orders.				Run ads.
Collateral			Literature reprints.		Upgrade fulfill-ment services.	
Public relations	Update press list, begin ongoing editorial liaison.					
		Place feature stories.			Draft news release.	
Trade shows	Book show.	Update booth graphics.			Order giveaways.	
Internet marketing		Web site development.			Web site testing.	

Figure 14.2   Sample combined marketing plan.

In-house personnel should give you their best estimate of when they can complete certain activities. Outside agencies must do the same. You will need this information when you put together your own schedule. Take into account other projects currently in the queue that may take priority and plan accordingly.

Online Promotional Plan

Eventually, you must let the world know you're open for business. The key areas of focus for online promotional activities follow (Figure 14.9).

Read Relevant Newsgroups

Perform keyword searches with a newsreader or at Dejanews, http://www.dejanews.com, to locate appropriate groups. Before you post your first message, make sure you read Frequently Asked Questions (FAQs). FAQs are documents regularly posted to news-groups to educate new users. FAQs will tell you whether or not you

can post announcements or news releases to selected newsgroups.
Plan your participation in each newsgroup accordingly. If a Web
site forbids formal announcements, you will have to find another
way to get the word out. Participate in discussions and include
your Web URL in your signature block. Some newsgroups do not
allow commercial posts, while others consist entirely of them
(Figure 14.3). For more information, go to http://www.fdma.com/
~news/advert.faq for a FAQ document on newsgroups and
advertising.

Join Relevant Mailing Lists

If you're looking for lists, or e-mail discussion groups, that cater
to selected individuals, find a site that catalogs mailing lists.
Search "lists of lists," such as Publicly Accessible Mailing Lists,
http://www.neosoft.com/internet/paml/, and Kim Bayne's Marketing Lists on the Internet, http://www.bayne.com/wolfBayne/
htmarcom/mktglist.html. Once you locate several appropriate

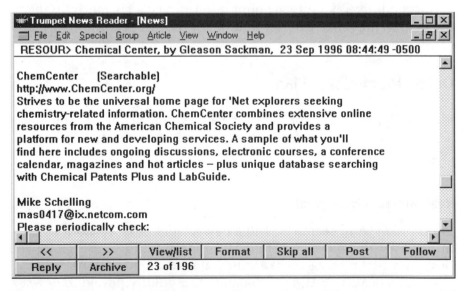

Figure 14.3 comp.internet.net-happenings allows commercial posts on Web page launches.

lists, send for their INFO and/or WELCOME files. Read the documents and determine if the list is for you. Join any relevant mailing lists. Before you post any message, lurk for a while. *Lurker marketing* can refer to reading posts before participating. When you see an opportunity to join in discussions, do so. Include your Web address in your signature block. If the list allows it, you can post your announcement (Figure 14.4).

Submit Your URL to Search Engines and Indexes

You can choose to register your Web page in various locations on the Web in one of several ways.

1. Visit individual directories, such as Lycos, http://www .lycos.com, or WebCrawler, http://www.webcrawler.com/ WebCrawler/SubmitURLS.html (Figure 14.5), and submit your URL to each site.

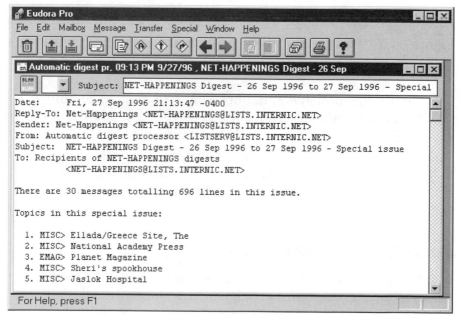

Figure 14.4 The Net-Happenings Digest compiles multiple Web site announcements into a digest for distribution via e-mail.

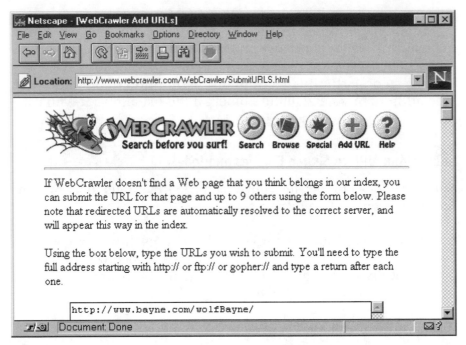

Figure 14.5 WebCrawler allows marketers to submit up to 10 URLs for cataloging at one time.

2. Visit a consolidated announcement site, such as Submit It!, http://www.submit-it.com/ (Figure 14.6), or 1 2 3 RegisterMe!, http://www.123registerme.com.

3. Hire a commercial Web site promoter, such as The PostMaster, http://www.netcreations.com/postmaster/ (Figure 14.7), and WebPromote, http://www .webpromote.com/.

Include Commercial Online Services

Don't forget to include other online services, such as America Online, CompuServe, and Prodigy in your promotional plans. These sites have separate forums dedicated to a variety of topics. If you don't have an account already, establish one. If you're using an outside service to promote your site, find out if it participates

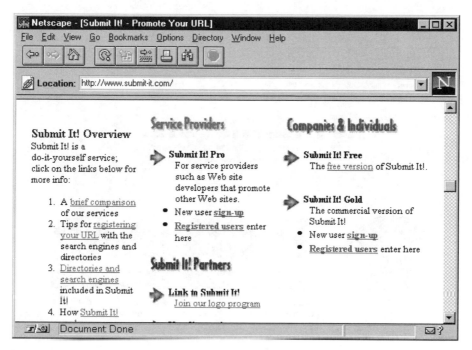

Figure 14.6 Submit It! offers both free and commercial services for registering your Web site address to multiple search indexes and directories.

in these other services as well. You can even arrange to trade promotional duties with another subscriber if you know someone who has an account.

Trade Reciprocal Links

Locate sites in your industry that would be willing to trade hyperlinks with you. Search for similar sites in your favorite search directory. Ivan Levison, editor of *The Levison Letter,* provides this tip to marketers who want to find out which sites are offering links to another site.

> You'd be amazed at how many Web sites out there are pointing people in your direction.

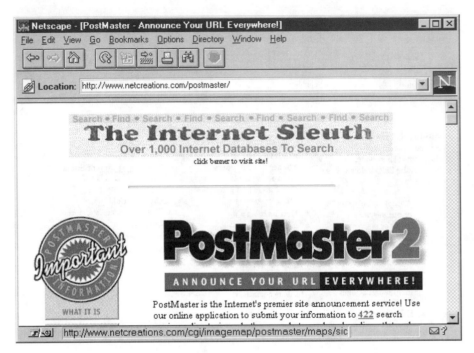

Figure 14.7 PostMaster submits your Web announcement to over 400 search engines and directories.

```
For a complete list of links to your home page (excluding your own site),
just follow these simple instructions. The whole process takes only a
minute. No kidding!

    1. Go to http://altavista.digital.com

    2. Enter the following in the empty search box. (Obviously, you have to
substitute your own Web site address in both places. I've used mine
[http://www.levison.com] as an example.)

    +link:http://www.levison.com/ -url:http://www.levison.com

    3. Press "submit" and in no time at all you'll get a complete list of
sites that link to yours!
```

Check your competitors' links and ask to be linked to the same general industry sites as well (Figure 14.8).

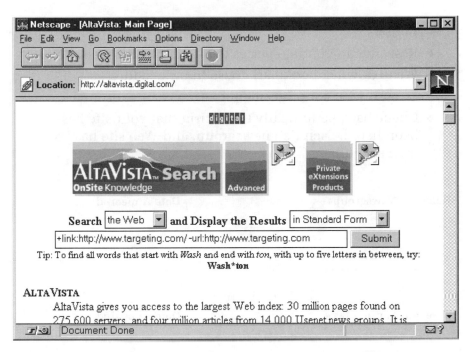

Figure 14.8   AltaVista provides access to over 30 million pages on the Internet, allowing you to locate several targets for reciprocal links.

Distribute the News

Along with all your other promotional activities, don't forget to send out a traditional news release. Keep your release short and simple, highlighting its key features. Distribute the release through a variety of media, including it with any other announcements your company may be sending out that week. Include your URL and e-mail address in the editor's notes on your other releases as well. If you decide to follow up with editors to encourage coverage of your site, please don't call them up and say, "Did you get my release?" Thousands of companies are announcing Web sites at the same time. Editors need to know how your announcement is unique, interesting, and fits into their current focus. Weave your Web site discussion into something else you're doing, and gear it toward whatever the editor happens to be writing about at the moment.

Instructions

- ◆ Research appropriate places to publicize your Web site.
- ◆ Write down or bookmark these Internet addresses.
- ◆ Submit your announcement to each online resource.
- ◆ Check back periodically to confirm that your site has been listed. Each list, newsgroup, and Web site has its own schedule.

Relevant Newsgroups   **Date Appeared**

_____   _____

_____   _____

_____   _____

_____   _____

Relevant Mailing Lists   **Date Appeared**

_____   _____

_____   _____

_____   _____

_____   _____

Search Engines and Indexes (choose one)

❑ Individual directories, indexes, and robots.

URL   **Date Appeared**

_____   _____

_____   _____

_____   _____

_____   _____

❑ Consolidated announcement site. Specify: _____

❑ Commercial Web site promoter. Cost: _____

Figure 14.9   Web promotion checklist.

Commercial Online Services (name appropriate forums)

America Online   Date Appeared

_____   _____
_____   _____
_____   _____
_____   _____

CompuServe   Date Appeared

_____   _____
_____   _____
_____   _____
_____   _____

Prodigy   Date Appeared

_____   _____
_____   _____
_____   _____
_____   _____

Other   Date Appeared

_____   _____
_____   _____
_____   _____
_____   _____

Reciprocal Links   Date Appeared

_____   _____
_____   _____
_____   _____
_____   _____

Figure 14.9   (*Continued*)

Hot and Cool Sites Date Appeared

_____ _____

_____ _____

_____ _____

_____ _____

News Release

❑ Draft copy.

❑ Route for approval.

❑ Distribute. Date distributed: _____

Distributed by: _____

_____

❑ Include follow-up with other editorial contact activities.

Publication Date Appeared

_____ _____

_____ _____

_____ _____

_____ _____

Figure 14.9 (_Continued_)

In the Future Everyone Will Be Famous for 15 Minutes

No better example of that famous forecast of fleeting fame exists than in those sites that promote the hottest and coolest: Cool Site of the Week, Cool Site of the Millennium, Hot Site of the Nanosecond, or Cool Site During the Bottom of My Manic-Depressive Cycle. In exchange for several hours of someone's time surfing the Web, a cute logo, and a willingness to review just about anything, anyone can become a bona fide site reviewer. And they most certainly do.

Whatever happens to suit someone's fancy that week, that day, or even that minute can suddenly become _the_ site to visit. Users love these rating sites. They love them so much that Yahoo! has even dedicated a category to them. I love them so much that I made a big deal out of receiving one when my daughter's Web site, Kaitlyn's Knock Knock Jokes and Riddles, was selected as the Safe for Kids Site of the Week for July. That was fun. Now for business.

How do cool and hot ratings apply to your Internet marketing program's bottom line? Well, they really don't. That's the point. Ratings are one of those Web elements that have nothing to do with why your competitor is online or why anyone at all is marketing on the Internet. At least, I hope not. Some Webcrafters live for this type of recognition and will do anything short of selling their soul to attain cool or hot status. These rewards are nice to get as secondary kudos for all your hard work.

These Web site awards won't convince people to buy your product or service. I don't mean that you shouldn't pursue Web site ratings. In some cases, being singled out as a cutting-edge site can enhance your Internet promotion. Just remember to be selective about the ones you pursue. You're judged by the company you keep.

PART THREE

Evaluation: Reviewing Achievements and Improving Future Performance

Measuring Internet Marketing Results

Review of Part 2: Implementation

In Part 2 of *The Internet Marketing Plan, Implementation: Fitting the Internet into Your Marketing Communications Mix,* you continued to draft portions of your Internet marketing plan directly related to individual marketing communications activities. These activities included advertising, collateral, corporate identity, market research, public relations, sales support, and trade shows. Finally, you covered the basic steps needed to announce your Internet marketing presence to the world.

In Part 3, *Evaluation: Reviewing Achievements and Improving Future Performance,* you will read a brief overview of methods for measuring activity in your Internet marketing program. There is one chapter in this section, Chapter 15, *Measuring Internet Marketing Results.*

Measurement is the only activity that will demonstrate the effectiveness of your Internet marketing program. Demonstrating increased sales is one form of measurement. Tracking positive media coverage is another. Your choice of measurement methods relates to your original goals: Why are you marketing on the Internet? This chapter will discuss the possibilities that exist for measuring your Internet marketing presence so you can make an informed decision about how to proceed. By the way, installing an Internet measurement function, whether it's software or an out-side analysis firm, is best done *before* you announce your Internet presence. Why did I put this chapter last? That's easy. You won't know how well you're meeting your goals until your Internet marketing presence has been launched.

Chapter 15.   Measuring Internet Marketing Results

Your Internet marketing plan is best supported by including data that reinforces your decision to market on the Internet. Section Six of your Internet marketing plan can be expanded by including any combination of the following:

- ◆ Suggestions for measurement implementation programs
- ◆ How selected measurement functions will demonstrate that you are meeting your Internet marketing plan objectives

Getting the Most out of This Chapter

Review the different options for Internet marketing measurement for applicability to your Internet marketing program. Select those activities that will accurately demonstrate Internet marketing's effectiveness and impact on your overall marketing communications program. Research Internet and marketing publications (Appendix C) for up-to-date reviews of software packages and measurement firms.

What Is Marketing Measurement?

Measurement is the closed loop of marketing. It gives you a sense of accomplishment and a sense of closure. Without it, you're operating in the dark. Too many times, marketers continue with their marketing programs based on instinct. Instinct is fine, especially if you've cut your marketing teeth in the trenches. You've got experience to support those views. In many cases, "marketing instinct" is nothing more than educated guessing. Most of the time, instinct is not enough. You need proof. You get that proof by producing numbers and analysis. In traditional marketing, this analysis can take any number of forms.

Let's focus in on one marketing area: PR. In public relations, you can measure the effectiveness of your media relations program by analyzing the final result: press clippings. First, you clip coverage and start looking at the trends. Then your coverage starts growing and you need some additional help. Perhaps you hire an outside firm to gather clippings for you. Service bureaus like Burrelle's Information Services, Bacon's Clipping Bureau, and Luce Press Clippings will track coverage in print and broadcast media for a fee. They'll provide you with copies of clippings so you can see the results yourself. You might select coverage on your company, its divisions, and parent companies. You might ask a firm to provide you with both editorial coverage and advertising for your competitors as well. On a regular basis, you review the coverage your company has received. Is is good? Is it bad? Who wrote it? How do you report this to management?

How to report is equally as important as knowing *what* to report. You can tell management that you received 12 clips in January and 9 in February. That would vaguely demonstrate that you are doing your job. If the press clippings are lukewarm reviews of your company and products, your report of the *number* of clippings didn't amount to much.

Before you implement a measurement program, you need to review your marketing objectives. For example, your overall objectives might include improving brand identification. A subset of that might be directly related to editorial coverage. Many companies analyze press clippings to indicate success from many different angles.

Advertising Equivalence

If your marketing goals include showing that public relations is producing as much interest in your products as advertising, you may wish to equate editorial mentions with advertising expenditures. This is one way to show a return on your PR investment.

Editorial Slant

Sales can be adversely affected by bad press. You'll want to recognize it early so you can proactively adjust. Effective public relations campaigns manage a company's identity in the marketplace. Presenting your company in the best light is a business marketing expectation. By analyzing your press coverage for fairness and tone, you'll understand how your market is forming its opinion of your services and products.

Key Message

Your company's image is governed by the primary messages it presents to the public. If you want the public to identify your company with a certain product or technology, you've got to create key messages. Getting your key messages out to the public is part of your job. Analyzing your press coverage for key messages demonstrates whether the public is receiving your messages at all and to what degree.

In the marketing communications area of advertising, you might measure readership retention to determine if your current advertising campaign is gaining recognition. In just about every aspect of marketing communications you have the choice of measuring the quantity of your results, measuring the quality of your results, or measuring both. The same applies to Internet marketing.

What to Measure in Your Internet Marketing Program

My favorite Internet marketing advertisement is one that appeared in the December 11, 1995, issue of *Brandweek* magazine. The full-page ad was placed by *Penthouse* magazine. It showed two bars side by side on a chart with the headline, "Ours is bigger than theirs." The first bar represented the number of hits that the *Playboy* Internet site was receiving. It was 800,000 Internet hits daily. The second bar represented the number of hits the *Penthouse* site was receiving. It was 2.9 million Internet hits daily. *Penthouse* wanted you to know that its site was worth exploring for advertising placement.

Webmasters look at their log-analysis reports on a daily or weekly basis to see how many hits were registered for a particular page. This is how they know whether a page is generating interest. When it comes time to reevaluate the content at their sites, the pages with low-hit reports will either be renamed, revamped, archived off-line, or deleted entirely. Pages with high-hit counts will be evaluated to determine what additional and similar content can be created to include in the site. In other words, if your visitors prefer one type of product or service information over another, you'll know immediately. You'll be able to compensate and mold your site to suit your market.

If you're counting hits at your site, you are roughly demonstrating activity level. Your measurement program won't be complete if that is your only yardstick. Hits show only quantity, not quality. Programs that count only the number of hits miss the overall picture and don't answer the following questions:

- Who is visiting this site?
- Are we reaching the right customer?
- How has the design of my site either helped or hindered the visitor's access to important information?

There are dozens of other questions about your Web site and its visitors you will want answered. The programs that measure just hits won't give you these answers. They're nice to look at, but as a business marketer trying to demonstrate a return on your Internet investment, you need more.

Where Did They Go and How Did They Get There?

Clickstream-analysis reports can show you a visitor's path through your site. This can be helpful, especially if you're trying to determine why that page announcing your new services isn't getting any play. You could analyze clickstream reports to determine if your site organization needs review. You can also use this data to determine how certain types of visitors navigate your site. If your site requires registration by company, job title, and/or industry, clickstream analysis will be worthwhile for you to review.

Knock, Knock. Who's There?

Are you trying to show management that your site has increased your company's international reach? Tracking the domain names and countries of your visitors will help. Again, this measurement by itself won't show quality. There might be quite a few students in that foreign country who are visiting your site. You may not have any way of knowing until you analyze a few more details. I wouldn't open up a sales office in another location based on this Internet measurement information alone.

How Many Browsers Does It Take To . . .

Browsers come in many different flavors. Some Internet users have a choice in how they view the Web, while many others do not. Meanwhile, Webmasters like to experiment. The latest and greatest HTML code extension, graphics trick, or applet can be incorporated into your site to make it look great. It does look great—to everyone *inside* your company. Too bad your customers are everywhere else. Just what are they using to access your site? If you track the types of browsers visitors are using to view your site, you can tell whether your market is seeing all your nifty work. You may find out that the majority of browsers out there are barfing everytime they click on your hyperlink. If that's the case, think about providing an alternative version of your site for the browser-impaired.

Yes, I Did See Your Web Address in That Ad!

Did your recent advertising campaign increase interest in your site? How about your latest news release? If you watch how your Web site activity has increased following a recent marketing launch, you'll know the impact of your programs. Analyzing your press coverage may produce some proof that your Internet presence has merit in supporting your regular PR activities.

Is It Sales Yet?

The easiest way to measure the success of your Internet marketing program includes tracking the sales generated by your Web site. If your sales leads management program is sophisticated enough to close the loop for you, then you're in good shape. If you don't have a good sales-leads program in place, now's the time to think this one through. If your Internet marketing goals don't include sales, then you'll have to measure your program in other ways.

Counting Beans and Other Pastimes

Log-analysis tools allow you to track page hits, time of visit, domain names, geography, and so forth. Most of the time they automate the tracking process by relieving you of the rigors of bean counting. Your Internet service provider may already have something in place that you can use. You may also need something more detailed in order to create a thorough report on your Internet marketing progress.

Compiling data to support a return on your investment can be tricky. Very few of the downloadable shareware programs analyze data. They certainly don't show the relationship of your hits to each other. Many of the shareware programs are inadequate for detailed marketing measurement purposes. Their reports are impossible to use when trying to link your Web activity to your marketing communications objectives.

A commercial package might be a better solution for you. Commercial software packages have the added feature of customization for your unique requirements (Figures 15.1 through 15.3). If accuracy in reporting is important to you and you can't live with ballpark figures, don't rely on the free log-analysis tools. Investigate one of the commercial ones.

Measurement Tracking Firms

Companies have been measuring marketing communications success long before the Internet became a marketing issue. Outside agencies use a combination of software and/or individuals to track, verify, and audit your site. They analyze the data and report back with management-appropriate reports (Figure 15.4). Outside service firms can also offer an objective view of your Internet marketing traffic, which makes log tools and reports inaccurate by

Figure 15.1   net.Analysis allows you to add custom
filters and time ranges to its reports.

comparison. Many of these firms will save you time in compiling
the results from your logs and do a better job of demonstrating
how well your program is performing.

Outside service firms can be expensive. Some require minimum contracts that could run into the thousands of dollars. If
you've spent thousands of dollars to launch an Internet marketing program, don't scrimp on this last part of your program.
Before you hire an outside firm, make sure that you have an
understanding of exactly what you're getting in return for your
marketing dollar.

If you are interested only in showing independent verification
of your site traffic, you can find a free measurement-tracking firm
on the Internet (Figure 15.5). These bureaus work by using a

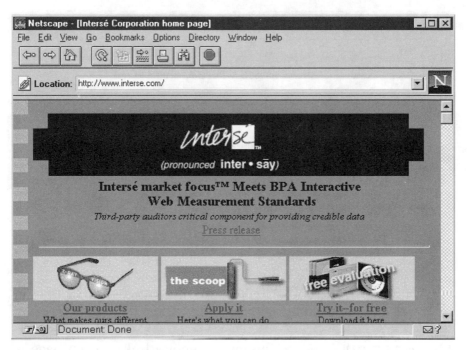

Figure 15.2   Intersé Corporation offers a free demo version of its product to interested Webmasters.

hyperlink inserted into your Web page and linked to their site. These bureaus may not be as useful as you'd like, since they are counting only hits.

Off-Line Tracking Methods

To track the effectiveness of your traditional marketing communications programs, assign different e-mail addresses or different Web page addresses to each activity. When I speak at trade shows and conferences, I provide a unique e-mail address for each event. This way, I know where my inquiries have originated. To keep track of reader inquiries from a particular magazine, assign a unique e-mail address to advertisements. This technique is similar to providing a toll-free number with an

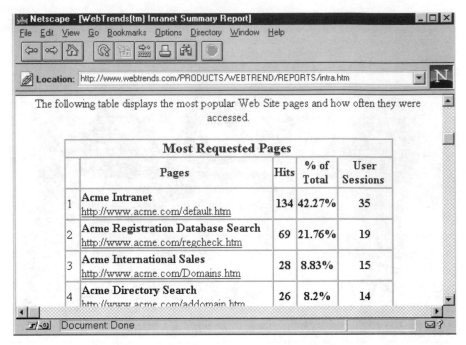

Figure 15.3 WebTrends' summary reports link to each page for reference.

extension. Your company switchboard knows how to route these calls, even if you don't have an extension with this number. As a marketer, you can identify how the customer obtained your telephone number.

Summary

Your Internet marketing program can be as simple or as complex as you would like to make it (Figure 15.6). It's difficult to estimate how well you've done on any size or type of marketing program unless you take steps to track your progress. Measurement is often an afterthought for many marketers. It shouldn't be. Measurement should be tied in from the very beginning as an essential part of your program. With measurement, you'll be able to ask for addi-

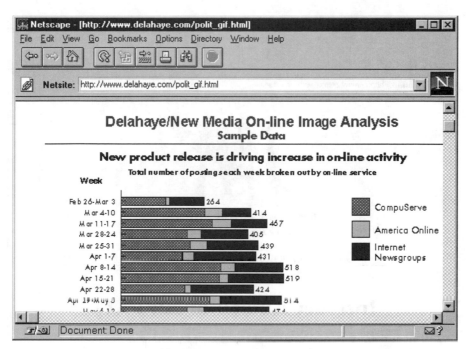

Figure 15.4 Delahaye's detailed analysis determines if a recent campaign has affected a company's Internet marketing activity.

tional revenues to continue your program into the next year. With measurement, you'll be able to demonstrate to management how well you are creating awareness through your Internet marketing program. With measurement, you can accurately show how your Internet marketing program is a powerful complement to your complete marketing and sales activities.

Your Internet Marketing Plan Summary

As a final step in completing your Internet marketing plan, include a summary. Your summary, which you'll include in Section Seven of your plan, should be brief, much like the summary in this book. I can't tell you what to put in your summary because

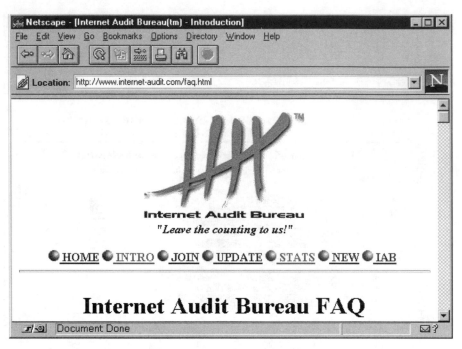

Figure 15.5 The Internet Audit Bureau provides free visitor statistics on its Web pages to registered sites.

I haven't seen your plan. I'll leave that one up to you. After all, this plan is your baby. Perhaps the closing statements in your written proposal should resemble a toast. Here's one, made during a party to celebrate a company's recent Internet launch:

> *Our competitors are there. Our partners are there. Our customers are there, too. And now we're on the Internet, as well. At the very least, we have harnessed this phenomenon called Internet marketing before it took us by surprise. Here's hoping we can capitalize on it to make our company grow. With planning, dedication, and the work of many talented people, we will prosper by our Internet marketing presence. Maybe not today, maybe not tomorrow, but eventually. We'll be patient. We'll be realistic. But most of all, we'll have fun. After all, it's not worth doing if we don't enjoy it. L'Chaim.*

Instructions
- ◆ Review the various measurement options for applicability to your program goals and budget.
- ◆ Rate each option for its relevance to your current needs.
- ◆ Duplicate this form for each software or firm under consideration.

Software or outside firm

_____

_____

_____

_____

Costs

_____

_____

_____

_____

Features or services

_____

_____

_____

_____

Ease of installation and use

_____

_____

_____

_____

Relevance of services or reports to Internet marketing objectives:

Irrelevant   **1**   **2**   **3**   **4**   **5**   **6**   **7**   **8**   **9**   **10**   Relevant

Notes: _____

_____

_____

_____

_____

_____

_____

_____

Figure 15.6   Internet marketing measurement options.

Internet Marketing Plan For (Company Name, Division) Submitted By (Your Name) (Today's Date)

This document is a basic template for your Internet marketing plan. To use this template, copy the disk file inetplan.txt. Use this duplicate to create your own written Internet marketing plan. Some sections of this plan may contain overlapping or duplicate information. The examples provided are suggestions. The exact placement of Internet marketing plan data is up to you. You may reorganize the final document in any way that makes sense to you. You may wish to rearrange it to match the organization of your traditional marketing communications plan, in which case it may change entirely.

Section One: Business Overview and Executive Summary

Instructions: Develop this section of your marketing plan from information you gathered while completing exercises in Chapter 2, *Preparing the Business Overview and Executive Summary.* Use your answers from the completed worksheet in Figure 2.5. Emphasize any element of your company background and future that will be affected by or will affect your Internet marketing plan.

1. Internet marketing plan introduction
   a. Briefly explain why you are writing an Internet marketing plan.
2. Company overview
   a. What are your company's goals, objectives, philosophies, and charter?
   b. Background and historical analysis
      (1) How long has your company been in existence?
      (2) State significant dates and events related to your company and its marketing programs.
   c. Future outlook
      (1) Mergers
      (2) Acquisitions
      (3) Joint ventures
      (4) Strategic alliances
3. Products and/or services overview: What type of business is your company engaged in?
   a. Products
      (1) Product line
      (2) Manufacturing capabilities
   b. Services
   c. Sales
      (1) Pricing
      (2) Volume
   d. Goals and objectives
   e. Future outlook
      (1) Research
      (2) Technology
      (3) Pricing
4. Market or industry
   a. Target definition
      (1) Customer
      (2) Industry

    b. Notable patterns or trends

    c. Competition

       (1) State other companies in your industry that are serious competitors.

       (2) Products

       (3) Strengths and weaknesses

    d. Market share

       (1) Company

       (2) Competition

  5. Section summary

    a. Risks in relying solely on traditional marketing activities

Section Two: Applicable Internet Market Statistics

Instructions: Develop this section of your marketing plan from information you gathered while completing exercises in Chapter 3, *Analyzing Internet Market Statistics.* Use your answers from selected research reports after you have completed the worksheet in Figure 3.6. Emphasize any element of both general and specific Internet market reports that support your plans for an Internet marketing program.

  1. Online users: numbers and percentages

    a. General Internet studies overview

       (1) Overall estimate of worldwide users, host

          (a) Browser, platform, and connection speeds

       (2) Internet business usage trends

          (a) Breakdown of domain name registrations

          (b) Purchasing behavior and revenue

    b. Market or industry-specific studies

       (1) Growth of Internet use within your industry

       (2) Demographic breakdowns

          (a) Average age of selected users

(b)   Internet users by gender

(c)   User profiles

—Purchasing influence and authority

—Computer and Internet proficiency among users

—Job titles

—Income

(d)   Other

2. Section summary

    a. How market reports advocate Internet marketing for your company

Section Three: Marketing Communications Strategies

Instructions: Develop this section of your marketing plan from information you gathered while completing exercises in Chapter 4, *Formulating Marketing Communications Strategies.* Use your answers from the completed worksheet in Figure 4.5. Emphasize any marketing communications strategy that will be affected by or will affect your Internet marketing plan.

1. Objectives and goals
2. Specific strategies for achieving these objectives and goals
3. Section summary

    a. Traditional and Internet marketing strategies, comparisons, and contrasts

    b. How use of the Internet will strengthen your overall marketing goals

Section Four: Internet Marketing Budget

Instructions: Develop this section of your marketing plan from cost information you gathered while completing worksheets in each of these chapters.

- ◆ Chapter 6.   Forming the Internet Marketing Task Force
- ◆ Chapter 7.   Designing Advertising and Direct-Mail Campaigns
- ◆ Chapter 8.   Utilizing Collateral Materials / Sales Literature
- ◆ Chapter 9.   Developing a Corporate Identity
- ◆ Chapter 10.   Conducting Market Research
- ◆ Chapter 11.   Executing Public Relations and Promotional Programs
- ◆ Chapter 12.   Incorporating Sales Support Functions
- ◆ Chapter 13.   Planning Trade Shows
- ◆ Chapter 14.   Launching Your Internet Marketing Program
- ◆ Chapter 15.   Measuring Internet Marketing Results

Do not go into too much detail in this section, other than to summarize budget line items. Remember, a complete description of each of these programs will be included in plan Section Five. Emphasize any element of your budget that will be affected by or will affect your Internet marketing plan.

1. Traditional marketing budget overview
   a. Insert your completed Internet marketing plan spreadsheet (disk file budget.xls) here.
2. Estimates on Internet marketing
   a. Internet service costs
      (1) Account setup or activation fee
      (2) Monthly service or usage
      (3) Upgrade expenses
         (a) Hardware
         (b) Software
   b. Purchasing, configuring, and operating an in-house Web server
      (1) Hardware
      (2) Software

      (3) Additional personnel

      (4) Telephone company service

   c. Internet marketing plan activity costs

      (1) Advertising and direct-mail campaigns

      (2) Collateral materials / sales literature

      (3) Corporate identity

      (4) Market research

      (5) Public relations and promotion

      (6) Sales support

      (7) Trade shows

      (8) Program launch

      (9) Measurement

         (a) Outside audit bureaus or agencies

         (b) Software tools

    (10) Other

3. Web development costs

4. Revenue opportunities

   a. Internet advertising placement / sponsorship

   b. Online sales

      (1) Products

      (2) Services and subscriptions

   c. Other

5. Section summary

   a. An assessment of the financial impact of your Internet marketing program on other traditional media expenditures

   b. Before and after charts: traditional and Internet marketing

      (1) Comparisons of marketing expenditures

      (2) Comparisons of sales revenue

   c. Recommendations for cost savings in traditional marketing communications functions

    d. Bids from outside vendors and suppliers

    e. Other recommendations and support for Internet marketing

Section Five: The Internet Marketing Task Force

Instructions: Develop this section of your marketing plan from information you gathered while completing exercises in Chapter 6, *Forming the Internet Marketing Task Force.* Use your answers from completed worksheets in this chapter. Emphasize any personnel or outside vendor issues that will be affected by or will affect your Internet marketing plan.

1. Task force overview
2. Details
    a. Task force leadership
    b. Current staffing options
       (1) Marketing
       (2) Sales
       (3) Customer service
       (4) Technical support for Internet operations
       (5) Other
    c. Temporary personnel agency
    d. Outside vendors and services
       (1) Internet service provider
       (2) Web developers
       (3) Interactive agencies
       (4) Consultants
       (5) Other
3. Section summary
    a. How Internet marketing will affect staff and operations
       (1) Efficiency improvements

b. In-house versus outsourcing considerations
   (1) Career opportunities for current employees
       (a) Training
   (2) Talent and capabilities comparisons
       (a) Agency review
   (3) Other

Section Six: Internet Marketing Program Implementation

Instructions: Develop this section of your marketing plan from program implementation information you gathered while completing exercises in the following chapters:

- ◆ Chapter 7. Designing Advertising and Direct-Mail Campaigns
- ◆ Chapter 8. Utilizing Collateral Materials / Sales Literature
- ◆ Chapter 9. Developing a Corporate Identity
- ◆ Chapter 10. Conducting Market Research
- ◆ Chapter 11. Executing Public Relations and Promotional Programs
- ◆ Chapter 12. Incorporating Sales Support Functions
- ◆ Chapter 13. Planning Trade Shows
- ◆ Chapter 14. Launching Your Internet Marketing Program
- ◆ Chapter 15. Measuring Internet Marketing Results

Use answers from the worksheets in each of these chapters. This section can also be supported by including data from any Chapter 3 market research report that includes references to impact of the Internet on other media, Internet business usage trends, and purchasing behavior and revenue. Emphasize any element of your marketing communications program that will be affected by or will affect your Internet marketing plan.

1. Implementation overview
2. Marketing communications

Each of the Internet marketing communications functions that follow can be described by including these items:

    a. Brief paragraphs on each Internet marketing communications activity

    b. Your rationale for individual program selection

    c. A discussion of how each Internet marketing activity complements and impacts your traditional program

    d. A plan of action for converting selected materials to the Internet

    e. Summary of activities that will include your Internet addresses for cross-promotional purposes

    f. Evaluations of outside vendors who might perform any or all of these functions

        (1) Advertising and direct-mail campaigns

        (2) Collateral materials / sales literature

        (3) Corporate identity

            (a) A preliminary draft of your corporate Internet style manual

        (4) Market research

        (5) Public relations and promotion

        (6) Sales support

        (7) Trade shows

        (8) Measurement

            (a) How selected measurement functions will demonstrate that you are meeting your Internet marketing plan objectives

        (9) Other

3. Program launch

    a. Launch summary

        (1) Brief overview of each element in your online promotional plan

  b. Month-by-month schedule
      (1) Timeline charts showing Internet marketing
           activities alongside traditional marketing
           activities
4. Section summary
  a. A summary of your entire marketing communications
      program, including how traditional and Internet
      activities will supplement each other

Section Seven: Internet Marketing Plan Summary

Instructions: Develop this section of your marketing plan by
reviewing your entire written Internet marketing plan. Summarize
any element of your overall traditional marketing communications program that will be affected by or will affect your overall
Internet marketing plan.

1. Overall recommendations for action
  a. Why your company should execute a new or
      enhanced Internet marketing program
  b. Why we should take action now: important timing
      considerations

Section Eight: Supporting Documents

Instructions: You may include supporting documents in Section
Seven or you may decide to weave them into your plan throughout as you discuss each section. The choice is up to you. Suggested materials for inclusion in this section are as follows:

1. Press clippings
2. Research reports
3. Other

appendix b

Marketing Plan Software

If you still need additional help in preparing marketing plans after you complete this book, here are several low-cost software packages. These programs are designed to take you through the step-by-step process of enhancing your company's marketing plan.

Sales and Marketing Success
Dynamic Pathways Program
180 Newport Center Dr., Suite 100
Newport Beach, CA 92660
Toll free (800) 543-7788
Tel. (714) 721-8601
Fax 714-644-1880
http://www.dynamicpathways.com

Marketing Plan Pro
Palo Alto Software, Inc.
144 E. 14th Ave.
Eugene, OR 97401
Toll free (800) 229-7526
Tel. (541) 683-6162
Fax 541-683-6250
http://pasware.com/

Marketing*Builder*
JIAN Tools for Sales Inc.
127 Second Street
Los Altos, CA 94002

Toll free (800) 346-5426
Tel. (415) 254-5600, ext. 110
Fax 415-941-9272
http://www.jianusa.com/

Plan to Succeed Software: Plan-A Marketing Plan Software
ICBB: Internet Capital Bulletin Board
1 Place du Commerce, Suite 350
Montreal, Canada H3E 1A4
Toll free (800) 644-4892
Fax 800-762-4650
Fax 514-762-3216
http://www.icbb.com/
icbb@accent.net

appendix c

Periodicals Covering the Internet and Marketing

Internet

Corporate Internet Strategies
(newsletter)
Cutter Information Group
37 Broadway, Suite 1
Arlington, MA 02174-5552
Fax 617-648-1950 or 800-888-
1816
http://www.cutter.com
lovering@cutter.com

Interactive Age
The newspaper for electronic
commerce, covering busi-
ness applications of the
Internet and online services
A CMP publication
http://www.interactiveage.com

Interactive Marketing News
(newsletter)

News and practical advice on
using interactive advertising
and marketing to sell your
products
Phillips Business Information,
Inc.
1201 Seven Locks Road
PO Box 61130
Potomac, MD 20859-1130
Tel. (301) 424-3338
Fax 301-309-3847
clientservices.pbi@phillips.com

Interactive PR News (newsletter)
The newsletter on new media
for communications professionals
Phillips Business Information,
Inc.

1201 Seven Locks Road
PO Box 61130
Potomac, MD 20859-1130
Tel. (301) 424-3338
Fax 301-309-3847
clientservices.pbi@phillips.com

Internet: What's Working for Business (newsletter)
Using online services to improve your bottom line
Computer Economics, Inc.
5841 Edison Place
Carlsbad, CA 92008
Tel. (619) 438-8836
Fax 619-438-5280
imt@compecon.com
http://www.computereconomics.com
http://www.intermarketing.org

Internet Marketing & Technology Report (newsletter)
Advising marketing, sales, and corporate executives on online opportunities
Computer Economics, Inc.
5841 Edison Place
Carlsbad, CA 92008
Tel. (619) 438-8836
Fax 619-438-5280
imt@compecon.com
http://www.computereconomics.com
http://www.intermarketing.org

Internet Week (newsletter)
News and analysis of Internet business opportunities

Phillips Business Information, Inc.
1201 Seven Locks Road
PO Box 60030
Potomac, MD 20859-1130
Tel. (301) 424-3338
Fax 301-309-3847
clientservices.pbi@phillips.com

Internet World (magazine)
The magazine for Internet users
Mecklermedia Corporation
20 Ketchum Street
Westport, CT 06880
http://www.iworld.com
info@mecklermedia.com

I-way (magazine)
Making the Internet easy
86 Elm St.
Peterborough, NH 03458
Tel. (603) 924-7271
Fax 603-924-6972
editors@iway.mv.com
http://www.cciweb.com/iway.html

Multimedia Week (newsletter)
Your business insight into emerging platforms, authoring tools, components, the Internet, and online services
Phillips Business Information, Inc.
1201 Seven Locks Road
PO Box 61130
Potomac, MD 20859-1130

Tel. (301) 424-3338
Fax 301-309-3847
clientservices.pbi@phillips.com

the net (magazine)
The high-intensity Internet
    magazine
Imagine Publishing, Inc.
1350 Old Bayshore Highway,
    Suite 210
Burlingame, CA 94010
Tel. (415) 696-1688
Fax 415-696-1678
subscribe@thenet-usa.com

New Media Week (newsletter)
Growing your electronic-
    content business
Phillips Business Information,
    Inc.
1201 Seven Locks Road
PO Box 61130
Potomac, MD 20859-1130
Tel. (301) 424-3338
Fax 301-309-3847
clientservices.pbi@phillips.com

Online Marketplace (newslet-
    ter)
Interactive transaction monthly
Jupiter Communications
627 Broadway
New York, NY 10012
Tel. (212) 780-6060
Fax 212-780-6075
http://www.jup.com

Online Tactics (newsletter)
Solutions for online/Web pio-
    neers

SIMBA Information Inc.
PO Box 7430
Wilton, CT 06897
Tel. (203) 834-0033, ext. 134
Fax 203-834-1771
SIMBA99@aol.com

Web Developer (magazine)
The number one technical
    magazine for Internet profes-
    sionals
Mecklermedia Corporation
20 Ketchum Street
Westport, CT 06880
wdservice@webdeveloper.com

WebMaster (magazine)
A supplement to *CIO Magazine*
CIO Communications, Inc.
5495 Beltline Rd., Suite 240
Dallas, TX 75240
Tel. (214) 239-5736
Fax 214-239-5734

Websight (magazine)
The World Wide Web magazine
Navigate Media Inc.
9520 Jefferson Boulevard
Culver City, CA 90232-2918
Tel. (310) 838-6200
Fax 310-838-0359
editors@websight.com
http://websight.com

WebWeek (magazine)
The newspaper of Web tech-
    nology and business strategy
Mecklermedia Corporation

20 Ketchum Street
Westport, CT 06880
http://www.iworld.com
info@mecklermedia.com

Wired (magazine)
520 3rd St., 4th Floor
San Francisco, CA 94107-1815
Tel. (415) 222-6200
info@wired.com

Yahoo! Internet Life (magazine)
Ziff-Davis Publishing Company
One Park Avenue
New York, NY 10016
Tel. (212) 503-4790
http://www.yil.com

Marketing Communications

Advertising Age (magazine)
Crain Communications
965 E. Jefferson
Detroit, MI 48207
Toll free (800) 678-9595
http://www.adage.com/

Brandweek (magazine)
The newsweekly of marketing
BPI Communications
1515 Broadway
New York, NY 10036
Toll free (800) 722-6658
Tel. (212) 536-5336

The Bulldog Reporter
   (newsletter)

The Media placement newsletter for PR professionals
1250 45th St.
Suite 200
Emergyville, CA 94608-2924
Tel. (800) 959-1059
Fax 510-596-9331

Creative (magazine)
The magazine of promotion
   and marketing
Magazines/Creative, Inc.
37 West 39th St.
New York, NY 10018
Tel. (212) 840-0160
Fax 212-819-0945
creativemag@comvision.com
http://www.creativemag.com

Developer Connect
User group and influencer marketing
User Group Connection
231 Technology Circle
Scotts Valley, CA 95066
Tel. (408) 461-5700
Fax 408-461-5701
ugc@ugconnection.org

Exhibitor (magazine)
The magazine for trade show
   and event marketing management
206 S. Broadway, Suite 745
Rochester, MN 55904-6565
Tel. (507) 289-6556
Toll free (888) 235-6155
Fax 507-289-5253

exmag@isl.net
http://www.exhibitornet.com

Gauge (newsletter)
The newsletter of communications effectiveness
The Delahaye Group, Inc.
117 Bow Street
Portsmouth, NH 03801
Tel. (603) 431-0111
Fax 603-431-0669
http://www.delahaye.com

The Levison Letter (newsletter)
Ideas for better direct mail and advertising
Ivan Levison & Associates
Marketing Communications
14 Los Cerros Dr.
Greenbrae, CA 94904
Tel. (415) 461-0672
Fax 415-461-7738
ivan@levison.com
http://www.levison.com

Marketing Tools (magazine)
Information-based tactics and techniques
Dow Jones & Company, Inc.
127 West State Street
Ithaca, NY 14850
Tel. (607) 273-6343
http://www.marketingtools.com/

PR News (newsletter)
The international weekly for public relations, public

affairs, and communications executives
Phillips Business Information, Inc.
1201 Seven Locks Road
PO Box 61130
Potomac, MD 20859-1130
Tel. (301) 424-3338
Fax 301-309-3847
clientservices.pbi@phillips.com

Public Relations Tactics (newsletter)
News, trends, and how-to information for public relations people
Public Relations Society of America
33 Irving Place
New York, NY 10003-2376
Tel. (212) 995-2230
Fax 212-995-0757

Publish (magazine)
The electronic publishing authority
501 Second Street
San Francisco, CA 94107

Sales and Marketing Strategies & News (magazine)
The nation's comprehensive news source for successful sales and marketing strategies
Hughes Communications Inc.
211 W. State St.
PO Box 197

Rockford, IL 61105
Tel. (815) 963-4000
Toll free (800) 435-2937
Fax 815-963-7773

Sales Lead Report (newsletter)
Increase sales through leads
  management
The Mac McIntosh Company,
  Inc.
1739 Havemeyer Lane
Redondo Beach, CA 90278-
  4716
Tel. (310) 376-1221
Fax 310-376-7722
mac4leads@aol.com

TradeShow & Exhibit Manager
  (magazine)

Goldstein & Associates Publishing, Inc.
1150 Yale Street, Suite 12
Santa Monica, CA 90403
Tel. (310) 828-1309
Fax 301-829-1169
http://www.tem.com/tem

**What's Working for American
  Companies in International
  Sales & Marketing** (newslet-
  ter)
Progressive Business Publica-
  tions
370 Technology Dr.
PO Box 3019
Malvern, PA 19355

index

Ad banners, 21, 156, 161, 170, 172
  dimensions and specifications of, 164
Ad placement and sales, 201–202
Ad premiums, 194–196
Ad-tracking service, 114
Advertising message, 167
Advertising placement, 156, 165
Advertising rate card, 180
Advertising rates' directory, 179
Advertising specialties, 194–196
Advertising, unsolicited, 171–172
ALT tags, 172–173
American Newspaper Network, 158
America Online, 197
  (see also AOL)
Anamorph site, 54
Animated graphics, 21
Annual reports, 4, 213, 214
AOL, 198, 276
AOL address, 137
Applet, 346
ASCII, 22
ASCII-based text files, 168
ASCII text, 169, 193
ASCII-to-HTML conversion, 125
Associated Press, 252
Audience, 184, 187
Audience targeting, 180
Audited site, 191

Autoresponder, 29, 280, 325
  applications for, 283–284
Autoresponse program, 08–00

Backup systems, 123
Banner design services, 177–178
Banner exchange directory, 170
Banner exchanges, 190
Banner Generator, The, 178
Bingos. See Reader service cards
Boilerplate company data, 253
Boilerplate documents, 22
Boilerplate layout, 242–243
Boilerplate paragraph, 29
Boilerplates, 168
Boilerplate signature block, 29
Bookmarks, 31, 253
Bounced messages, 160
Boutiques, 125
Brainstorming, 103–107, 187
Browser market, 33
Browsers, 21, 164, 168, 206, 253
  designing for, 246
  frames and, 287
  kinds of, 346
  text colors and, 245
  use on Internet, 212
Bulk e-mail houses, 199
Bundled Internet startup package, 118

Business directories, 258
Business Marketing, 264
Business Marketing Association (BMA),
    31, 242
Business overview and executive sum-
    mary, 27–36
    drafting of, 43–47
    (*see also* Company overview)
Business-to-business advertising, 176
Bytes, 243

Campaign launch, 321, 322–327
CD-ROM drives, 121, 123
CGI scripting, 133
Clickable images, 210, 211
Clickstream analysis, 345
Clickstream log analysis, 161
Clickstreams, 160, 166
Clickthrough ratios, 165–66
Clipping services, 252, 343
Collateral material, 203–220, 283
    integration with Internet, 204–205
    and Web publishing options, 210–211
Colors, 244–245
Comdex technology expos, 310–311
Commercial posts, 328
Common Internet File Formats, 212
Communications strategies, 5
Company history, 33–36
Company identity, 30 (*see also* Company
    name)
Company literature list, 216–217
Company logo, 224, 243
    application of, 239
    ASCII text version, 243
Company name, 30–33
Company overview, 28–36
    company history and, 33–36
    image management and, 30–33
Company profile, 4
CompuServe, 264
Computer systems, 123
Computing services, 136
Conferences. *See* Trade shows
Consolidated search sites, 257
ConsultantSee Network, 141
Controllers, 123
Cookies, 163
Copyright, 148
Copywriting, Internet, 176–177
Corning's Telecommunications Products
    Division, 91

Corporate identity, 212, 221–246
    applying principles of, 222–223
    drafting a style manual, 234–246
    Internet elements of, 239–240
    off-line image applications, 224, 226
    trademark confusion on Net, 226–234
    using guidelines online, 223–224
    See also Company identity
Corporate plan, 146
Customer incentives, 194–196
CyberAtlas, 178
Cyberspace ads, 20

Data-base development, 136
Decisive Surveys, 261
DejaNews, 131, 256, 265, 327
Delta Business Directory, 135
Demographic profiles, 78
Demographics, 160, 187
    organizations and associations, 68–69
    resources for, 62–70
    trade magazines and, 69–70
    See also Internet demographics
Design elements, 21
Dictionary of Occupational Titles (DOT)
    Index, 131
Direct mail, 196–200
Direct-mail list brokers, 198
Document formats, 212
Domain name, 34, 63, 119, 323, 324, 326
    brainstorming for a, 230, 231–234
    extensions, 228
    ownership issues of, 226–234
    promoting Internet presence and, 296,
    298
    registration of, 228–230
DOT Web site, 131, 134

Editorial contact, 270–272
Electronic Engineering Times, 264
Electronic magazine (e-zine), 158
Electronic newsletters, 160
E-mail, 14–15
    bulk-distributed surveys by, 259–261
E-mail account, 280
E-mail address, duplicate, 58
E-mail address lists, 15
E-mail address, vanity, 30
E-mail archives, 15
E-mail autoresponder. *See* Autoresponder
E-mail autoresponse program, 169, 193
E-mail comment form, 3

E-mail discussion groups. *See* Mailing lists
E-mail leads, 285–286
E-mail lists, bulk, 199–200
E-mail marketing, 41
E-mail, unsolicited, 197–200
E-mails, untargeted, 171
Embot, 284–285
Exhibitor magazine, 309
Exhibitor services firms, 301–302
EXPOguide, 300, 301
Expositions. *See* Trade shows

FAQs (Frequently Asked Questions),
   327–328
Fee-based advertisements, 193–194
File suffixes, 212
Financial data, 213
Frames, 286–287, 290
FTP, 9, 257
FTP directories, 98, 162
FTP files, 168
FTP site, 22, 98

Gender targeting, 62
GIFs, 207, 208
Gopher area, 119
Grabber, 167
Graphic artists, 147–148
Graphics-based advertising, 167–169

Hard-disk space, 212
Headers, 166
High-Tech Marketing Communications.
   See HTMARCOM
Horizontal rule, 244
Hotels on the Net international directory,
   306, 307
HTMARCOM, 100
HTML, 21, 133, 135, 212, 324
   ad banners and, 164, 165
   World Wide Web documents in, 224
HTML editor, 22, 125
HTML extensions, 12, 346
HTML source code, 172
HTML-to-mail function, 120, 324
Hyperlinked banner, 165
Hyperlinked banner ads, 175
Hyperlinks, 21, 211, 220
Hyperlinks trading, 331–333 (*see also*
   Reciprocal links)
HyperNews, 147
Hypertext features, 212

Hypertext links, 168, 215
HyperText Markup Language. *See* HTML

Icons, 244
ILE logo, 164
Image management, 30 (*see also* Public
   relations)
Implementation strategies, 8–23
   design creativity and, 20–22
   e-mail and, 14–15
   repurposing for, 19–20
Independent ISPs, 58
Indexes, 329
In-house resources, 132–134
In-house Web servers, 117–122
InReference, Inc., 256
Interactive demonstrations, 311–313
Interactive software, 155
International Directory of Women Web
   Designers, 135
International ISPs, 120
Internauts, 146
Internet access, 114
Internet access provider, 140
Internet ad brokers, 163
Internet address, 204
Internet advertising, 158, 159–163,
   170–202
   ad agencies, 173–174
   banner design services, 177–178
   financial issues and, 173
   in-house ad creation, 174–175
   placing ad space, 187–193
   responsible marketing and, 171–172
   site sponsorship, 179–186, 201–202
Internet Audit Bureau, 160
Internet consultancy firms, 135
Internet demographics, 53, 62 (*see also*
   Demographics)
Internet etiquette, 171
Internet files, updating, 22
Internet launch, 19
Internet leads, 286, 287
Internet Link Exchange (ILE), 164, 172
Internet Literacy Consultants, 212
Internet marketers, 102 (*see also* Mar-
   keters; Marketing consultants)
Internet marketing, active, 51–52
Internet marketing, international, 61–62
Internet marketing mix, 279
Internet marketing, passive, 51–52 (*see
   also* Reactive marketing)

Internet marketing plan, 2–8, 249 (*see also* Marketing, online; Marketing principles)
  creation of, 4–6
  elements of, 2–3
  evaluation and measurement of, 7–8 (*see also* Market statistics)
  implementation of, 6–7 (*see also* Marketing plan)
  See also Internet marketing program; Internet statistics; Market statistics
Internet marketing plan template, 355–364
  budgeting, 358–361
  business overview and executive summary, 355–357
  communications strategies, 358
  forming a task force, 361–362
  program implementation, 362–364
  statistics, 357–358
  summarizing, 364
  supporting documents, 364
Internet marketing program, 350–353 (*see also* Internet marketing plan)
Internet MCI, 11
Internet PR, 260
Internet presence, 10, 11, 49, 112, 155
  corporate identity and, 230, 241
  developing the, 128–129
  goal-setting and, 23–24
  hardware needs, 123
  market-targeting with, 81, 91
  See also Marketing presence; Online presence; Web presence
Internet properties, 179, 189
Internet service options, 116–120
  cost worksheet, 118–120
  See also Internet service providers; ISPs
Internet service providers (ISPs), 4, 116–120, 347
  evaluation of, 137–139
  resource list, 122–123
  See also Internet service options; ISPs
Internet statistics, 53–62
  evaluation, 71–77
  Internet growth measurement and, 59–61, 63
  methodology, 54
  worldwide user estimates, 56–59
  See also Internet marketing plan; Market statistics
Internet style, 224, 225

Internet style manual, 224, 234–246, 323
Internet travel agents, 303–304
InterNIC, 229
Intranet, 3
ISP list, 117
ISPs, 118 (*see also* Internet service options; Internet service providers)

Java, 147, 181, 191, 220, 286, 290
Java scripting, 133, 135
Java scripts, 21, 168
Junk e-mail. *See* E-mail, unsolicited

Key message, 344
Keywords, 40, 45, 209, 256, 287
  advertising slant and, 37–39
  market research by, 260, 265
Keyword search, 89

LAN administrator, 109
LAN support, 136
Launch, the. *See* Campaign launch
Leads management firms, 286, 288–290
Levinson Letter, The, 177, 331
Link exchanges, 189
List messages, 162, 189
List owner, 167
Literature, company, 18–19
Log analysis, 345, 347
Log-analysis tools, 163
Lurker marketing, 51, 329

Magazinedata, 158
Mailbot address, 253
Mailbots, 22, 169, 193, 253, 280
  applications for, 283–285
  See also Autoresponders
Mailbot script, 168
Mailing and clipping services, 274, 276
Mailing list digest, 156
Mailing lists, 166, 256–257, 328–329
Mail robots. *See* Mailbots
Market awareness, 90
Marketers, 136, 140, 173, 200, 259, 295
  as copywriters, 176
  corporate identity issues and, 212, 224, 230
  measuring program results, 342, 350
  See also Internet marketers; Marketing consultants
Marketing agency evaluation, 141–145

Marketing benefits, 188
Marketing budget, 4, 5
Marketing budget plan:
    company sales and, 112–113
    determining priorities, 111
    measurable results of, 115
    reallocating funds for, 113
Marketing calendar, 322
Marketing case studies, 107–108
Marketing communications mix, 193–194
Marketing communications program, 204
Marketing consultants, 137–141
Marketing evaluation, 341–351
    defining measurement programs,
        342–343
    delineating measurement parameters,
        344–350
    measurement options in, 353
    measurement tracking firms, 347–351
Marketing goals, 181
Marketing materials checklist, 42
Marketing, online, 34 (*see also* Internet
    marketing plan)
Marketing plan, 154, 327 (*see also* Internet
    marketing plan)
Marketing plan software, 365–366
Marketing presence, 200, 279
    See also Internet presence; Online pres-
    ence; Web presence
Marketing principles, 81, 84–103
    false, 85–103
    image-management and, 89–92
    Internet *vs.* traditional marketing,
        95–103
    market research and, 94
    in use of computing services, 94–95
    Web site costs and, 86–87
    in Web site design, 87–89, 92–94
    See also Internet marketing plan
Marketing program schedule, 323–325
Marketing risks, 188
Marketing specialist, 131
Marketing strategy phrasing, 104–107
Marketing task force, 6, 110, 323
    forming the, 148–149
    outsourcing *vs.* in-house, 128–131,
        134–136
Marketing team manager, 95
Marketing, traditional, 34
Market research, 49–50, 62–70, 249–261, 283
    business ethics and the Net, 250–251
    e-mail surveys for, 259–261

    through newsgroups, mailing lists,
        255–257
    strategies for, 252–253
    See also Demographics; Internet demo-
    graphics
Market research firms, 178 (*see also*·Mea-
    surement tracking firms)
Market statistics, 4, 5
    analyzation of, 49–52
    application of, 78–79
    See also Internet statistics; Internet mar-
    keting plan
Master PR document list, 275
Measurement tracking firms, 347–351 (*see
    also* Market research firms)
Media buyer, 183
Media directories, 157, 274, 276
Media-kit library, 158
Media list, 158
Media planning, 157–158
Media Professionals, 158
META HTML tag, 39, 40
Mirsky's Worst of the Web, 87–88
MIS, 136
MIS manager, 109
Modems, 121, 123

Navigational links, 244
Netscape, 12, 33
Netscape 3.0, 246
Newsbytes, 252
News distribution services, 276
Newsgroups, 9, 14, 119, 168
    the campaign launch and, 327–328
    market research and, 252, 255–256, 260
News release, traditional, 333

Objectives, 82–83, 85, 103–107, 189, 193,
    343
Off-line image, 224, 226
Off-line media, 9–10
Off-line tracking, 349–350
Old marketers' tales, 9–10, 85–103
    See also Marketing principles, false
Online advertising:
    fee-based options, 170
    free and low-cost options, 169–170
    See also Online promotion
Online directory, 88, 168
Online document library, 20
Online document update, 326
Online market, 189

Online marketers, 15
Online media, 9–10
Online monitor, 51
Online news library, 266
Online order form, 287
Online ordering, 91
Online presence, 10, 16, 295–296
    (*See also* Internet presence; Online presence; Web presence)
Online promotion, 42, 135, 327–336
    commercial services and, 330–331
    hyperlinks trading and, 331–333
    mailing lists and, 328–329
    news distribution checklist, 334–336
    See also Online advertising
Online sales literature, 13
Online services, commercial, 330–331
Online world, 3
Online world features, 21
Order processing, 285

Pagefolio Consultants Directory, 135
Passwords, 163
Password management software, 219
Password-protected sites, 218–220
PC Week, 227
Periodicals, Internet, 367–370
Periodicals, marketing, 370–372
Planning software, 158
Portable Document Format (PDF), 212
PostMaster, 332
PostMaster Direct, 199
PostScript, 212
PR Checklist, 273–274
Presence page, 146
Press coverage, 344, 346
Press release, 268–269
Print advertising, 158–163
PR News, 213
Public relations, 30, 90, 263–277, 284
    news releases online, 266–267
    risks and opportunities in, 265
    See also Image management
Publicly Accessible Mailing Lists, 328
Publishing tools, nonstandard, 212

Reactive marketing, 51 (*see also* Internet marketing, passive)
Readers, 212
Reader service cards, 286
Reciprocal links, 331–333
Reference links, 212

Remotes, 287, 290
Remote windows, 21
Repurposing, 19–20, 28, 29, 174
Reuters newswire, 11
Reuters Online, 252
Revenue-generating advertising, 194
RFP (request for proposal), 17

Sales literature, 203–220, 281–282
    distribution of, 209–210
    formatting documents, 212
    restricting online access to, 218–220
Sales support, 279–291
    autoresponders as, 280, 283–285
    leads management for, 285–290
Scanner, 213, 216
Screen captures, 210, 211
Scrolling text, 168
Search capability, 209–210
Search engines, 21, 29, 35, 39, 329, 332
    and consolidated search sites, 257
    for online news library, 266
Search index, 40
Search strategy, 252–255
Secure payments, 291
Seminars. *See* Trade shows
Servers, secure, 285
Servers, unsecure, 285
Service providers, commercial, 58
SGML, 212
Shareware, 347
Signage, 245
Signature blocks, 168, 171, 324, 328, 329
    establishing recognition with, 193, 242–243
Site links, reciprocal, 195
Site statistics, 187
Small business plan, 146
Software customization, 347–350
Spam, 197 (*see also* E-mail, unsolicited)
Spamming, 197–198
Sponsorship, 193
Strategies, 82–84, 85, 103
Subscriber-restricted database, 253
Surfing the Net, 252–253
Sweetened text, 39 (*see also* Advertising slant)
Systems operator, 109

Tactics, 82–84, 85
Tag lines, 29

TeleCard, 281
Text-based advertising, 167–168
Text-based message, 156
T-1 line connections, 307
Trademark protection, 226–234
Trade Show Central, 299–300
Trade show directories, 299–301
Trade shows, 195, 293–319
    accommodations and travel for, 303–308
    brainstorming for, 314–316
    Internet-related applications for,
        295–298
    selecting the, 299–301
    virtual, 310–314, 318–319
Traditional advertising, 203
Traditional marketing, 114
Traffic, 184
Travel reservations online, 303–306
Turnkey site, 125
Typeface, 225, 244

Uniform Resource Locator. See URL
UNIX system, 204
URL, 17, 31, 164, 195, 245, 324
    cataloging of, 329–330
    in sales promotion, 281, 296, 298
User traffic, 117
User-transparent software, 160

Virtual catalog, 146
Virtual trade shows, 310–314, 318–319
Voice mailboxes, 14
VRML, 133, 135, 181, 191, 220

Wallpapers, 208
Web address, 295, 329, 346
Web ads, 162
Web boutique, 141, 146–147
Web browsers, 88, 172 (see also Browsers)

Web Consultants Showcase, 135
Web design, 4, 63, 93, 235, 287
Web design boutiques, 125 (see also Web
    design services)
Web design services, 120, 135, 178, 323
    (see also Web design boutiques)
Web development costs, 114
Web directory, 158
Web embargos, 267
Web formats, 212
Web hosting services, 120, 126
Web log analysis, 120
Webmasters, 1, 93, 167, 172, 287
    as Internet publishers, 158
    and marketing analysis, 345, 346
    and online advertising, 161, 163, 164
Web page code, 165
Web page launch, 328
Web page placement, 60
Web presence, 21, 226
    See also Internet presence; Online pres-
    ence
Web presence development, 105
Web server, 109
    cost worksheet, 121–122
Web site cost, 86–87
Web site ad banners, 190
Web site announcement, 329
Web site design, 19
    worksheet for, 124–126
Web site graveyard, 326
Web site, PR-oriented, 90–91
Web site ratings, 336–337
Web sites, 324
WebTrack's Ad Space Locator, 179
Web visitors, 18
Windowpanes, 287
Work-for-hire agreement, 147
World Wide Web (WWW), 3, 212, 257, 299